Wes Humble has woven together perti daily words of comfort, invitation, and light for the journey through the entir aimed at the academic but at the common seeker and follower of Jesus Christ. The vernacular language of the insights and prayers invites us into a place of comfort and familiarity, where we can find food for our soul. Flowing from the heart of a loving pastor and wise teacher, these entries will encourage many toward a deep fellowship with the One Who guides us ever onward.

– Russ Clark –
Retired United Methodist Pastor

He Restores My Soul is an awesome devotional from God's man who is gifted with insight about the church and the days we live in.

– John Moffatt –
Senior Pastor, Springs Valley Wesleyan Church.

We worship and serve a Living God and are blessed by His Living Word. Truly, there is life in following God and living by His Word. I am thankful for Pastor Wes Humble and his insightful devotions. It has been a pleasure and a privilege to regularly receive his well-prepared devotions.
Many of his daily writings reveal insights and allow you to first dip your toe in the surface and then become immersed in the depth and breadth of the wisdom found in God's Word.
I heartily endorse Wes Humble's devotional, *He Restores My Soul.*

– Steven L. Yashnik –
Attorney

"How often we need reminding that God is always there on our best and worst days. It's up to us to be still and know. Through this devotional you'll be encouraged about the journey that God has set before you and how He's there to help guide you every step of the way."

– Darin and Brooke Aldridge –
Award-winning Americana/Country/Bluegrass duo that has toured the world & plays regularly on the Grand Ole Opry

Try to read just one per day, if you can! I believe you will be drawn to read ahead. These messages speak to the real challenges, the real monotony and the real gladness that make up our everyday existences. . . so be encouraged by reading them every day to see that he is with us every step of our ways.

– JENNIFER SMITH –
COMPUTER PROGRAMMING TEACHER, GIRARD HIGH SCHOOL,
GIRARD, OHIO
KAIROS PRISON MINISTRY VOLUNTEER

I have known Wes since he was a young man serving the Lord as a teenager. I watched him grow up spiritually and physically from a boy to a man. He later became my pastor. He is a great communicator. His devotionals are very inspiring and speak to the heart of our generation. He encourages the readers to read the Word and to be honest before the Lord so that he can guide us through these troubled times in which we are living. I have personally been blessed and received encouragement and know that you will be too You will see his writings come from his heart for God and ministry and his desire to help people make it to heaven. You will not want to miss one of these devotionals. They will speak into your life.

– LEONARD KUHNS –
CO-FOUNDER OF KUHNS BROS. SAWMILL AND LOG HOMES

Wes is a Spirit-filled Christian leader and that comes through in these daily devotionals. Grounded in biblical foundation, inspired by the Word, these daily readings will provide guidance, inspiration, and hope in these challenging times for Christians.

– JUDGE KELLY COTTRILL –
COMMON PLEAS COURT OF MUSKINGUM COUNTY OHIO

It is a gift from God to be able to connect with people as Wes does. His transparency, humor, and humility allow him to speak into others' lives. I have witnessed this many times in the 43 years I have known him. Most of all, God helps him to expound and explain truth from the Scriptures and make it understandable for everyday living.

– VERLYN MELHORN –
PRESIDENT, KLEEN MIST CAR WASHES INC.

As you read through this devotional book, *He Restores My Soul,* you will experience the outstanding communication skills of Wes Humble woven into each "thought of the day." He has a unique ability to take the Scripture and provide application and inspiration to help face the challenges of our Christian journey. As a life-long friend and ministry partner in various settings, it is my privilege to recommend this book to you!

– DON GESSNER –

GESSNER MINISTRIES AND EXECUTIVE PASTOR AT WESTSIDE CHURCH OF THE NAZARENE IN INDIANAPOLIS, INDIANA

The endorsements for this book have come from people that have been a part of my life in different seasons and circumstances. You may not know them by name but in their own way they are serving Jesus Christ and living out their faith daily. I deeply appreciate their kind and supportive words and the lasting and enduring friendships. Here is a synopsis of my relationship with them.

Michael Avery: Dr. Avery and I go back to my college days at God's Bible School and College in Cincinnati, Ohio. I was starting college and he was finished or just finishing. I attended his church and built a bond of friendship centered on love for God and his promises for holy living. We also share an appreciation for history and the art of leadership. I love what he is doing with his life post college presidential leadership and his continual love for sharing God's message with the church around the world.

Russ Clark: Russ has been a pastor and district superintendent in the United Methodist Church. He also has been an advocate for veterans and their spiritual, emotional, and overall health. I was honored to be his pastor for several years and felt his support from the second row every time I opened God's Word. I have much respect for his service in the military and his efforts to lead others to a working faith and knowledge of God's Word.

Steve LeMasters: Steve and his wife, Karen, have been a friend to my family for years. They have loved when it was tough to love and been gracious and generous with God's grace to me personally. Steve and I meet together on a regular basis and he has been a brother, friend, and encourager no matter what was going on in my life or his. I cherish the times we spend together.

John Moffatt: John is the pastor of the first church I was privileged to pastor right out of college, located in French Lick, Indiana. God has enabled him to do an amazing work at this church. He is truly a pastor to the community and a respected leader. Most of all he has been a friend and encouragement to me the last seven years or so. Some of the things I am doing in ministry now are because of his unwavering encouragement to get back in the fight. I believe God has used in him in my life in a great way. I am thankful for his voice and friendship.

Edward Cook: I have utilized Edward's graphic design skills for many projects over the years. He is a long time employee at County Pines Printing and I go all the way back to their beginning days in the 1980s. I have a lot of appreciation for him as a godly man and for his knowledge of God's Word and efforts to share the message of holiness around the world. I am delighted that he found this devotional to contain content that he could recommend.

Darin and Brooke Aldridge: I enjoy all kinds of music but have a real love for listening to and playing bluegrass. A few years ago, I was able to interact with the larger bluegrass community in a very personal and up close way. Of all the people I met, these two impressed me because of their consistent walk with Jesus and their willingness to share their faith unashamedly. God has blessed them with opportunities, awards, and a great fan base. He continues to open doors to perform including multiple appearances on the Grand Ole Opry. I am thankful for their gift of music and support of this book.

Don Gessner: I have known Don and Shirl since I was in high school. He has worked developing ministry around the country and at the local church level. Besides singing and leading worship, he has also served as an executive pastor. We were privileged to work together for six years in a growing and dynamic church. When my life took an unexpected turn, Don was a consistent help and friend, not by endorsing my failure but by lovingly investing his time in what has turned out to be a nearly daily phone conversation. Many times those early conversations in 2015 were life saving for me. He continues to lead others to Jesus and I am thankful for his friendship.

Leonard Kuhns: I have served with Leonard in church and college leadership roles, and I was once his pastor. When I was in high school I spent time working on Saturdays at the Kuhn's Brothers Sawmill for him and his brother Larry. I've watched him walk through the ups and downs of life, including the loss of his youngest daughter. When I walked through my own valley of failure, he was a friend that never quit being a friend and extended forgiveness with no hesitation. In some ways, I have always felt like I was an unofficial part of the extended Kuhn's family.

Steve Yashnik: Steve is a dynamic follower of Jesus Christ. He is passionate about his faith and the Word of God. Whenever I am with him for extended conversations, he makes me want to be a better Christian. I am thankful our paths have crossed and that we work together on a regular basis. I love to hear him pray.

Mike Holbrook: I have known Mike my entire life. Our families, brought together by a local church community before I was born, spent many holidays together. The closeness of our parents almost made us like blood relatives. I am so thankful for his continuing friendship and for the spiritual leadership he has exhibited within his own family and now the Churches of Christ in Christian Union. He is great at relationship building and possesses a steady hand at leadership.

Verlyn Melhorn: Verlyn is another one of my closest friends. I have traveled with him and served with him on the DayMedia board. Through the years, we have enjoyed go-cart racing, laughter and long talks about our faith and life in general. He is one of those people that not only has led a successful family business but also possessed the quiet strength of natural leadership to help grow and sustain that business through all economic challenges. I am thankful for this enduring friendship.

Kelly Cottrill: Kelly is a recent acquaintance. I've known him less than a year but have great confidence in his faith and walk with Jesus. From successful entrepreneur and franchise restaurants owner to going back to school and securing a law degree, he is an example of courage and intentionality. Now he serves faithfully as a judge in Muskingham County, Ohio, and even there he seeks the wisdom of the Word and prayerfully executes his duties on a daily basis.

Ron Reese: Ron Reese is a longtime family friend. I have traveled around the United States with him numerous times for ministry and even leadership training. We worked together at the Global Ministry Center of the Churches of Christ in Christian Union and forged a relationship based on our love for God, sermons, law-enforcement chaplaincy, old trucks, food, and even dumb jokes (the dumber the better). I am grateful for our continuing friendship and for his influence in my life.

Drudy Abel: I asked Drudy to write the introduction for this book because she has been the person I report to at Liberty HealthShare for the last couple of years. I also asked her to write it because I don't believe I have ever worked for anyone above me more supportive of my ministry role than her. We share a lot of the same friends on social media and the same faith background so we know a lot of the same people. Our paths did not cross until 2018. I have great confidence in her daily reliance on God for guidance and support. I have watched her lead with a compassion that can only come from a relationship with Jesus. I am very grateful for her support and the support of Liberty HealthShare for this project.

HE RESTORES MY SOUL

Devotional Insights for
Every Day of the Year

Wes Humble

He Restores My Soul

Published by Whispering Pines Publishers, Shoals, Indiana

ISBN 978-1-948362-58-0

Scripture quotations marked (NLT) are taken from the Holy Bible, New Living Translation, copyright ©1996, 2004, 2015 by Tyndale House Foundation. Used by permission of Tyndale House Publishers, Carol Stream, Illinois 60188. All rights reserved.

Scripture quotations marked MSG are taken from THE MESSAGE, copyright © 1993, 2002, 2018 by Eugene H. Peterson. Used by permission of NavPress, represented by Tyndale House Publishers. All rights reserved.

Scripture quotations marked NKJV are taken from the New King James Version®. Copyright © 1982 by Thomas Nelson. Used by permission. All rights reserved.

Scripture quotations marked (NIV) are taken from the Holy Bible, New International Version®, NIV®. Copyright © 1973, 1978, 1984, 2011 by Biblica, Inc.™ Used by permission of Zondervan. All rights reserved worldwide. www.zondervan.com. The "NIV" and "New International Version" are trademarks registered in the United States Patent and Trademark Office by Biblica, Inc.™

Printed by Country Pines, Inc., Shoals, Indiana

Preface

He Restores My Soul is a collection of devotions most of which were written for the members and employees of Liberty HealthShare in Canton, Ohio. There are also devotions that were written for a church staff and leadership development; and if you look carefully, you may find a sermon outline or two.

I love the Bible and the fact that you can read it repeatedly and still find new treasures to mine if you are willing to spend the time and make the effort. My attempt to make comments about the Scriptures are nothing more than my effort to push others to apply the truth of God's Word to their everyday lives.

The Bible is our roadmap for life on this planet. God's Word contains commandments, laws, principles to live by, relationship advice, and most of all it reveals the gospel and the story of Jesus Christ, who came to be the Savior of the world. It is in his Word that we find spiritual life and health. I hope that this devotional will provoke you to search deeper into the Scriptures on your own. I desire it to provide you with enough of a thought each day to draw you closer to Jesus.

I do want to thank a few people for their help and encouragement along the way. Thanks to my team members at Liberty HealthShare for encouraging me to keep writing. This would include Drudy Abel, Deanna Albrecht, Steve Yashnik, Terri Ipson, Steve Furst, Mike Fairless, Bob Kintigh, and others who have responded when receiving some of the devotions weekly with personal stories and anecdotes of how they were touched by the Scriptures. I would like to thank Paula Pulskamp for helping me keep the devotions organized each month and for doing some Scripture counting and additional proofreading as well.

I would like to thank my family for providing me with the drive to keep serving Jesus and to do whatever it takes to know his Word better. Francene Humble, thanks for helping me by writing the last few prayers that were needed to bring the book to completion and for encouraging me along the way. Your confidence, support, and belief in God's call in my life never wanes and I feel it every day. I would not be back in ministry today without you by my side.

I am thankful for my spiritual heritage and for exposure to great sermons, great books, and the community of faith. Growing up, I knew there was no better way to live than following Jesus Christ. I am grateful for his grace, mercy, and forgiveness in my life.

Wes Humble
Liberty HealthShare
Executive Director of Ministry
and Community Relations

Wes Humble served in ministry for more than 31 years before coming to Liberty HealthShare. He pastored churches in Ohio, Indiana, and Pennsylvania. For seven years he served as Director of Communications for The Churches of Christ in Christian Union. He also served as the office editor of the *Evangelical Advocate* and the *Holiness Digest* magazines. He spent five years at Ohio Christian University as Director of Institutional Advancement. His last church was in Newark, Ohio, and was a multi-site church with three locations and six services each weekend. Wes continues to serve as the Chaplain for the Licking County Sheriff's Office, which includes serving as a member of the LCSO SWAT. He has been the Executive Director of Ministry and Community Relations at Liberty HealthShare since 2018. He also serves part-time as Director of Ministry Development for Bridge City Church in Newark, Ohio. He is married to Francene, and between them they enjoy seven children and seven grandchildren. He is passionate about sharing the hope found in the love and grace of Jesus Christ through writing, speaking, and social media.

Foreword

Writing is about the arrangement of words that communicate thoughts, emotions, warnings, directives, and a hundred other expressions of creativity. In the nearly 40 years that I have known Wesley, he has demonstrated the skill of pen and paper. Now he has put together a collection of scriptural gems that will prove to be a means of grace for the reader. You will find them devotional, inspirational, challenging, and so very salubrious for those in need of a tender touch.

RON REESE
RETIRED PASTOR, EVANGELIST, DISTRICT SUPERINTENDENT
THE CHURCHES OF CHRIST IN CHRISTIAN UNION

Introduction

Often people come into our lives who have little to no effect on us. Sometimes God sends someone whose impact will leave a lasting and measurable impression. The latter is my experience with Wes Humble.

More than once, God has confirmed that He sent Wes to be the Director of Ministry at Liberty HealthShare and that my time working with him is by his design. While I was privately praying for direction, Wes would often share a verse in a meeting or an email that spoke directly to that issue. At first, I would quickly express my feeling of surprise, although I know nothing God does should surprise me; however, I soon felt reassurance in the role God had given him.

In our years together at LHS, not only do I sense God's presence in his life, I am often awed at the insightful yet uncomplicated way in which Wes shares God's Word. He has a gift of putting words to paper that speaks intimately to the reader. I believe that these devotionals will both challenge and inspire you to a deeper, more personal walk with Christ.

Wes prepares the devotionals for our board meetings and on our employee home page. We were thrilled when he agreed to put his devotions into a book to share with our members. On behalf of Liberty Health-Share, it is my pleasure to endorse *He Restores My Soul.*

DRUDY ABEL
LIBERTY HEALTHSHARE CEO

Working for God

Work willingly at whatever you do, as though you were working for the Lord rather than for people. Remember that the Lord will give you an inheritance as your reward, and that the Master you are serving is Christ." Colossians 3:23-24 NLT

A large part of our days are spent at work. We have routines on either side of our workday. We wake up and prepare to spend the day away from home and interacting with the people we work with and around. Christians most often pray in the morning, but not always. While we may be allowed to pray while we work, it should never be a conflict or keep us from working. When we pray, we pray to the Lord; but the apostle Paul is suggesting that when we work, we should offer our day to God as well. Maybe you don't pray in the morning, but I wonder how different your day might look as you interact and guide those around you if you offered your day and skill to God on your way to work? Remind yourself during the day or maybe even whisper a prayer of surrender to God affirming that this day is his as are you.

PRAYER

Lord, I give this day to you. Give me the wisdom I need to lead or work, and fill me with your kindness and compassion even when things don't go the way I want them to. I need your help every day, God, and so I am reminding you and myself that this day belongs to you and that I am working for you today. Amen.

Light of the World

You are the light of the world—like a city on a hilltop that cannot be hidden. No one lights a lamp and then puts it under a basket. Instead, a lamp is placed on a stand, where it gives light to everyone in the house. In the same way, let your good deeds shine out for all to see, so that everyone will praise your heavenly Father.
Matthew 5:14-16 NLT

All of us are called to light the way for people around us. When we do good things or good deeds it encourages and motivates those around us to do the same. Some call this paying it forward, but Jesus taught it was normal practice for those that bore his name. In fact, he took it a step forward and said when we do good deeds it brings praise to our heavenly Father. Sometimes we are tempted to act in a positive way because of what others will think of us, but in reality all of our actions should be dedicated to our heavenly Father if we are Christians.

Let your light shine grace to those that need grace this week.
Let your light shine goodness on those that are struggling.
Let your light shine and guard those that need protection from themselves or others.
Let your light shine gentleness where kindness is needed.
Let your light shine generosity on those around you that are in need.

We have the unique opportunity to influence those around us to be better people. Let the Light of the World shine through you today.

PRAYER

Lord, let me live in such a way that your light can shine through me today. Don't let my actions or reactions inhibit your ability to use me to share your light with my world. Amen.

Real Joy...

Oh, the joys of those who do not follow the advice of the wicked, or stand around with sinners, or join in with mockers. But they delight in the law of the LORD, meditating on it day and night. They are like trees planted along the riverbank, bearing fruit each season. Their leaves never wither, and they prosper in all they do.
Psalm 1:1-3 NLT

Avoid this: Avoid following the advice of ungodly people or even joining in the negative activities that they may engage in. This is not saying Christians should never be around non-Christians. It is, I believe, clearly stating that there are some lines that if crossed will be devastating to our own faith.

Add this: Delight in God's Word! Meditate on it day and night. The Word of God is a powerful force that can help all of us on a daily basis. The Bible says we should "hide it in our heart." It's not about how many chapters you read a day, but can you take a phrase or a verse and let it speak and work in your heart and mind on a daily basis.

Attain this: "They are like trees planted along the riverbank, bearing fruit each season. Their leaves never wither, and they prosper in all they do." What a promise and metaphor! Trees are always stronger along the water source. Prospering in all we do is not about money, but even the poorest of the poor flourish when they abide in the presence of the Lord daily. Our lives prosper in the things that matter most.

PRAYER

Lord, may I stand strong like a tree planted by the river. May my life be filled with your wisdom as I express your love to those around me. Prosper me with your presence that my joy may be full. Amen.

God Will Always Rescue

I will exalt you, Lord, for you rescued me. You refused to let my enemies triumph over me. O Lord my God, I cried to you for help, and you restored my health. You brought me up from the grave, O Lord. You kept me from falling into the pit of death. Psalm 30:1-3 NLT

Many of us watched with great fascination a few years ago as a soccer team in Thailand was rescued from the cave they were trapped in. They were there a whole week before anyone could even locate them and verify that they were still alive. It then took another week to rescue them. It was a global effort, and some very brave and strong people effected the rescue. One elite member of the armed forces died in the process. I imagine there was great fear that first week when they had no idea if they would be found or rescued.

Sometimes we get into caves in our lives, and if we are serving Christ we have one that never leaves us or walks away. Practically speaking the psalmist calls all Christians to worship the Lord, and he gives us some reasons that we should remember. As a man or woman of faith you will have some things to always praise God for. They have been consistent since the beginning of time. God never changes, and the Bible says that Jesus Christ is the same yesterday, today, and forever. Let's look at three quick reasons that the psalmist suggested.

God rescued me

When you become a Christian it is because Jesus Christ came to this earth to rescue you. He came to deliver you from the devastating effects of sin in your life and to offer grace, mercy, and forgiveness.

God refused to let my enemies win

If you have served God for any length of time, you will know that once he is on your side he is really on your side. We will always have challenges as long as we are in this imperfect world, but God will triumph in our lives if we keep everything surrendered to him.

God restored my health

There are times when God heals us physically, but in this case I believe the writer was writing about the health of his situation. He was rescued and God didn't let his enemies win. By the way, God is willing to heal us mentally and emotionally if we will let him. Why shouldn't we honor and praise a God like our God?

PRAYER

Lord, thank you for your presence in my life. You never leave me or forsake me, even in the roughest times. You may not always spare me pain and suffering, but you walk with me and strengthen my heart and faith during tough times. When I get into the caves of life and start to despair, help me to never give up on you and to always believe that you know right where I am. Help me to remember that you gave your life to rescue and restore me and that you never give up on me. Amen.

Who's Thinking About You?

For I know the thoughts that I think toward you, says the Lord,
thoughts of peace and not of evil, to give you a future and a hope.
Jeremiah 29:11 NKJV

It's an amazing thing to realize that God has thoughts about each one of us. He is thinking about you, and not just today but your whole life. He actually has a plan for each of our lives. It's individual and personal. Have you discovered your plan? Do you have any idea why you are here and what God really wants to do with your life in the time you have left on this planet?

So what is God thinking about you today? In this verse, we learn three things for sure:

Peace: We all desire peace. Peace at home, peace at work, peace in our families, and even peace in our world. Know today that God has thoughts of peace toward and for you.

Future: Wouldn't it be great if we could see the future? Probably not! We would worry and fret about the circumstances still yet to come into our lives. How amazing is it that God is thinking about our future and wants to make sure we know we have one! He is God that wants to be in relationship with us more than anything, and he invites us into his story daily.

Hope: There is nothing worse than having no hope. The Word of God is filled with hope. There is hope for you no matter how bleak things may look at the moment. This very day God is thinking about you and giving you a hope that is like none other.

PRAYER

Lord, today give me the ability to sense your peace in my life. Al-
low me to trust you with my future, and fill me with the hope that
only comes from you. Let me extend these good thoughts to others
around me to enable them to also walk in your peace. Amen.

God Will Cover You...

He will cover you with his feathers. He will shelter you with his wings. His faithful promises are your armor and protection. Psalm 91:4 NLT

A terrifying wildfire swept across Northern California killing five people although dozens were reported missing. Among the stories of the deceased is the story of a seventy-year-old great grandmother and two great grandchildren—James (5) and Emily (4)—that perished in the fire. The great grandfather received a call from five-year-old James shortly after he left to get supplies. The boy asked him to come home because they needed help. The fire was closing in. He was not allowed to go back because of the wall of fire. It was devastating news, and the families are grieving with deep sorrow; but the report that caught my attention was this quote: "Grandma did everything she could to save them. She hovered over them with a wet blanket."

That picture is the picture of motherly love. It is the picture of someone doing everything they can to save those around them. Sometimes the best efforts are not enough. While we may not be walking through an actual fire, things will surface in our lives that threaten to upset our peace and even security. That is why we place ourselves in God's hands. That is why we rely on his promises and walk in his ways. Even this is not a guarantee that we will not suffer, because things happen on this planet. There are tragedies that strike. Our bodies are fragile, and sickness can threaten and even take our lives. Evil people can do harm to others. In the midst of everything, we read the above verse and realize that God, like a mother hen, will cover and shelter us with his promises and protection.

He knows about you and your situation today. Don't be afraid to trust him. Let him give you peace and even joy in the midst of turmoil. Christians aren't protected from the things that happen to everyone else, but we have a loving and powerful God that promises to help us and walk beside us even through the devastation. Put your hand in his today. Allow yourself to feel the covering of his wings and the warmth of his presence in your life.

PRAYER

Dear God, you know everything about my life. You know my circumstances and how much I need you today. I want to trust you with my life and the people I love. Help me walk close to you and to accept your protection, love, and care today. Amen.

Help Is on the Way

I waited patiently for the Lord to help me, and he turned to me and heard my cry. He lifted me out of the pit of despair, out of the mud and the mire. He set my feet on solid ground and steadied me as I walked along. He has given me a new song to sing, a hymn of praise to our God. Many will see what he has done and be amazed. They will put their trust in the Lord. Psalm 40:1-3 NLT

God lifts us out of our despair.
"He lifted me out of the pit of despair."

God stands us on a rock of deliverance.
"He set my feet on solid ground and steadied me as I walked along."

God teaches us a song of devotion.
"He has given me a new song to sing, a hymn of praise to our God."

No matter what you may be facing today, God promises to help. The psalmist did say that he waited patiently, and that can often challenge us. Someone once said, "God's clock keeps perfect time." You will find that he is never early and never late, although at times it may seem like he didn't answer in a timely manner or even the way we wanted him to.

Don't give up. He is coming to help. He will lift you out of your despair. He will place you on solid ground so that you need not worry about falling or failing. Best of all, he will give you a new song to sing. We sing regardless of our circumstances because God gives us a song in our hearts. We sing because he is Lord and he is on our side. We praise him for his help in our times of trouble.

PRAYER

Lord, please teach me a new song today. Let me sing praise to you no matter what may be happening around me. I will wait for you.

When You Pray

When you pray, don't be like the hypocrites who love to pray publicly on street corners and in the synagogues where everyone can see them.... When you pray, don't babble on and on as people of other religions do.... Don't be like them, for your Father knows exactly what you need even before you ask him! Pray like this: "Our Father in heaven, may your name be kept holy. May your Kingdom come soon. May your will be done on earth, as it is in heaven. Give us today the food we need, and forgive us our sins, as we have forgiven those who sin against us. And don't let us yield to temptation, but rescue us from the evil one. Matthew 6:5-13 NLT

Recently I attended a church where the pastor called the whole church to the altar to kneel and pray in the first part of the service. He said, "C'mon church. Let's come and pray and square things with God." It was a profound moment.

There are many kinds of prayer. There is petitioning prayer, silent prayer, intercessory prayer, thanksgiving prayer, warfare prayer, even what some call "listening prayer." At its heart, prayer is nothing more or less then opening up your heart and mind to Christ.

Prayer is the language, the channel, and the evidence of intimacy. Prayer could be as simple as a quick breath at a stoplight or a prolonged season of intercession. Prayer is transparent; but more than anything, prayer is alignment. I like to think of it like this:

1. **We align in prayer for perspective.**
"Our Father in heaven, may your name be kept holy." Matthew 6:9 NLT
2. **We align in prayer for purpose.**
"May your Kingdom come soon. May your will be done on earth, as it is in heaven." Matthew 6:10 NLT
3. **We align in prayer for provision.**
"Give us today the food we need" Matthew 6:11 NLT

4. **We align in prayer for partnership.**

"*. . . and forgive us our sins, as we have forgiven those who sin against us.*" Matthew 6:12 NLT

5. **We align in prayer for petition.**

"*And don't let us yield to temptation, but rescue us from the evil one.*" Matthew 6:13 NLT

Alignment is something that is necessary to maintain regarding our vehicles, and if we ignore it eventually it does damage to our tires. Prayer is the alignment of our souls on a regular—hopefully daily—basis.

PRAYER

Lord, teach me to pray. Let me learn to converse with you today and accept the fact that you want to hear from me. Give me ears to hear your voice in prayer when you whisper into my heart. Amen.

A Withered Hand

On another Sabbath day, a man with a deformed right hand was in the synagogue while Jesus was teaching. The teachers of religious law and the Pharisees watched Jesus closely. If he healed the man's hand, they planned to accuse him of working on the Sabbath. But Jesus knew their thoughts. He said to the man with the deformed hand, "Come and stand in front of everyone." So the man came forward. Then Jesus said to his critics, "I have a question for you. Does the law permit good deeds on the Sabbath, or is it a day for doing evil? Is this a day to save life or to destroy it?" He looked around at them one by one and then said to the man, "Hold out your hand." So the man held out his hand, and it was restored! At this, the enemies of Jesus were wild with rage and began to discuss what to do with him. Luke 6:6-12 NLT

This short story from Luke could be addressed from several angles. There is the judgment and criticism directed at Jesus, which is the context for the story; but I am choosing to remind you of the man and his withered or deformed hand. This hand represents the things in our lives that are broken—the stuck places and things that seem to hold us back from being 100 percent in our faith. Look at the progression of the story in this outline:

- **The man had a desire to be with Jesus.**
  When we desire to be with Jesus and to make him the focus of our lives, we are moving in the right direction. James 4:8 says, "Draw near to God and he will draw near to you."

- **The man had a visible difficulty.**
  He could have tried to hide it; but he really wanted help, so he put himself in the middle of a public event with Jesus and the religious leaders. Just remember, none of our brokenness shocks God. He knows about us before we seek his help.

- **The man had to make a decision.**

  When Jesus said, "Hold out your hand," he could have easily refused and run away; but he decided to go through with it and submitted his problem to Jesus, even with others watching.

- **The man was distinctly different.**

  In the NKJV verse 10 says, "and his hand was restored as whole as the other." Be assured today that if you will trust God with your difficulties or whatever your "deformed hand" may be or represent, He will hear your cry and restore you today.

PRAYER

Dear Jesus, Please come my way today. You know the areas of my life that need You so desperately. I long for you to make a difference in my life today. Amen

No Fear

God is our refuge and strength, always ready to help in times of trouble. So we will not fear when earthquakes come and the mountains crumble into the sea. Let the oceans roar and foam. Let the mountains tremble as the waters surge! Psalm 46:1-3 NLT

The words used to describe God in these verses should bring a sense of calm and trust in our times of challenge. God never talks about avoiding or the absence of calamity in our lives. Things are going to happen. When things are crumbling and our world is shaken, God has not failed us. He has promised to be with us in the middle of tragedy. We sometimes think that when we find ourselves in difficult circumstances that God has abandoned us, but this is not the case.

God Leads His Dear Children Along is a song written by George Young after his home was burned to the ground. If you don't know the song, treat it as poetic verse but with a purpose.

> *In shady, green pastures, so rich and so sweet*
> *God leads His dear children along*
> *Where the water's cool flow bathes the weary one's feet*
> *God leads His dear children along.*
>
> *Sometimes on the mount where the sun shines so bright*
> *God leads His dear children along*
> *Sometimes in the valley, in darkest of night*
> *God leads His dear children along*
>
> *Though sorrows befall us and evils oppose*
> *God leads His dear children along*
> *Through grace we can conquer, defeat all our foes*
> *God leads His dear children along*
>
> *Some through the waters, some through the flood*
> *Some through the fire, but all through the blood*
> *Some through great sorrow, but God gives a song*
> *In the night season and all the day long.*

God will give us his presence when the winds and waves of life threaten us. Hold on to your faith and keep singing the song that God will give you.

PRAYER

Dear God, Please help me to not be afraid of the dark places in my life or the storms that come my way. You are my refuge and strength! Amen

A Fortress and a Fountain

Whoever fears the Lord has a secure fortress, and for their children it will be a refuge. The fear of the Lord is a fountain of life, turning a person from the snares of death. Proverbs 14:26-27 NIV

Tim Keller writes, "God is both a fortress and a fountain, because evil not only attacks us but attracts us." When we fear God and recognize him as our fortress for protection and our fountain of provision, it leaves a legacy for those around us to follow. I'm thinking of our children and the life that we live in front of them or others that are watching us as we make decisions. Every decision we make and every attitude we possess affects those in our spheres of influence.

Fortress of security: God is our fortress and protection. When we pray, we invoke his help and security for our families and those we love. We live in a scary world, and we need God's protection both in our walk with him and in our daily lives as we live them out in a fallen and broken world.

Fountain of life: There is nothing that will satisfy the hole inside of us except a relationship with Jesus Christ. He is the fountain of life and of life eternal. He is the provision our weary soul searches for daily. So many times people are tempted to think that material things or entertainment will bring joy or happiness, but it is a fickle joy that is not sustaining.

And so we come back to our fortress and fountain. Our God protects and provides!

PRAYER

Lord, today I am thankful for your protection. You are my fortress that I run to, and you are the fountain of life that gives life-giving water that causes us to never thirst again. May I always look to you. Amen.

God Wants to Move In!

Jesus replied, "All who love me will do what I say. My Father will love them, and we will come and make our home with each of them. John 14:23 NLT

Jesus was preparing his disciples' hearts and minds for his cross, death, and resurrection. He also wanted them to know that he was leaving the earth with the promise to return someday. In the heart of these last life lessons, he inserts the words found in today's Scripture. He is making promises to them and to us.

The promises are based on our love and obedience to God. This is much deeper than an every now and then visit to church or a worship service. When we sign on to do what he says and to love God, we are signing on to a life-altering, life-changing activity. It will come with lows and highs, burdens and blessings, and everything else that humanity experiences—but with one difference.

Jesus said, "My Father will love them, and we will come and make our home with each of them."

Are you ready for God the Father, the Son, and the Holy Spirit to come and live in and through you? This is the relationship God has always longed for out of the humans he created. Very few actually step up and genuinely take him up on the offer.

Too often, we commit to God but fail to surrender. When we commit, we decide how little or much and where to draw the line in the relationship; but when we surrender, we take our hands off and let God draw the lines. Consider this and your relationship with God. Have you allowed him to make your heart his home? Open up and let him in today.

PRAYER

Dear God, I may not have loved you as much as I could have in the past. I have been guarded and careful about how much I let you into my life. Please help me love you in a way that makes you feel welcome into my life on a daily basis. Amen.

He Is My Shepherd

Yes, the Sovereign Lord is coming in power. He will rule with a powerful arm. See, he brings his reward with him as he comes. He will feed his flock like a shepherd. He will carry the lambs in his arms, holding them close to his heart. He will gently lead the mother sheep with their young. Isaiah 40:10-11 NLT

There are many references to God being a shepherd scattered throughout the Bible. This reference is the coming of the Son of God that Isaiah saw in his prophetic mind. It is descriptive of the Messiah or Christ who came as the Good Shepherd. Jesus often referred to or used this metaphor to describe his relationship to the church or individual followers. When you look at these verses closely, you find that there are some characteristics that may be encouraging.

He will feed his flock like a shepherd.
    He supplies our daily needs.
He will carry the lambs in his arms...
    He is strength for our weaknesses.
... holding them close to his heart.
    He is security when we are afraid.
He will gently lead...
    He shares in our need for direction and guidance

Take time to really ponder the above outline. Personalize it to where you are today as you read this. You may not need him for all of these things today; but you will find yourself with basic human needs every day, and our Sovereign Lord in his awesome power comes to our aid as a comforting shepherd but also one that knows no fear. Often in the Old Testament there are references to God's mighty arm being made bare for protection and even judgment. The idea is that he rolls up his sleeves and gets to work on our behalf. Here Isaiah reminds us of that strong arm: "He will rule with a powerful arm." Lean on his arm today. Let him guide you and supply you with what you need the most.

PRAYER

God, today I recognize you as my Shepherd. You are my source for strength and security. You supply my needs and share in my life when I invite you to. I need you today, Lord. Amen.

Be Still and Know...

Be still and know that I am God! Psalm 46:10 NLT

"Be still."

It sounds like something a parent would say to a child. Usually it is prompted because we are talking too much, talking out of turn, or even being disrespectful. This command comes from God the Father, and I don't believe it is spoken in discipline as much as encouragement. It is as though he is saying, "You want to know me? Do you want to understand who I am? Then be quiet for a while and listen to my voice." Being still is a great goal and you should practice it today. Turn all the noise off and just be still. Be quiet and listen to God's whisper in your heart.

What happens when we are still? This verse says we will come to know that he is God. That means we may have our breath taken away when we really internalize this fact. He is God! There is nothing too hard for him. There is nothing too little for him to care about. There are no secrets that he is not aware of. He knows you better than you know yourself, and now here is your chance to know him.

Prayer is a beautiful thing, especially if you practice the listening side of this interactivity with God. We are great at talking in prayer and poor most of the time at listening. Jesus reminded us that he is the Good Shepherd and that his sheep know his voice. Here are a few suggestions to try today:

- Find a quiet place with little to no outside noise.
- Still your body. Try to keep your movements to a minimum.
- Breathe deeply and whisper your desire to God to know him and that he is God.
- Worship him with thoughts of adoration and praise.
- Welcome him to fill your thoughts and heart with his presence.
- Listen...
- Write down your thoughts and then pray about them.
- Be still and know that he is God

He wants you to hear his voice today. You are not seeking to hear an audible voice but the soft voice of the Spirit of God who speaks into our souls.

PRAYER

Lord, I will be still today to the best of my ability. I will try to listen earnestly to you and talk less when I am in your presence. Speak, Lord, and I will listen and hear it with my heart. Amen.

He Hears My Voice

I love the Lord because he hears my voice and my prayer for mercy. Because he bends down to listen, I will pray as long as I have breath! Death wrapped its ropes around me; the terrors of the grave overtook me. I saw only trouble and sorrow. Then I called on the name of the Lord: "Please, Lord, save me!" How kind the Lord is! How good he is! So merciful, this God of ours! The Lord protects those of childlike faith; I was facing death, and he saved me. Let my soul be at rest again, for the Lord has been good to me. Psalm 116:1-7 NLT

There are times in our lives when we need to speak our confidence and faith in God. Most of the time we wait until we are in a crisis, but hopefully we remember his faithfulness during the good times as well.

Looking at these verses today, celebrate who God is and what he does when you cry out to him.

He hears me: *He hears my voice and my prayer for mercy.*
He hovers over me: *He bends down to listen.*
He honors me: *How kind the* Lord *is! How good he is!*
He helps me: *So merciful, this God of ours.*
He harbors me: *The Lord protects...*
He heals me: *I was facing death, and he saved me.*

He listens to your words and hears your prayers. He hovers over you and bends down in your direction to make sure he doesn't miss a word. His kindness and goodness honors you because you are so important to him. He helps you when you need mercy, because we all need that from time to time. He protects you like a harbor for a ship in the time of storm. He saves you even from death at times, and of course the irony is that the perfect healing for time and eternity is death itself. What a mighty God we serve!

PRAYER

Lord, you are looking out for me even though I can't see you. I know and believe that you are near. Your love for me is hard to comprehend. Thank you for loving me so well. Amen.

Children of God

But to all who believed him and accepted him, he gave the right to become children of God. They are reborn—not with a physical birth resulting from human passion or plan, but a birth that comes from God. John 1:12-13 NLT

Being born once is significant, although none of us have the capacity to remember it. We may have been present at someone else's birth, or maybe you even carried and delivered a baby. It is a big deal. Jesus came along and began talking about being born again. At first, this was confusing to some; but eventually the message was communicated to the hearts of men and women.

We are born broken. We are born in sin and carrying the capacity to sin from a very young age. God calls us to follow him. He calls us to adoption into his family. All of this is made possible by the sacrificial work of Jesus Christ. John 1 is all about the coming of Jesus and the gospel of good news he brought to humanity.

Believe and accept him. Become the children of God.

As God's children, we submit ourselves to our heavenly Father. We are adopted into his family, and everything about us will change because of it. Slowly and surely, we take on the nature of our God. Today, let your heavenly Father work through you and in you. Today, love him for all he's done for you. Earthly mothers and fathers pass away and leave us, but he never changes. He knows you because if you've let him, he has made you one of his kids.

"So you have not received a spirit that makes you fearful slaves. Instead, you received God's Spirit when he adopted you as his own children. Now we call him, 'Abba, Father'" (Romans 8:15 NLT).

PRAYER

Lord, thank you for providing a way to become one of your children. You are my guide and provider, and I am listening to you as a child listens for their parent's voice. Amen.

Come and Talk With Me

Hear me as I pray, O LORD. Be merciful and answer me! My heart has heard you say, "Come and talk with me." And my heart responds, "LORD, I am coming." Psalm 27:7-8 NLT

Prayer sometimes comes easy and other times it is hard. Sometimes we feel drawn to it, and sometimes we may be tempted to feel that we just don't have the time or energy for it. We don't know the circumstances that are behind the words found in Psalm 27 but we have all been there for one reason or the other.

There is a distance between God and us for whatever reason, but now we need him and we call out to him. Hear me, Lord! Be merciful to me, Lord! Answer me, Lord! We may feel desperate, and we call out to him with everything we can muster.

The psalmist reminds us that God has said, "Come and talk with me." That is an amazing invitation. This call has been the source of many moments of help and comfort for people all over the world and from every time period in history. The writer says that he heard this call in his heart and he responded with the most appropriate and proper response: "Lord I am coming."

God is calling out to you today. He is looking forward to hearing from you. I wonder if he ever gets weary of people who only come when they are in dire need. Why not respond today and tell him how thankful you are for all the blessings in your life? If you are in need, don't hesitate to tell him that and ask for help. Sometimes all we need is to have a friend that says, "Come and talk with me." The songwriter reminds us of this:

> What a friend we have in Jesus,
>   All our sins and griefs to bear!
> What a privilege to carry
>   Everything to God in prayer!
> Oh, what peace we often forfeit,
>   Oh, what needless pain we bear,
> All because we do not carry,
>   Everything to God in prayer!

Can we find a friend so faithful?
   Who will all our sorrows share?
Jesus knows our every weakness,
   Take it to the Lord in prayer.

PRAYER

Lord, this invitation to come and talk with you is more important to me than I probably even know. I value this opportunity and will speak with you throughout this day. Amen.

24/7

But Jesus replied, "My Father is always working, and so am I." John 5:17 NLT

I think this qualifies as 24/7 coverage from God the Father and God the Son ... they never stop. No vacations, no breaks, no time off. They are always working.

When Jesus spoke these words he was responding to criticism for healing a man on the Jewish Sabbath. What we know about Jesus and what he is doing on a daily basis can be found in the familiar words of Romans 8:17. It says: "Who then will condemn us? No one—for Christ Jesus died for us and was raised to life for us, and he is sitting in the place of honor at God's right hand, pleading for us."

The KJV says that he is interceding for us. He is praying for us, and not just causally praying but pleading and interceding, which suggests an earnestness only to be found in deep love and caring. Every day Jesus is pleading for you in prayer, and he is sitting at the right hand of God the Father. This should give us pause and cause us to reflect on what is happening on our behalf today.

Another reference to his work is found in the story of the stoning death of Stephen in the book of Acts.

"The Jewish leaders were infuriated by Stephen's accusation, and they shook their fists at him in rage. But Stephen, full of the Holy Spirit, gazed steadily into heaven and saw the glory of God, and he saw Jesus standing in the place of honor at God's right hand. And he told them, 'Look, I see the heavens opened and the Son of Man standing in the place of honor at God's right hand!'" (Acts 7:54-56 NLT).

Just moments before he is martyred for his faith, Stephen is allowed to see into heaven and Luke records that he saw Jesus standing at God's right hand. It would not take too much of an imagination to understand that while Jesus may often sit and pray for us, there are times when life is pressing and in his compassion he may stand at what is about to take place.

Sitting or standing, he is working for you today. He is engaged. He is aware of all the circumstances that make up your life on a very broken planet called earth. He cares and is all about you today. He knows what is happening in the urban centers of our world, the rural towns, the countryside, and in the nations that live with daily suffering. He is praying for us all. He is working for us today.

PRAYER

Lord, while I know and believe you are praying for me, I need you to know how thankful I am. I am thankful that you are praying for me every day. Your prayer for me is a source of strength in my life. Amen.

Good News? Great News!

As the Scriptures say, "People are like grass; their beauty is like a flower in the field. The grass withers and the flower fades. But the word of the Lord remains forever." And that word is the Good News that was preached to you. 1 Peter 1:24-25 NLT

God's Word endures forever. It is this Good News that was preached to us. This is the Word that changes our lives on a daily basis when we read it, study it, and follow it. I remember the Good News that I have received in my lifetime. From my earliest days of sitting in church until now and in reading God's Word in about every situation imaginable, his Word has spoken. God says his Word will not return empty or void. What have you heard his Word say to you?

Here's a partial list of some of the Good News we have received. Think of other things you have received from God's Good News and thank him for them today.

Eternal life	Hope	Help	Grace
Mercy	Forgiveness	Salvation	Promises
Wisdom	Conviction	Obedience	Correction
Courage	Mission	Comfort	Direction
Faith	Hope	Love	How to Pray
Invitation	Songs	Leadership	Sacrifice
Examples	Suffering	Inspiration	Encouragement
Joy	Truth	Guidance	Peace

Pick up your Bible today and let the Word of God speak into your soul. Life is short. Read it and let it live inside of you. You won't regret it. God wants to share His Good News with you today.

PRAYER

Lord, thank you for your Word. It is in your Word that I find the food that sustains my spiritual life and dedication to you. May I always study it and follow it all the days of my life. Amen.

What Makes You So Confident?

Hezekiah trusted in the Lord, the God of Israel. There was no one like him among all the kings of Judah, either before or after his time. He remained faithful to the Lord in everything, and he carefully obeyed all the commands the Lord had given Moses. So the Lord was with him, and Hezekiah was successful in everything he did. 2 Kings 18:5-7 NLT

"This is what the great king of Assyria says: What are you trusting in that makes you so confident? 2 Kings 18:19 NLT

King Hezekiah should be in the Old Testament Leadership Hall of Fame. First and foremost, he trusted God and remained faithful to him. We read that he carefully obeyed all of the commands given by God to Moses. God was so pleased with him that he was with him in all his endeavors and he was successful in everything he did.

In 2 Kings 18:19, we find Hezekiah and his kingdom in a standoff with the king of Assyria. Threats are made and King Hezekiah's standard response is to rely on the living God. The king of Assyria asks the question, "What are you trusting in that makes you so confident?"

What a great question for all of us to consider. Who do we trust? Who do we trust with our past, present, and future? Who do we trust when things happen around us that are out of our control? Take it from Hezekiah's story, we can't go wrong trusting God with our lives.

In the following chapters of 2 Kings you find that Hezekiah was afraid. He experienced enough fear to take a copy of the threats and spread them out before God in the temple and ask for God's help and for deliverance from the surrounding army. God responded! That very night the angel of the Lord went through the camp of the Assyrians and killed 185,000 soldiers. The next morning the king of Assyria decided he had had enough. You have to know when you read this story that Hezekiah did not know the outcome. He had to trust. Even when the prophet Isaiah reached out to him and told him God was going to answer his prayer, he still had to make it through the night.

Stand strong. Be faithful to God. Do the right things and trust God with the rest. He knows what is happening, and he knows your fears. He also has the power to help you through the challenges of this life when they come. Stay on God's side.

PRAYER

God, help me to trust you with the big stuff today. You know my fears, but I ask that you turn my fear to faith. I want to always be on your side. Amen.

If I Only Knew Where to Find God

"But he knows where I am going. And when he tests me, I will come out as pure as gold. For I have stayed on God's paths; I have followed his ways and not turned aside. I have not departed from his commands, but have treasured his words more than daily food. Job 23:10-12 NLT

If you are familiar with the story of Job, you know that he was a man truly tested by God. He lost everything, including his fortune and his family. When he uttered these words, he was in the middle of a long siege of struggles mentally, emotionally, and physically. What Job is commended for more than anything else is that he never lost faith and trust in God.

It's not as though he was immune to discouragement. In the second and third verses of this chapter, Job remarks, "My complaint today is still a bitter one, and I try hard not to groan aloud. If only I knew where to find God, I would go to his court, I would lay out my case."

When you look at his comments in verses 10 and 12 you see that he is answering his own questioning. He is unsure about his circumstances, but there are some things he is very sure of:

Confident in his future in God:
   "But he knows where I am going."
Confident in his own faithfulness:
   "And when he tests me, I will come out as pure as gold."

His four reasons for this confidence should inspire and motivate us to stay close to God so that when we don't have the strength to endure life or maybe even the desire to persevere we will still stand strong.

- I have stayed on God's paths.
- I have followed his ways and not turned aside.
- I have not departed from his commands.
- I have treasured his words more than daily food.

PRAYER

Dear Lord, give me the courage to persevere and to stay on your path. Don't let me turn aside to depart from your commands. May your words be my daily spiritual food. Amen.

It's Probably not as Bad as it Looks

It can happen for a variety of reasons, but we are told that depression increases for many people around the holidays. What are you supposed to do when that feeling begins to come over you like a suffocating blanket of hopelessness? Even reality doesn't really look like reality, and the things that might depress you look far worse than they are. It is scary and dangerous to indulge these emotions without God's help.

The psalmist addressed some of this in Psalm 143: *Come quickly, Lord, and answer me, for my depression deepens. Don't turn away from me, or I will die. Let me hear of your unfailing love each morning, for I am trusting you. Show me where to walk, for I give myself to you. Rescue me from my enemies, Lord; I run to you to hide me. Teach me to do your will, for you are my God. May your gracious Spirit lead me forward on a firm footing.* Psalm 143:7-10 NTL .

In his desperation, he cries out for help from God. There are times when the Psalmist will be very clear in what he needs and these verses are no exception. Most of us can relate to these prayers:

"Come quickly, Lord, and answer me."
"Let me hear of your unfailing love."
"Show me where to walk."
"Rescue me from my enemies."
"Teach me to do your will."
"Lead me forward."

Pressures at work, at home, and other places sometimes cause us to want to give up and run the other direction. Find your help in God. Press close to him and lean on him. He will show up and find you when you least expect him.

PRAYER

Lord Jesus, allow me to be strong today. Help me to not buy into the lies that try to drag me down. Lead me, Lord, and I will follow. Amen.

Just Have Faith

But Jesus overheard them and said to Jairus, "Don't be afraid. Just have faith." Mark 5:36 NLT

Jairus had come to Jesus asking for him to come and heal his daughter who was very sick. News had just arrived that it was too late—his daughter was dead. This is what Jesus overheard.

"Coming to Jesus" with our needs, wants, and concerns is sometimes an emotional roller coaster. While I believe without any doubt that Jesus can do anything about everything, I have no idea why he chooses to do what he does or doesn't do. In this story, he goes on to raise this little girl from the dead, but at the point of this conversation no one saw that coming.

Sometimes God heals us. Sometimes he does not. Sometimes we get our prayers answered the way we want, and sometimes we do not. As followers of Christ, we are encouraged to have blind faith in the God we cannot see. We are taught to believe that he has our best interest at heart. There are times when this is easier to believe than others, but I never want to doubt. I want to always believe that he is for me and with me, as he is also with you.

And so today, we hear him say these words to us, "Don't be afraid. Just have faith." I admonish you and encourage you to read them over and over and ask God to increase your faith. Don't believe the lies that fear tells you, but believe in the God that sticks closer than a brother as the Bible says.

You may be in the deepest challenge of your life, but truly let faith triumph over fear. Keep holding on to his hand. Keep trusting that live or die, sink or swim, he is for you and will not leave or forsake you.

PRAYER

Dear Jesus, you know. You know it all and all about it. Sometimes I get tired of asking, but here I am again. This time I am asking that you would make my faith strong and deliver me from the fear that tries to take me down. Amen

Love Is a Command!

Love means doing what God has commanded us, and he has commanded us to love one another, just as you heard from the beginning. 2 John 6 NLT

There are times in our lives when we may come across someone who is hard to love. Even within the faith community you may find that you have a personality conflict, or you may find someone that is not returning love for love. People that are judgmental and find all the faults of other people may be hard to love. Family members that appear to be users and takers of the kindness of family members may be hard to love.

What John writes here is really significant and should be viewed with seriousness. Of course, our love for God is expressed in keeping his commands. That alone should be thought through and embraced as a way to live daily. I always find it interesting when people use their salvation as an excuse to sin or disobey God's commands. Sin matters. God doesn't take it lightly. Yes, Jesus offers forgiveness for our sins, but God clearly wants his people to lean into holy living and not sinful living. He wants us to love God and love one another.

Why not think of someone today that you have difficulty loving and find a way to express God's love to him or her in a tangible way? Practice loving others at church, or the store, or at work. Be intentional and consistent, and it may become a habit. Love like Jesus loves you.

PRAYER

Dear Jesus, I do struggle at times to love like you want me to love. Please give me the grace and guidance to love well in all my relationships. Amen.

He Will Care For You All Year Long

I have cared for you since you were born. Yes, I carried you before you were born. I will be your God throughout your lifetime—until your hair is white with age. I made you, and I will care for you. I will carry you along and save you. Isaiah 46:3b-4 NLT

These words were originally spoken by God to Israel as a reminder of his promises to this nation and people. With the advent of Jesus Christ to this world, these promises transferred to all people everywhere. More importantly, they transfer to you if you acknowledge God as your Lord.

When we face the prospect of a new year we are filled with anticipation and expectancy. Most of the time those thoughts are positive and hopeful. Often in the back of our minds we realize that a new year may also bring new challenges. We fear the loss of a loved one, a serious medical diagnosis, the phone call in the middle of the night, emerging problems with our children, and a myriad of other things. All of our human condition and experience can be surrendered to God because he promises to be with us our entire life.

He is part of our past: "I have cared for you since you were born. Yes, I carried you before you were born."

He is part of our present: "I will be your God throughout your lifetime."

He is part of our future: "...until your hair is white with age."

His promises include every stage of our life and certainly every stage of a new year. Here is what he offers for you and I today: "I made you, and I will care for you. I will carry you along and save you."

What a God! All he ever asks from any of us is for us to put our lives and loves into his hands and management. Allow him to lead your life. Pursue your relationship with God at a new level of trust and closeness. Live in the security of his promises to you.

Here is a great prayer to make a daily prayer adapted from Psalm 31:14-15a:

PRAYER

Dear God, "But I am trusting you, O LORD, saying, 'You are my God!' My future is in your hands." And so it is in your hands, Lord. I will leave it there all year long. Amen.

In Christ We Find Peace

I have told you all this so that you may have peace in me. Here on earth you will have many trials and sorrows. But take heart, because I have overcome the world." John 16:33 NLT

Shortly before Jesus died, he conducted what we might refer to accurately as a cram session for his disciples. He knew his time had come and these were the things he really wanted them to take away from the three years they spent following him, listening to him, and watching him work.

It is not unusual when someone knows they are dying to try to say all the things they need to say before dying. This verse is the wrap-up verse to this session of teaching. The disciples were upset with what he was saying, mostly because he talked about suffering and his coming death and the fact that he was going away.

Into this moment he says, "I have told you all this so that you may have peace in me."

It is important that we see the last two words. Peace is an elusive pursuit. Nations seek it. Families long for it. Individuals often desire it. More often than not, peace is not found because we look for it in the wrong places.

Jesus is honest with them and says, "Here on earth you will have many trials and sorrows," and most of us can attest to that truth; but his offer of peace is wrapped up in the words "in me."

It is in him that we find peace. It is in him alone that we find the desires of our heart. It is in him that we find the love that satisfies our loneliness. It is in him that we find a friend that sticks closer than a brother. It is in him that we find someone to bring calm in the storm. It is in him that we find comfort in our afflictions. It is in him we find shelter. It is in him we find a rock to build upon.

Don't waste your time pursing the wrong things. Don't be foolish and look in all the wrong places for peace. The need for peace is real, but the answer is only and always in Jesus.

"Take heart, because I have overcome the world." – Jesus Christ

PRAYER

Dear Jesus, I long for peace. I wish I could live in a peaceful world. I need peace in my heart, my family, and even at work and at home. I will look for this peace in you and in you alone. Amen.

The Great Exchange

"Anyone who belongs to Christ has become a new person. The old life is gone; a new life has begun! 2 Corinthians 5:17 NLT

What an exchange! Those who accept Jesus Christ as their Savior will be changed. Whatever you were before will not be who you are now. The life of an authentic follower of Jesus will run counter to most of what this culture will tell you that you need to be.

For most of us, the trade of our old lives for a new one centered in Christ was the best thing that ever happened to us. Our priorities change. Our passions change. Our personal plans may look very different. There is something so amazing about fresh starts and do overs. This is what Jesus came to offer for men and women of all time.

No matter where you are or what you have done, it is always the right time for a new start. God knows you better than you know yourself. He knows your circumstances and your emotions. He knows your past, present, and future. Why not pause today and make sure that you genuinely belong to Christ. It's not about a church, a ritual, or a pastor. It's about you and Jesus.

What things would you like to trade in for a do over today? What would you do with a new life in Christ? You would love, live, and lead like Jesus. You would be able to pray to one that you honor with your life. You would gain the benefit of knowing that you are right with God and walking and living out the life he (our Creator) intended us to live.

Lean into Jesus today and allow him into your life. Align your life in him.

Then Jesus said, "Come to me, all of you who are weary and carry heavy burdens, and I will give you rest" (Matthew 11:28 NLT).

PRAYER

Lord, more than anything, I want you in my life. I want the world to see that I am a new person and that old things have passed away. I am coming to you today. I give myself to you today. I will rest in you. Amen.

Hold On!

Do everything without complaining and arguing, so that no one can criticize you. Live clean, innocent lives as children of God, shining like bright lights in a world full of crooked and perverse people. Hold firmly to the word of life. Philippians 2:14-16 NLT

These words were written to a group of first century believers discipled by the apostle Paul. He wrote this letter to encourage them to stay strong in their faith during his absence. The verses above are filled with a worthy admonition for all of us to consider.

He said:

Keep it positive and peaceful:
Within the body of Christ, we should be known for our positive attitudes and for being able to live at peace with one another. Fighting, arguing, and bickering at one another is contrary to everything the New Testament teaches us to be. The ability to not let others affect us is truly a gift from God and a result of our continual focus on him and his Word.

Keep it pure:
"Live clean, innocent lives as Children of God," he writes. Living clean means that we live our lives with nothing to hide. We are what we say we are. Who we really are is who we are when no one is looking. God must be more than a Sunday-only God to the authentic follower of Christ. He will factor into all of your daily walk, public and private. Keep it clean.

Keep up the pursuit:
"Hold firmly to the word of life." Our time on this planet is very short. Every person that lives past fifty begins to look back and wonder where time has gone. They look ahead and wonder where and how fast time will go. Eternity looms large and is where all of our investments should be made. Pursue God every day. Hold tenaciously to his Word and lean into him for strength and support.

We all live our lives with the same amount of time daily and we choose how we are going to live. Everyone makes choices every day to follow God's way or not. You can do it! You can live your life with eternity in view and what a difference that may make!

PRAYER

Dear Lord, while my life might not mirror those early Christians and their challenges, I don't plan on trusting my life with anything or anyone but you. I will keep things positive and I will do my best to live a pure life while pursuing you with all my heart. Amen.

Make the Right Call

Seek the LORD while you can find him. Call on him now while he is near. Let the wicked change their ways and banish the very thought of doing wrong. Let them turn to the LORD that he may have mercy on them. Yes, turn to our God, for he will forgive generously. Isaiah 55:6-7 NLT

The one thing God never stopped doing in the Old Testament is inviting his people to turn from their selfish and evil ways and to return to him. Sometimes he allowed them to get themselves into real trouble by their actions, but it was always followed up with an invitation to return.

So too with us. God's standards are high and very clear. He demands total allegiance and instructs us not to allow anyone or anything to come between our relationship with him. When it happens, we find ourselves with a choice: continue to live apart from God's abiding presence or turn back to accept his offer of mercy and forgiveness.

If you are feeling God stirring your heart, seek him while you can find him and call to him while he is near. Banish the wrong and turn to him. His mercy will find you and his forgiveness will overwhelm you.

He will forgive generously. He will forgive *you.* He will welcome you and restore you and your faith. Don't wait. Don't put it off. Press in toward Him today. Here are your action steps straight from Isaiah 55:6-7:

Seek
Call
Change
Banish
Turn

PRAYER

Dear God, thanks for including this invitation to seek you and follow you. Teach me to do this daily. Show me your ways and give me a hunger to know you more. Amen.

Lord, If Only...

When Martha got word that Jesus was coming, she went to meet him. But Mary stayed in the house. Martha said to Jesus, "Lord, if only you had been here, my brother would not have died. But even now I know that God will give you whatever you ask." John 11:20-22 NLT

Mary, Martha, and their brother, Lazarus, were best friends of Jesus. When Lazarus was apparently deathly ill, the two sisters sent word to Jesus; and yet the Bible records that he seemingly delayed his trip to their home. By the time he did appear, Lazarus was deceased and buried. His sisters were devastated and both of them said the same thing to Jesus: "Lord, if only you had been here..."

How many times have you and I thought how different things might have turned out if Jesus had been more visible and in the middle of our circumstances? He is always around. He knows everything that happens in our lives, and yet we still long for him to be more present.

What is it that you have walked through or are walking through right now? At one time or the other, we all go through situations that test our faith. They threaten to overwhelm us. At the time we think there is no way we can endure or make it through it. We long in those moments for a God with skin that can sit across from us and talk or show up at the hospital or even funeral home.

The good news is that he is there. He never leaves us or forsakes us. He does show up. He shows up in our hearts. He shows up in our prayer times alone with him. He shows up and whispers his peace, which is a comfort like none other. It's okay to feel the human frustration that Mary and Martha both felt, but don't give up on your faith. Press closer to him and trust him even when things look hopeless.

Jesus said, "I have told you all this so that you may have peace in me. Here on earth you will have many trials and sorrows. But take heart, because I have overcome the world."

You will overcome! You can do this. Keep trusting. Keep longing for him. You are loved, and Jesus knows all about it.

PRAYER

Lord, I am so thankful that you care for me like you do. Even when life offers more questions than answers I will still do my best to believe that you are in the middle of it all. I trust you and love you, Lord. Amen.

Knowing God Better

*May God give you more and more grace and peace as you grow in
your knowledge of God and Jesus our Lord.* 2 Peter 1:2 NLT

This verse is part of a greeting in a letter from the apostle Peter, written to a first century church. He is praying that they receive more grace and peace, and he connects it with their growing knowledge of God.

Every Christian should want to grow in their knowledge of God. What do you know about him? How well do you know him? When we are building a relationship with someone, we try to learn everything we can about them. We learn their likes and dislikes. We study their mannerisms and their interests. How much more should we seek to know God and everything we can about him?

Peter seems to link this growing knowledge with the grace and peace of God in our lives. It's simple really. The more you know about God the more grace and peace you will experience. When things happen that challenge us and threaten to impede our faith, what will hold us steady is the knowledge of God's goodness, mercy, compassion, and faithfulness.

A working knowledge of God's attributes alone would give us great measures of grace and peace. In your own quest to know him better, look up these verses describing his attributes.

He is infinite: "And he is before all things, and in him all things hold together" (Colossians 1:17).

He is immutable: "I the Lord do not change. So you, the descendants of Jacob, are not destroyed" (Malachi 3:6).

He is self-sufficient: "For as the Father has life in himself, so he has granted the Son also to have life in himself" (John 5:26).

He is all powerful or omnipotent: "By the word of the LORD the heavens were made, their starry host by the breath of his mouth" (Psalm 33:6).

He is all-knowing or omniscient: Isaiah 46:9-10.

He is omnipresent: Psalm 139:7-10.

He is all-wise: Romans 11:23.

He is faithful: Deuteronomy 7:9.

He is good: Psalm 34:8.

He is just: Deuteronomy 32:4.

What we come to know about God shapes our beliefs and deepens our faith. Know him. Study him. Never give up your hunger and thirst to know him better. May your life be filled with "more and more grace and peace."

PRAYER

Dear God, I want to know you more! I realize the more I know you the more my faith will be strengthened. Fill my life with your grace and peace! Amen.

A Victory Parade

In the Messiah, in Christ, God leads us from place to place in one perpetual victory parade. Through us, he brings knowledge of Christ. Everywhere we go, people breathe in the exquisite fragrance. Because of Christ, we give off a sweet scent rising to God, which is recognized by those on the way of salvation—an aroma redolent with life. 2 Corinthians 2:14-15 MSG

There is no substitute for authenticity when it comes to following Christ. When people speak of the church, they often speak of hypocrisy, hate, and generally an attitude of judgment and negativity.

This is far from what Christ intended when he launched the church, his body, to be his hands and feet in the world. The apostle Paul knew this, and he knew what Christ would do with devout followers. His language is descriptive. It is personal. It is convicting.

If we are truly walking with Christ, we are part of a "perpetual victory parade" like none other. It is through our lives of devotion and love for God that others come to know Christ. As if that is not enough, Paul says that everywhere we go people will "breathe in the exquisite fragrance."

What aroma comes from us on a daily basis? What parade are we marching in, and who is leading the parade? Smart people are very careful who they follow. Here's an outline and another way of understanding it:

We move in the right direction: "God leads us from place to place in one perpetual victory parade."

We motivate others to make the right decisions: "Through us, he brings knowledge of Christ."

We minister with the right devotion: "Because of Christ, we give off a sweet scent rising to God, which is recognized by those on the way of salvation—an aroma redolent with life."

This life should have more appeal than any other we might choose to live. Join God's parade of grace and goodness. Be a part of his story and let those around you breathe in the mercy of God from your life on this day!

Dear Jesus, please lead me in your parade every day! Let me be so close to you that others see and think of you when they watch me live my life. Fill me with your grace I pray. Amen.

God's Severe Tender Love

In the midst of personal trials, heartbreaks, and sorrow we often turn to God and ask why. We may even wonder if God is punishing us for something. Historically God has used some big moments and events to get people's attention. I don't believe God causes most of the things that happen in our lives, but I do believe he uses them to try to speak to us because we are more attentive when life is upside down. We tend to be more willing to search for answers and turn toward God when circumstances are not what we desire them to be.

The writer of the book of Lamentations in the Old Testament had this in mind when he wrote the following: *Don't run from trouble. Take it full-face. The "worst" is never the worst. Why? Because the Master won't ever walk out and fail to return. If he works severely, he also works tenderly. His stockpiles of loyal love are immense. He takes no pleasure in making life hard, in throwing roadblocks in the way.* Lamentations 3:31-33 MSG

I love this phrase: "If he works severely, he also works tenderly." It very well may be that God is using something happening or not happening in your life to help you choose to return to him or connect with him in a deeper way.

Remember these words from this Scripture:

"His stockpiles of loyal love are immense."

"He takes no pleasure in making life hard."

God's love for you never wavers; and when life is hard, you have the opportunity to draw close to him and lean on him for support, compassion, and mercy. Don't give up. Don't allow your faith to weaken. Press forward and draw close to God no matter what it takes. Because he is the Good Shepherd, he will not leave you or forsake you. He is with you and for you today!

PRAYER

Dear Jesus, I want to trust you with my life. I don't want to run from trouble but learn that you are always present. Sometimes I just need to feel your love. Today is one of those days. Amen.

The Lord Is for Me

In my distress, I prayed to the LORD, and the LORD answered me and set me free. The LORD is for me, so I will have no fear. What can mere people do to me? Psalm 118:5-6 NLT

Freedom from fear is a much sought after and desired strength. From the time we are young we learn to fear people. We fear that we won't be accepted or fit in on the playground. We fear that we might not have friends because we don't wear the right clothes or belong to the right group of kids at school. Later in life, this fear can be both gripping and expensive. We may fear others' rejections because of the car we drive, the house and neighborhood we live in, and because we can't afford to shop in the right stores. If we are not careful this fear may even drive us to live above our means by spending money we don't have to gain the approval of people.

For the followers of Christ around the world this fear of people often has much more serious threats and overtones. Many Christians find themselves in fear for their lives every day because of their faith in Jesus Christ. They live with the threat of death daily.

When God sets us free it does not always mean deliverance from people or things that cause fear. Many followers of Christ in the last two thousand years have died for their faith. Many others have faced people or situations that were threatening in some way.

This freedom he gives us is bigger than just deliverance. It is a complete trusting in God that no matter what is happening or what the outcome of our circumstances, we trust him; and because of that, we are free from fear. "The Lord is for me, so I will have no fear." You may not be there today, but you can get there in your heart; and when you do, you will find that fear has fled. God is bigger than the things or people that have caused you to be afraid. Remember, he is for you today.

PRAYER

Dear Lord, I find great comfort and peace today knowing that you are for me. Without you I am nothing, but with you I feel strong and invincible. Thank you for being there day after day. Amen.

I Will Bow Down

Start with GOD—the first step in learning is bowing down to GOD; only fools thumb their noses at such wisdom and learning. Proverbs 1:7 MSG

If God is God and you believe that he is, the first step in the rest of your life is to acknowledge it as a fact. The second step is to learn to remember it every day and live like it.

That's what God has always looked for in his relationships with humans. He has always wanted us to love and trust him for who he is. When we shape our lives around the strong belief that God is the only God and sovereign Lord of all, we will find ourselves on a journey beyond what we could imagine.

"Bowing down to God" means that his will is more important than ours. It means on a daily basis that we put God first above the culture, our family, and our friends. His Word and his commands are more important than our very lives. In fact, Christianity has a long history of men and women who lost their lives for believing in Jesus Christ and it continues today around the world.

Bowing down to God is not so much a physical act as it is an act of the heart and mind. It is an act of surrender to him. It is an act of reverence that allows his will to be played out in our lives. With all of your heart let God work in and through you. With absolute resolve bow down to him and trust him in every season of your life. Trust him today. Love him alone today. If need be, take a knee.

PRAYER

Dear God, I am humbled by the opportunity you give us to submit our lives to your sweet control and guidance. I want you. I need you and I will seek you daily. I will take a knee. Amen.

God's Family

Jesus replied, "My mother and my brothers are all those who hear God's word and obey it." Luke 8:21 NLT

One day when Jesus was teaching, he was told that his mother and brothers couldn't get in because of the crowd. His response was interesting but it reminds us how important obedience is in God's eyes.

This is not being disrespectful to his family, but rather it is being inclusive to those who hear and obey his teaching. These words were uttered at the end of Luke's narrative in this chapter and followed by stories about Jesus from a different day. I am sure he wasn't running or hiding from his mother and brothers. He probably greeted them at the conclusion of his teaching.

Mostly he wanted the crowd to know how important they were in the kingdom of God if they truly were followers. If you and I truly hear God's Word and obey it we are adopted into his family. The Bible refers to us being adopted into God's family. We become sons and daughters of God. We have the right to call him Father if we hear and obey.

God has always wanted us to be obedient to his Word. Jesus taught us to obey, and the Holy Spirit was given to us that we might be "guided into all truth." Jesus said, "If you love me, obey my commandments." Today, focus on hearing and obeying God's Word. You've been adopted into God's family; now you have to act like it.

PRAYER

Heavenly Father, thank you for adopting me as one of your children. Help me to hear your voice today and to obey. Give me the courage to desire to live like you want me to live. Amen.

When God Speaks

And Samuel replied, "Speak, your servant is listening." 1 Samuel 3:10 NLT

Samuel was a young man whose mother had dedicated him to the Lord for service. She did this by literally allowing him to live and serve the old prophet, Eli. It is a fascinating story, and I would recommend you read it often. God came calling one day by calling Samuel's name. Samuel's reply is our focus today: "Speak, your servant is listening."

When God tries to communicate with us it is best to listen. Listening is hard, especially when we don't have the privilege of actually hearing his audible voice. Sometimes, like Samuel, we may not even recognize that it is God trying to speak to us. When we figure it out or think that it may be God, then it is time to listen.

Be quiet.
Be focused.
Be ready to hear.
Be hungry to hear.
Invite Him to speak.

God had something to say to Samuel, and he often wants to say things to us. He leads us and nudges us toward doing his will and being more like him daily. Do everything you can to find and follow his voice.

PRAYER

Lord, nothing would bring me more peace today than to be able to know that you have spoken into my life. Help me to hear you today in my heart. Fill my mind and heart with your presence. And if I hear, give me the grace and ability to do what you say. Amen.

When God Calls

"Now get up and stand on your feet. I have appeared to you to appoint you as a servant and as a witness of what you have seen and will see of me." Acts 26:16 NKJV

The context for this Scripture is the apostle Paul relating the story of his conversion to Christ on the Damascus road. It was a life-changing moment. This encounter was God pursuing Saul, who was at the time the enemy of Christianity. He would change his name to Paul and become a prolific first century leader and lead author in the New Testament. God is always looking for men and women who will carry out his plan on this earth. We are called to love and lead like Jesus. We are valuable to God, but that doesn't mean he won't call us to some tough tasks.

There will always be a place where we realize our worth.

For Paul it was the command to stand on his feet. God had something for him to do. Have you ever heard this call or received an understanding of your value to God?

There will always be a purpose that calls us to our work.

The voice from heaven gave him his purpose. It was a clear call to be a servant and a witness. There is a work for all of us to do. It is as unique as we are. There is no one like you in this world.

There will always be passion to witness and serve others.

It's an ongoing call. God never seeks to discover what we want to do but rather to reveal what he wants from us. He invites us into his story on earth. What an amazing opportunity.

Wouldn't you love to hear from God today? Don't ask if you don't want to know. When Paul encountered God on this road he asked this question: "What shall I do, Lord?" Don't be afraid to pray that prayer daily. Allow God to work through you today beyond what you can see. Allow God to do great things in and through you this week. His power is greater than any earthly challenge.

"Now all glory to God, who is able, through his mighty power at work within us, to accomplish infinitely more than we might ask or think" (Ephesians 3:20 NLT).

PRAYER

Dear Jesus, if you can use me today, I sure want to be available. Let me hear your call on my life, and let me daily be used by you. Amen.

What Have You Done?

Then the Lord God asked the woman, "What have you done?"
Genesis 3:13 NLT

When Adam and Eve sinned, God came looking for them. He confronted them, chastised them, and clothed them. It was Eve that disobeyed first, and then she invited Adam to join her in her actions. They were both equally guilty, but God singled her out because she was the one who took that devastating first bite. It was not only devastating for them but for all humans born afterwards. Her actions came with eternal consequences.

I can imagine God asking this question with the bewilderment of a parent when a child does something really baffling that comes with a heavy price. There is that shaking of the head in confusion, and the question comes, "What have you done?" A good follow up is, "How could you do this?"

There will be moments and seasons in our lives when we may hear God ask this question. Things happen that upon later reflection we shake our own heads and wonder how or why we did them. I'm sure Eve rehearsed that conversation with her tempter many times over the rest of her life. I imagine she also thought about the fact that there was only one rule to keep and observe in the Garden of Eden and she along with Adam managed to break it.

When you hear God ask you this question, know that he comes with the love of a heavenly Father. There will be consequences to all of our decisions, of course, but there is also redemption.

Our God comes to seek and save those that are lost. Our God sent his only Son into our world to rescue us from the curse brought about by sin. We are blessed because we have a Savior, and he invites us to follow him to heaven. He knows the way and shows the way.

Have you failed at something? Do you long for a do over? Are you bound by the chains of guilt?

Begin again by listening to the voice of your heavenly Father. Listen carefully to his voice

Prayer

Dear God, you know all things; and you know things I have done and things I have left undone. Please give me the courage and strength to do what is right and pleasing to you. Amen.

Waiting on the Lord

Wait patiently for the Lord. *Be brave and courageous. Yes, wait patiently for the* Lord. Psalm 27:14 NLT

Sometimes life demands that we just wait. We would love to do something else, but waiting seems to be the only answer. It's not easy for most people to wait. We wait in lines, but not very patiently. We wait at traffic lights and wonder why it takes so long for the light to change. We wait for the call from the doctor's office and wonder why it takes a week or more to get results back from a test.

Maybe one of the hardest waits of all is waiting for God to answer a prayer or give us direction in our lives. I've known people that have prayed for their husbands or wives to accept Christ and become a follower. Sometimes their prayers have lasted decades. We wait on God because we believe in him. We believe he knows everything about us and that he has the power to change our circumstances or help us through difficult times.

The psalmist gives us two actions to help us while we wait on God. "Be brave and courageous," he wrote. If you trust God, you can be brave. If you believe that he has your best interest in mind, you can be courageous even in the face of what looks like certain defeat and ruin. Be strong today and confident in the mighty power and love of God. Wait for it ... wait for his help to come. He will come and help you.

PRAYER

Dear God, waiting is so hard, but I know I need to wait on you. Give me the ability to be brave and courageous. Help me to be patient. Help me to always trust no matter what. Amen.

Mourning and Comfort

God blesses those who mourn for they shall be comforted. Matthew 5:4 NLT

The world loves to laugh. We enjoy and feel comforted by laughter. As with so much of Jesus' teaching, this runs counter to the accepted norms of society. Nobody I know would go into mourning in order to seek comfort.

No one really likes to cry do they? Is there anyone who enjoys bad news and looks forward to that phone call or knock on the door that leads to genuine brokenness? I think all of us live with the notion that in a second of time a normal day or a normal life can be turned upside down.

Jesus knew that to live on this earth would mean that we would all face sorrow and grief. We grieve death, divorce, loss of a job, personal injury or illness, the actions of our children, change in health of a family member, change in our finances, and a hundred other things. You may be mourning something today. It may be about you, or it could even be about something in the world around you because sometimes the actions of others can cause genuine sorrow. We should all grieve for people that go without food or clean water around our world. Mourning is a quality that I think Jesus wants in us. It's not so much about the devastations that come our way personally, but can you mourn for others? Can you carry a sorrow or burden in you for the people around you? If so, you will be comforted by God himself. He will help you bear your burden and season of mourning. He is offering you comfort today. Take him at his word and receive this blessing.

PRAYER

Dear Lord, thank you for your blessings. Today I would really love to feel and sense comfort from you. Too many times I look for comfort from other people or things. Help me find comfort in you more often. Amen.

Enjoy Some Rest

Then Jesus said, "Let's go off by ourselves to a quiet place and rest awhile." Mark 6:31 NLT

The context of this Scripture is that Jesus was simply worn out or wearing out from the continual interaction with people. In his case, the crowds were in the thousands and his teaching and healing of people were happening whenever and wherever they could find him.

Immediately after Jesus made this statement to the disciples, they climbed into a boat and headed for "a quiet place where they could be alone." Then we read this:

"But many people recognized them and saw them leaving, and people from many towns ran ahead along the shore and got there ahead of them. Jesus saw the huge crowd as he stepped from the boat, and he had compassion on them because they were like sheep without a shepherd. So he began teaching them many things" (Mark 6:33-34 NLT).

The decision to step from the boat out of compassion led to feeding 5,000 with a few fish and some bread. He did eventually send the disciples away in the boat while he went into the hills alone to pray. Of course, the disciples needed him later in the night in the middle of a storm, so Jesus came walking on the water to provide them with the security they needed.

If Jesus needed rest from interacting with and leading people, we also need to recognize the importance of this. As leaders, there will be times when we are exhausted from continually giving out to others. We teach, we train, we model and encourage others to grow as people and leaders. We cast vision and we make it happen. We engage in conversations and problem solve when called upon. Sometimes we discover the problems and work with others to resolve them.

Leadership is exhausting. People, even well-meaning ones, can drain and tax our emotional well-being. So what can we learn from Jesus' example?

- We need margin in our life that allows us to recover mentally, emotionally, physically, and spiritually.

- Retreat is not about vacation as much as it is about preserving ourselves to work and lead another day.
- Make time.
- Schedule blackout days occasionally and do nothing or don't allow yourself to be interrupted on those days.
- Read a good book. It will give your mind some rest.
- Practice hitting the pause button during the day. Even a five or ten minute shut down is helpful at times.

Remember our Creator built a day of rest into our human manual for living. It's called a Sabbath, and it is a day for rest and recovery.

An archaeologist once hired some Inca tribesmen to lead him to an archaeological site deep in the mountains. After they had been moving for some time, the tribesmen stopped and insisted they would go no further. The archaeologist grew impatient and then angry. However, no matter how much he cajoled, the tribesmen would not go any further. Then all of a sudden the tribesmen changed their attitude. They picked up the gear and set off once more. When the bewildered archaeologist asked why they had stopped and refused to move for so long, the tribesmen answered, "We had been moving too fast and had to wait for our souls to catch up with our bodies."

PRAYER

Dear God, please give me the ability to slow down and take time to rest. Help me see the importance of this and help me observe a weekly Sabbath. Amen.

Hearing God's Call

Simon Peter said, "I'm going fishing." John 21:3 NLT

The apostle Peter was one of the first disciples called by Jesus. He was a fisherman who was promised to become a fisher of men and women. He was enlisted to fish for souls and help them come to know Christ. He failed. He faltered in his faith just prior to the crucifixion of Jesus and then repeatedly denied that he ever knew him.

When Jesus resurrected, Peter heard about it and was one of the first ones to run to the open grave. The Bible says: "Stooping, he peered in and saw the empty linen wrappings; then he went home again, wondering what had happened" (Luke 24:12 NLT).

Peter was on the wrong side of things but still had a heart for Jesus. He was lost and no doubt afraid when he decided to go back to his fishing profession. It's what he knew and so it's what he returned to.

Jesus found him there and called him again to rejoin the disciples and the work that was about to happen. It was a simple call. There was no inquisition or questioning except four words: "Do you love me?" Peter answered three times, "Lord, you know I love you," and just like that he was back and recalled to service.

We complicate it sometimes. We too often don't believe it's his voice calling us back when we have landed on the wrong side of things; but it is what Jesus does. He came to seek and to save the lost. No matter where you might be in your faith journey, don't give up. Listen for his voice because he will come looking for you. Fish for a while if you need to, but Jesus will come looking for you. Be ready. Love him and he will lead you in the direction you need to go.

Brennan Manning, a recipient of God's repeated love and forgiveness, wrote, "I could more easily contain Niagara Falls in a tea cup than I can comprehend the wild, uncontainable love of God."

PRAYER

Dear Jesus, when I go off on my own, please gently lead me back to hearing your voice and answering your call. Thank you for never giving up on me. Amen.

Keep Fighting for your Faith

Finishing is better than starting. Patience is better than pride. Ecclesiastes 7:8 NLT

Most of us have heard the phrase, "finish strong." Often it is easier said than done. I don't think this phrase should just be ascribed to retirement or the end of our lives. I really believe we can incorporate it into our days, weeks, and months. We can apply it to raising our children, finishing projects, and a host of other real life scenarios.

King Solomon, who is thought to be the wisest man who ever lived, wrote these words a long time ago. At first I wondered what finishing had to do with patience and pride, but I think they go together.

There are times when we start things that seem harder to finish the longer we go. As time goes along, we can be tempted to check out or give up when the grind becomes tough. We might be tempted to quit early and take the credit for a great beginning instead of staying patient and pushing through to the finish.

The Message Bible translated this verse this way: "Endings are better than beginnings. Sticking to it is better than standing out" (Ecclesiastes 7:8 MSG).

Keep fighting and moving forward. Don't give up without a fight. Allow God to be God and work through you and in you. Even if you fail, don't quit. With God all things are possible.

The finish or ending is always better if you see it through to the end. Whether work, projects, relationships, parenting, or life, be patient and finish strong or well.

One day all will stand before the great Judge and our work will be tested. We will all be there. Lady Gaga and Donald Trump. Bill Gates and Mother Teresa. Adolf Hitler and Billy Graham. You may wind up standing next to Abraham Lincoln or Moses, but rest assured we will all be there. The questions will come: How did you finish? Did you finish?

"I have fought the good fight, I have finished the race, and I have remained faithful" (2 Timothy 4:7 NLT).

PRAYER

Dear Lord, may I always fight to finish well in my faith journey with you. If I falter or even fail, give me the grace to fall forward and reaching for you instead of turning away. Please keep me headed in the right direction daily. Amen.

The Greatest of These Is Love

Three things will last forever—faith, hope, and love—and the greatest of these is love. 1 Corinthians 13:13 NLT

This verse appears at the end of what has been traditionally referred to as the "Love Chapter." Because of the poetic and profound words in the other twelve verses of this chapter, they have been used in wedding ceremonies around the world. I don't think that is necessarily what the apostle Paul had in mind when he penned these words, but they are certainly appropriate within the context of a wedding. His conclusion is found in verse 13.

There are moments and seasons in our life when we may ask, "What's left?" We consider losses so big that we lose focus on the realities that are still there. The positives seem hard to find and yet the writer reminds us that there are three things that will last forever. Some translations say: "These three things remain." This is what we have left:

Faith: Faith is the gift of God; and if you ask him, he will give you enough faith and enough of his presence to sustain you when life seems to be blowing up right in front of you. He promises to never leave us or forsake us.

Hope: Hope always remains as long as we are drawing a breath. We have the hope of the next moment, hour, day, month, or year. Hope gives us the courage to face our biggest challenges and fears in a positive way based on the strength we find in Christ.

Love: There is God's love of course, and that is the best love of all. There will always be family love to support and sustain us through the toughest of times. There is the love of our faith community. Other than God's love, all other loves are imperfect and may fail us, but know that his love always remains.

Walk by faith today filled with the hope of new things and new days. Accept the love that God offers to you and be encouraged and blessed.

PRAYER

Dear Jesus, sometimes I wonder what I really have to call my own. Today I am reminded that I have faith, hope, and love. Thank you for loving me with a love that never fails. Your love gives me hope today! Amen.

Let Me See and Hear

But blessed are your eyes, because they see; and your ears, because they hear. Matthew 13:16 NLT

Jesus spoke these words when the disciples asked why he taught with parables. The fact is, they were the first disciples and were taught by Jesus himself. They were hearing his teaching firsthand. They had front row seats and saw and heard all Jesus had to say. He followed up with these words, "Many prophets and righteous people longed to see what you see, but they didn't see it. And they longed to hear what you hear, but they didn't hear it."

Fast forward to our time. We see and we hear. We are inundated with opportunity to see and hear about Jesus. We enjoy two thousand plus years of church history. Right now, on any given day, you can watch church services around the world take place on social media. We have the Bible, we have teaching, preaching, and churches. We have worship and opportunities that generations before us never had.

Pause today and ponder how blessed you are to have the access you do to God and his Word. Thank him for giving you the opportunity to live your life in a way that touches others with his love. The ancient prophets caught glimpses of a coming Messiah, but we can see so much more.

Jesus is just as real today as he was when he was walking the earth. Open up the eyes of your heart and listen closely as you go through this day. Listen closely as you read his Word and you will hear what he wants you to hear. You will find him and you will know that he is engaged in your life.

PRAYER

Lord, thank you for the blessing of seeing and hearing you daily. Help us to see what you see, hear what you hear, and do what you do. Amen.

A Strong Fortress

The name of the LORD is a strong fortress; the godly run to him and are safe. The rich think of their wealth as a strong defense, they imagine it to be a high wall of safety. Proverbs 18:10-11 NLT

Walls, forts, fortifications were places of safety in ancient times. What is being suggested is that we all have places to run and hide. You may pick a place of your own choosing, or you can pick the Lord. You may choose to trust in your own knowledge, gifts, skills, talents, education, wealth, strength, or a host of other things, but ultimately they will fail you.

There is only one place to run and find true safety. The Lord is our strong fortress! We run to him! Notice it is not just "the Lord," but "the name of the Lord." When all around is sinking sand, run to the name of the Lord. When storms and winds are blowing in your life that are shaking you to your core, run to the name of the Lord.

Get to know God and his strengths and attributes. The more you know about him the more you will run to his name. You will call on his power, his wisdom, and his sovereignty.

Have you allowed anything else to become your source of safety other than the name of the Lord? Run hard toward his name today and find true and abiding safety.

PRAYER

Dear Lord, today I call out your name. It is you that I seek and need to be my protection. I need you today, Lord. I need a strong defense and a high wall of safety. Thank you for your promises. Amen.

Put God First

*And you must love the L*ORD *your God with all your heart, all your soul, and all your strength.* Deuteronomy 6:5 NLT

This verse from the Old Testament was also spoken by Jesus when he came to this earth and began to call and teach his disciples. It has been God's standard and measurement of our commitment from the beginning.

Do you love God in this way?

Let's examine it closer and let God examine us in the process. Ask yourself these questions.

Do I love him with all of my heart?

The heart is who you are on the inside. It is your inner man or woman, your mind and will. It controls your likes and dislikes. It determines what you treasure and value. In Matthew 6:21 we are reminded that, "Wherever your treasure is, there the desires of your heart will also be." Only you can answer where your heart is and what you have given it to.

Do I love him with all of my soul?

This means your life, self, person, desire, passions, appetites, and emotions. Your soul is the part of you that will make it to eternity where you will live forever. It is in your soul that you will be bitter or better. We are told by Jesus to not fear those that can kill our body but to fear God who can destroy both our soul and body in hell. What or who you give your soul to is pretty important. As Jesus faced the cross he was deeply troubled in his soul. Peter wrote that the reward for trusting him would be the salvation of our souls.

"And what do you benefit if you gain the whole world but lose your own soul? Is anything worth more than your soul?" (Matthew 16:26 NLT).

Do I love him with all of my strength?

What kind of an effort are you giving your relationship with God? Rate the effort and attention you are giving to your spiritual walk. I doubt that anyone reading this will need to dial it down a notch or two. Throw yourself into serving God with every ounce of strength you have. Put him first. Seriously. Try it for a day or a week if you are really brave.

According to Scripture, God will give you the strength you need to follow him, fight for him, and to have great faith in him.

Apply yourself like you do to other things that don't really matter when eternity is the goal.

Our spiritual walk really comes down to putting God first. It is simple yet profound. Think about it as you walk through this day. Think about him and what it would mean to put God first as you come to each decision, action, reaction, and events throughout this day. Put God first! Love him with all your heart, soul, and strength.

PRAYER

Dear God, may I always put you first in my life. I pray for this day. I am asking for help in putting you first today. Amen.

Follow Me!

Later, as Jesus left the town, he saw a tax collector named Levi sitting at his tax collector's booth. "Follow me and be my disciple," Jesus said to him. So Levi got up, left everything, and followed him. Luke 5:27 -28 NLT

Jesus calls and invites everyone in the world to follow him. When he was calling his first disciples, he called them from some of the most unlikely places. He did not go to seminaries or religious institutions but walked the streets and the seashores calling some very unusual people.

One of them was Levi, later to be known as Matthew. He was a tax collector, which meant he was hated by most people because of his profession. The call was simple yet deeply profound.

Jesus said, "Follow me and be my disciple."

It's the same thing he says to us when he calls us. It's just six words but takes a lifetime to understand and unpack.

Levi's response is a classic response we should make a big deal of because it holds the secret to everlasting life. Are you ready to read it? Are you ready to do what Levi did? It will cost you everything and take every ounce of strength you have but the exchange is well worth it.

"So Levi got up, left everything, and followed him."

It seems like a simple formula:

Get up from wherever you've been living figuratively speaking.
Leave all the bad stuff behind.
Follow him.

Accepting Christ as one's Savior is only the beginning of a lifetime of battles, trust, testing, mountains, and valleys. Sometimes we will struggle beyond what we can imagine or think we can overcome. Sometimes God will be closer to us than a brother.

If you have heard his call but not really responded the way you should, why not get up and leave everything and truly follow him? Even if you have failed him in the past, he is patiently waiting for you to respond again and trust him with your past, present, and future.

Dear Jesus, I believe that you have called me and want me to follow you. Give me the courage today to get up and leave the past behind. Lead me, Lord, and I will follow you. Amen.

Don't Give Up

Let your compassion quickly meet our needs, for we are on the brink of despair. Psalm 79:8b NLT

Thankfully, most people don't feel that they are on the brink of despair every day, but when you are walking through a season of challenge you might be tempted to despair. For the Christian, despair should never be something we experience because of the power and strength of our God. In theory, we are supposed to trust him with our lives and all things that happen to us in our lifetimes.

There are times when like the psalmist you may feel as though you are on the brink of despair. There are no answers in sight. You have prayed and tried to muster your faith, but things in your life remain the same with no change that you can see. It is in these moments that despair may loom as an option. Don't give in to despair. When you despair, you have given up and are no longer trusting God. Despair allows us to seek other answers besides God. We take things into our own hands; and more often than not, we wind up with greater challenge and problems.

Being "on the brink of despair" is not despair. If you relate to this phrase because of something at home or work, don't give up. Remind yourself like the psalmist did of God's compassion, and appeal to him today on that basis. Remind him of his compassion and immerse yourself in who God is. Remember that he has your best interest in mind.

There is nothing that can compare to God's compassion. Allow him to work. Stay strong. Wait on the Lord and he will strengthen your heart. Don't give up today. Keep fighting and see the salvation of our God.

PRAYER

Dear Lord, I don't ever want to give up in my walk with you. There are days when I don't have answers for sure, but I still want to trust you. Amen.

God's Hand Will Go to Work for You

And now, Lord, look upon their threats and grant to your servants to continue to speak your word with all boldness, while you stretch out your hand to heal, and signs and wonders are performed through the name of your holy servant Jesus. Acts 4:29-30 ESV

This was a prayer by Peter and John after they were released from being called out for preaching and teaching about Jesus. They were excited to be used by God and they weren't afraid of the threats. A few days later they were arrested for the same behavior, and this time they were beaten before being released. The Bible says they rejoiced to be counted worthy to suffer for the cause of Christ.

In reading this prayer over many times, it seems to be a good pattern for us to follow when we find ourselves in challenging times. They were concerned that God would see what they were seeing or hearing, but in the same breath they ask for him to give them boldness as they spoke. They could have ended the prayer, but they once again circle back to God and say, "...while you stretch out your hand..."

They were going to do what God called them to do no matter what, but they wanted him to see and be aware do it *while* he was involved in working alongside them.

What would you like for God to stretch out his hand and do for you or with you? When God is stretching out his hand, it is not for a hand-out, but it is for a hand up or hand of support. He is about to go to work for you. I would not want to go through this life relying on myself and not have a powerful and sovereign God who offers his hands to work with ours.

When Nehemiah asked his king to be able to go back and rebuild the temple in Jerusalem, this is what he said, "And the king granted these requests, because the gracious hand of God was on me" (Nehemiah 2:8).

"And the gracious hand of our God protected us and saved us from enemies and bandits along the way" (Ezra 8:31).

Someday the hand of God will wipe away the tears from our eyes. Let his hand work on your behalf today. While writing this, the words to a song I haven't heard in years came to mind.

Put your hand in the hand of the man who stilled the water
Put your hand in the hand of the man who calmed the sea
Take a look at yourself and you can look at others differently
Put your hand in the hand of the man from Galilee.

PRAYER

Dear God, I am reaching for your hand today to work beside me and for me. You know better than me what I need today. Please, Lord, let your healing hand work in my life and the life of my family. Amen.

Avoid the Fall

Hebrews 11 is known as the faith chapter because it lists the stories of heroic acts of faith by Old Testament men and women. Their stories are inspiring and you and I should read them often. The verses following chapter 11 are a continuation of what has been written before, even though it is now labeled chapter 12. They should be read together. The writer pushes forward with these urgent words:

Therefore, since we are surrounded by such a huge crowd of witnesses to the life of faith, let us strip off every weight that slows us down, especially the sin that so easily trips us up. And let us run with endurance the race God has set before us. We do this by keeping our eyes on Jesus, the champion who initiates and perfects our faith. Hebrews 12:1-2 NLT

Feeling bogged down by life and circumstances? Overcome and overwhelmed by things you never saw coming and that you don't have answers for? Has some sinful behavior entered your life and you feel trapped and without hope?

Go back to these verses and break them down for three action steps to getting back on track.

- **Strip off every weight ... especially the sin.**
- **Run with endurance.**
- **Keep your eyes on Jesus.**

You can do this! Start with whatever or whoever has taken you away from following Christ and remove yourself from it or them. It may not be sin. It may be a lack of priorities, but that is easily fixed by making sure Christ is first in your life.

This life is a long run. It will not always be fast but it will be steady. You may walk; you may crawl; but stay in the race and on the course that God has set before you.

Never take your eyes off of Jesus. Distractions will call for your time and attention; but put the phone down, lay aside the laptop, turn off the TV, take the headphones out of your ears and unplug. Give God the best and first minutes of your day. Reach for him every day and not the devices and distractions we all are attached to.

Sounds simple, but it will take courage, determination, and desire. You can have as much of God as you want. Draw close to him and he will draw near to you. It will be worth the effort when we stand before God some day and face the eternity that is coming for all of us.

Let him be the champion, initiator, and the one who perfects your faith!

PRAYER

Dear God, help me today to remember those that have had great faith before me. Help me live a simple life of surrender to you and for you. Give me the courage to let go of anything or anyone that is hindering my walk with You. Amen.

A Clean Heart

Create in me a clean heart, O God. Psalm 51:10 NLT

Who wouldn't want a clean heart? The clean heart that the Psalmist David was praying for was a heart that was washed and cleansed from the guilt of sins. For him, it meant that the residue left over from sinful choices would be gone. It would be a new start. A new day! It would be as though nothing bad had ever happened in his life to darken and stain his soul.

Sin always leaves a mark. Men and women struggle with sin and can easily be overcome by the culture and their own desires. The Bible warns us to flee temptation and to avoid actions that would damage and destroy our hearts and lives, but many times we push on hoping for something that is illusive and disguised cleverly by the enemy of our souls. In the end we are left dirty and disheartened because sin does what it always does, it stains our life and leaves us discouraged and filled with doubt.

For David, it was adultery and murder. It was some pretty big stuff that marred and marked his heart. The good news is that he cried out to God and threw himself upon the altar of God's mercy. He took responsibility and asked for God to create in him a new heart. He followed up this prayer with a request for God to renew and restore, and that is exactly what God did!

Somehow David found the strength to trust that God heard his prayer, and he received what he was asking for! His heart was cleansed from it all! He was renewed with a right spirit, and God restored the joy of his salvation.

Pray and ask God to create in you a clean heart! Allow him to wash your heart and to give you another chance to start over. It's what he does. He loves to help us get it right. He is a God of many opportunities, and he is waiting to hear from you today.

PRAYER

Dear God, can I say it any better than David did? I need a clean heart. I need a do over and a fresh start. Please cleanse me and help me start over today. Amen.

Peter's Invitation

Peter said, "Change your life. Turn to God and be baptized, each of you, in the name of Jesus Christ, so your sins are forgiven...." He went on in this vein for a long time, urging them over and over, "Get out while you can; get out of this sick and stupid culture!" That day about three thousand took him at his word, and were baptized. Acts 2:38, 40-41 MSG

It was the day of Pentecost and the disciples were filled with the Holy Spirit. The city was full of travelers and they observed this commotion of 120 Christ followers rejoicing and praising God. The disciple Peter, now forgiven and restored, stood up and preached about Jesus. The message was simple, but apparently he preached for quite a while

The message? Change your life! Turn to God! Be baptized! Let Christ forgive your sins.

He offered them a chance to truly enter into the kingdom of God on this day. He wasn't offering membership to a church or denomination. He wasn't encouraging them to think about Jesus every now and then when they are in trouble. He was calling them to full-on discipleship—committing their lives and loves to Jesus and his teaching.

Could this message be for you today? It's an appealing call. Why wouldn't you want every part of your life to be given and surrendered to Christ? He will come back someday and we will face a judgment for how we lived and what we did with our lives.

On this day, about 3,000 took him at his word and believed. Even all these years later it is still the best invitation ever.

PRAYER

Dear Jesus, I believe that today I needed to hear this invitation. Change my life, O God. Change my heart, O God. Let me hear your call and follow you all the days of my life. Amen.

God is Always Going to Be There

"But there is a God in heaven." Daniel 2:28 NLT

"But there is a God in heaven" was uttered by a young man taken captive from his homeland and pressed into the service of a wicked king. Because of his commitment to God, Daniel was highly favored and promoted in unusual ways for a political prisoner of war.

When the king tried to find one of his wise advisors that could interpret his disturbing dream, not one of them could. He issued an order to kill them all. When Daniel heard it, he asked to be given the chance to interpret it. After much prayer, he did indeed give the king the answers he wanted regarding his dream.

This is what he said to King Nebuchadnezzar, "There are no wise men, enchanters, magicians, or fortune-tellers who can reveal the king's secret. But there is a God in heaven who reveals secrets, and he has shown King Nebuchadnezzar what will happen in the future."

Maybe today it is not a dream that you are struggling with, but something is happening and you don't know where to turn. Life can sometimes leave us with more questions than answers, and we are tempted to be frustrated and discouraged.

Today think about and mediate on this phrase: "But there is a God in heaven."

There is a God in heaven who knows exactly where you are.

There is a God in heaven who loves you beyond your comprehension.

There is a God in heaven who has the power to help you overcome.

There is a God in heaven who wants to be in the middle of everything you do.

There is a God in heaven who will lead you like a shepherd.

There is a God in heaven who sticks closer than a brother.

There is a God in heaven today and he is praying for you.

Walk today with confidence that God is on your side and that he cares for you and loves you.

PRAYER

Dear God, I know and believe you are in heaven and that you know exactly where I am today. Please help me never forget that you are there and that you are here with me every day. Amen.

He Is the Vine

"Abide in me, and I in you." John 15:4 ESV

I've been working on a thirty-day devotional based on Jesus' teaching in John 15 and other verses from the Bible that teach the importance of abiding in him. A few hours before his death, Jesus told his disciples that he was the Vine and they were the branches; and the point was that unless they remained or kept abiding in him, their work and worth would be useless.

Would you say that you are abiding in the Vine, Jesus?

In the face of recent events, many of us have had our faith shaken or at least questioned. We've asked ourselves what we really believe. Who do we really believe in? We've been reminded how fragile life is and how quickly our comfortable first world lifestyle can be challenged and turned upside down—almost overnight.

There is only one hope. This life is a vapor that disappears quickly. We live our lives, work our jobs, build our relationships, and one day wake up to realize that we have fewer years to be alive than the years we have already lived on this earth. Morbid thoughts? I don't think so. I prefer to think of them as words of reality. These words should cause us to focus on what really matters and what we will wish we had prioritized when we stand before God someday.

Jesus gave us the plan. "Abide in me." That was it. Stay connected to Jesus. Give him your full attention every day, and let him work in you and through you. Branches bear fruit if they stay connected. What a great day to think about what is going on in your world and more importantly in your life.

PRAYER

Dear Lord, you know better than anyone how connected we are. I don't want to be a branch on my own. I long to be connected to you and to be used by you. Help me to understand this, and show me the way. Amen.

Chariots and Horses

Some trust in chariots, and some in horses; but we will remember the name of the LORD our God. Psalm 20:7 NKJV

What or who are you trusting today? When this psalm was written, chariots and horses represented the power of armies and defense. If you had horses, you were considered wealthy because of the ability to have transportation and farm, which would feed your family.

Recently in our world we have come to understand just how fragile life can be, not just because of a virus, but we have learned also how quickly food and product shortages can happen. We have learned that people are willing to do whatever they need to do to take care of themselves first. Some of us have wondered what we would do if we didn't have a paycheck. How would we survive if the economy was shattered, and what would happen to our homes, families, and life in general?

For me, the "horses and chariots" represent the government and its programs. No matter how benevolent their intent, governments are not always able to save everyone and protect them. Stimulus checks sent out by the billions or trillions make no sense when our government is already in mind-blowing debt. So what do you trust in?

The Bible is clear, and God is clear about calling us to trust him with our very lives. We read in the Word of God that perilous times will come. Our earth and world will be shaken, but we are instructed to keep our faith strong in God. This means pursue your relationship with him now, not when the world is falling apart. Be loyal and faithful to him now so you are treating him as a parachute to use in case the plane is crashing.

In Luke 21, shortly before going to the cross, Jesus gave his followers some dire warnings. Through it all he told them to hang on to their faith and to keep their eyes on him. "Be always on the watch, and pray that you may be able to escape all that is about to happen, and that you may be able to stand before the Son of Man" (Luke 21:36 NIV).

Like the psalmist says, "We will remember the name of the Lord our God." Trust in God over government. He will be all that matters in the end.

PRAYER

Dear God, sometimes I am very afraid because I don't know what is going to happen next. Our world needs to turn to you. Please hear the prayers of those who trust you. Please hear my prayer. Amen.

Living in Harmony

May God, who gives this patience and encouragement, help you live in complete harmony with each other, as is fitting for followers of Christ Jesus. Romans 15:5 NLT

Have you broken the law lately? Probably. Before you react in horror at this accusation, remember that even going over the speed limit is breaking the law. Sometimes laws are hard to keep. Many times, we are tempted to give ourselves permission to break a law because we may feel entitled in some way. We see this most often when people purposely drive through red lights because they feel their time is more important and pressing, so they willingly break a law and put others in danger.

Here is some good news. Here are some things you can do and not have to worry about breaking any laws. The apostle Paul says when the Holy Spirit is producing fruit in our lives it will come out in these ways:

Love

Joy

Peace

Patience

Kindness

Goodness

Faithfulness

Gentleness

Self-control

Take these one at a time and measure your life. Work them into your life with the help of the Holy Spirit. Make a new start today in relationships at home and at work. Allow God to love through you. There is no law against these things!

PRAYER

Dear Jesus, examine my life and show me how to love those that I interact with today. Fill me with your presence that I might love like you love. Amen.

Be Careful With Your Heart

Be careful then, dear brothers and sisters. Make sure that your own hearts are not evil and unbelieving, turning you away from the living God. You must warn each other every day, while it is still "today," so that none of you will be deceived by sin and hardened against God. Hebrews 3:12-13 NLT

Recently we celebrated Valentine's Day and as always there was a lot of interest in hearts. Candy hearts, chocolate hearts, paper hearts, cut-out hearts, and balloon hearts were everywhere. The Hebrew writer was also very interested in our hearts or the seat of our affections and emotions.

The world we live in does its best daily to destroy our hearts. We are bombarded with information, advertising, entertainment, and temptations that are aimed at our affections. They are purposeful and often calculated to pull us in one direction or the other. Even people can have that effect on us as well.

We must guard our hearts if we are to remain faithful to God. Our hearts are not to be trusted, and so the writer says "be careful" and "make sure." Be sure of your heart and its affections. Test it and prove it daily. Be honest so that you can move back toward God if you need to. Don't be afraid to do the examination.

Jeremiah the prophet wrote these words: "The human heart is the most deceitful of all things, and desperately wicked. Who really knows how bad it is? But I, the Lord, search all hearts and examine secret motives" (Jeremiah 17:9-10 NLT).

Pause every day and truly examine your heart. Allow the Holy Spirit to show you your motives. Do everything you can to defeat the influence and pull of anything that moves you away from God. Love God first and foremost. Put God first on the throne of your heart. Pray this prayer often:

Search me, O God, and know my heart; test me and know my anxious thoughts. Point out anything in me that offends you, and lead me along the path of everlasting life. Psalm 139:23-24 NLT

Amen

He Supplies All Our Needs

And this same God who takes care of me will supply all your needs from his glorious riches, which have been given to us in Christ Jesus. Philippians 4:19 NLT

In the closing words of this letter written to the Christians and the church at Philippi, the apostle Paul reminds them of the God they are serving and his care. He expressed great thankfulness to them for their care of himself and professed that he currently had no needs.

He wrote these words earlier in the conclusion of this letter, "I know how to live on almost nothing or with everything. I have learned the secret of living in every situation, whether it is with a full stomach or empty, with plenty or little. For I can do everything through Christ, who gives me strength."

Here is the real backstory. He was in a Roman prison and chained between two Roman soldiers all day long!

The point is that no matter what you and I face, when our trust is in God we can learn to handle it with grace and peace. This is huge! Most people, even Christians (at least in North America), are nearly rendered helpless with the smallest of losses. Usually our first thought is, "Why is God doing this to me."

Make sure you are truly connected to God each day.

Trust him with your life and all your life experiences.

All humans experience adversity in their lives.

Be ready with a strong faith.

Pray often, all day long.

Remember, God will supply all your needs through Jesus Christ.

PRAYER

Dear Jesus, just as you were with the apostle Paul in prison, I believe that you will be with me today. I am so grateful for this promise and your presence. Amen.

I Will Trust Jesus

Jesus shouted to the crowds, "If you trust me, you are trusting not only me, but also God who sent me. For when you see me, you are seeing the one who sent me. I have come as a light to shine in this dark world, so that all who put their trust in me will no longer remain in the dark." John 11:44-46 NLT

Are you afraid of the dark? You don't have to answer that out loud, but most people prefer to have access to light, especially in an unknown place. Most of us would admit to how differently things appear when there is no light or how mysterious things can seem when the lights are off.

Within the context of our lives, we need light. We need to be able to see what is happing around us and to process it clearly. There is no question that we live in a dark world. Jesus said in the above verses that he came as a light to shine in a dark world.

For sure, our world is not getting any brighter. Sin and disobedience to God's Word is everywhere; and due to the onslaught of social media, entertainment media, and other forces at work, our children and grandchildren are facing an even darker world.

We need the Light. We need to be the light. Jesus is the Light, and he also taught that we as his followers would be a light for the world around us.

"You are the light of the world—like a city on a hilltop that cannot be hidden.... In the same way, let your good deeds shine out for all to see, so that everyone will praise your heavenly Father" (Matthew 5:14,16 NLT).

No matter what is happening in your world,

No matter what is happening at your work,

No matter what is happening in your homes, families, or neighborhoods,

No matter what is happening in your churches, your relationships, your personal life, or anywhere else ... put your trust in Jesus, and as he says, "All who put their trust in me will no longer remain in the dark."

Believe in him and trust him today. Tell him you trust him. Speak it out in prayer, and then live it out by faith. There can be no darkness when we are walking with Jesus.

PRAYER

Dear Jesus, you promised to bring us from darkness to light. You are the only light I need even when all around me seems dark. Teach me to trust you, Lord. Teach me to let your light shine through me. Amen.

He Never Changes

I am the Lord, *and I do not change.* Malachi 3:6 NLT

This scriptural reference is God responding to a wayward people that have chosen to go their own way and make their own choices. Israel totally disregarded God's Word and commandments and became very agitated when they had to pay the consequences of ignoring God and his sovereignty.

So who is this God that doesn't change? What are some things we need to know about him?

He is longsuffering.

He is merciful.

He is demanding.

He is holy.

He wants us to follow him 100 percent.

He accepts our repentance.

He knows everything.

He sees everything.

He is all powerful.

He will give wisdom to those that ask for it.

He can heal you physically, mentally, and emotionally.

He is forgiving.

He is just.

He is compassionate.

He will judge us all someday, but our time on this earth is our chance to follow him and determine our eternal home.

The Hebrew writer reminds us that, "Jesus Christ is the same yesterday, today, and forever." With that in mind, do everything you can to know this God. Find a way to push past the voices of our culture and press into knowing him and walking with him. Let him be your friend and constant companion. Allow him to change you from the inside out. Let him do his work through you to effect change in the world around you. This God longs to be in a relationship with you. Let him be the Lord of your life.

Lord, you are unchanging, and that brings me comfort today. Allow me to know you better and follow you more. Teach me who you really are and what you really want from me. Amen.

A Love Story

Intreat me not to leave thee, or to return from following after thee: for whither thou goest, I will go; and where thou lodgest, I will lodge: thy people shall be my people, And thy God my God: Where thou diest, will I die, and there will I be buried: the Lord do so to me, and more also, if ought but death part thee and me. Ruth 1:16-17 KJV

Rarely do I use the Kings James Version but these words have been part of my life and story so I share them with you today.

When my dad asked my mom to marry him they were students at a Christian college in Cincinnati, Ohio. She said nothing but ran away and didn't speak to him for two days! At the end of the two days, she pressed a piece of paper into his hand with these words from the book of Ruth and in doing so gave him her answer.

These words were spoken by a young widow named Ruth and were spoken to her mother-in-law who was encouraging her to go back to her own country and people. For whatever reason, this young woman wanted to stay and take care of Naomi even though she had no more sons. In fact she had very little to offer, but Ruth was determined to not forsake her.

It's an incredibly inspiring story of loyalty, love, and a willingness to give unselfishly to someone else. In fact, Ruth was giving up much of her own life and future because of love. Of course, you should read the rest of the story because she would eventually be blessed beyond her wildest dreams with a future and a husband.

Ruth's willingness to sacrifice her immediate happiness actually led to a beautiful future.

Practice loyalty today, first and foremost to God and then to others.

PRAYER

Lord, help me to love others around me today with a love that is pleasing to you. Please give me the grace to love people that might not be easy to love. Help me to love like you love me. Amen.

God's Ways

As you do not know the way the spirit comes to the bones in the womb of a woman with child, so you do not know the work of God who makes everything. Ecclesiastes 11:5 ESV

It is clear in the Scriptures that God's ways are higher than our ways. He is the Creator of all and the giver of life. He alone knows the mystery of how he breathes life into the baby in the womb. This verse alone should cause us to grieve for the thousands of babies whose lives end in their mothers' wombs. It is apparent that God is at work breathing life and his will into this sacred place.

We do not know the work of God. Behind the scenes in our lives, he is at work. Unseen to us, Jesus sits at the right hand of God praying for us as we manage our lives on this planet and navigate the difficulties and challenges that inevitably come our way.

Today, God knows exactly what you are thinking about, dealing with, scared of, or running from. He knows where you are in life and what he wants from you. God is at work in you. Stay close enough to him that you can see it and know it. Rely on him daily. The God who provides breath and spirit to the bones in the womb can do big things on your behalf. Don't stop trusting.

PRAYER

Dear God, I can't even fathom your ways. Help me to believe with all of my heart that you really do know about me. You know and you care. I may not be able to see answers, but I believe that you have the answers. Your ways are above me, but I believe. Amen.

Anger Is Never a Good Option

People with understanding control their anger; a hot temper shows great foolishness. Proverbs 14:29 NLT

Anger is something all of us have dealt with at some point in our lives. Anger can produce fear, it can be raging, it can be quiet and sullen, and it can cause both physical and emotional pain. Anger can easily get out of control.

Road rage, threatening messages, murder, destruction, and fighting are just some of the things that can be associated with anger. A correction officer once told me that some of the nicest people are on death row. They were good people that lost control of their anger and killed someone in the moment.

The writer is warning us to be understanding about this emotion called anger. We are to practice patience and self-control. The psalmist wrote, "Refrain from anger and give up your rage" (Psalm 37:8).

Why not practice self-control when it comes to things that make you angry? Better yet, ask God to help you and to soften your heart daily. In Proverbs 15:1 we read, "A gentle answer turns away anger but a harsh word stirs up wrath."

Recently I attended a children's event at a major arena. While going through security, I lost an expensive pocketknife. I was not happy. It seemed ridiculous. Most of all I was surprised how much it bothered me for several minutes afterward. Thankfully, I kept my mouth shut (for the most part), although I'm pretty sure I rolled my eyes. Processing my response made me aware that I still have work to do on the inside.

PRAYER

God, thank you for your Word that deals with us personally on so many issues. Don't let my anger be a factor in my relationships or encounters with others today. Let me walk with your peace in my heart. Amen.

Giving God Our Best

Then you ask, "How have we defiled the sacrifices?" You defile them by saying the altar of the Lord deserves no respect. When you give blind animals as sacrifices, isn't that wrong? And isn't it wrong to offer animals that are crippled and diseased? Try giving gifts like that to your governor, and see how pleased he is! Malachi 1:7-8 NLT

During the time of sacrifices in the Old Testament, God always asked his people to sacrifice their best animals in their acts of worship. From the beginning it was to be the best lamb, without spot or blemish, that they would offer to God with respect and honor.

Over time, and a lot of backsliding, the people got sloppy and careless with God's rules and desires. Most of the time they completely ignored what God had to say and their history. When they found themselves in trouble or a stuck place they would turn to God and offer some kind of sacrificial offering. Obviously, they weren't taking God seriously and would offer blemished, blind, or unhealthy animals, which in reality were no sacrifice at all.

I wonder if we ever offer God our worst instead of our best. I wonder if we offer him our second best in hopes that it will be enough.

The only way God expects us to live is to offer him our firsts of everything. He is God and he wants to be first in our lives. Recently, I stood for nearly a half an hour during worship at church. This normally doesn't bother me, but for some reason I wanted to sit down. I was quickly reminded in my heart that I had stood at a restaurant the night before for over an hour waiting on a table.

Giving God the best of our time, talents, and treasures is the best way to live. Keep him first in your life. Don't allow yourself to slip into sloppy and questionable practices no matter what others may be doing around you. Surrender yourself often to his ways and allow God to shape you and mold you as you prepare for eternity.

PRAYER

Dear Lord, please don't let me slip in my devotion and worship to you. All that I have and all that I am I surrender to you. Help me today to be conscious of my time and all that I offer to you. Amen.

Dangerous Drifting

So we must listen very carefully to the truth we have heard, or we may drift away from it. Hebrews 2:1 NLT

When it comes to our faith and walking with Christ, drifting has been a problem for most humans. We are encouraged in the Bible to fix our eyes on the goal and to not grow weary in well doing, and yet there are times when we find ourselves drifting away from God and his Word.

Drifting means we go with the flow instead of going in the direction we should be going. Drifting happens when we stop rowing, figuratively speaking. It means you just drift with the current trends and winds that more often than not blow you completely off course. Drifting happens, and we must be very careful to evaluate who or what is driving our lives.

The writer of Hebrews suggests that to avoid this common phenomenon we must focus our attention on the truth we have heard. We must guard our hearts and stay the course that God has set before us. This becomes increasingly hard when others around us may choose to drift in their walk and faith.

One of the biggest challenges for Christians is to resist the temptation to follow what others are doing or not doing around them instead of following what they believe and know to be the truth. Water always seeks the lowest level, and unfortunately so does humanity.

Pay attention today and make every effort to hear the truth, know the truth, and understand the truth as you live out your day. Purpose in your heart that you won't allow anything or anyone to sidetrack you from doing what God wants and expects from you.

PRAYER

Dear God, I admit I have at times drifted in my faith. I have allowed circumstances to dictate my course instead of trusting you to guide me and sustain me in difficult times. Please show me your ways and give me the courage to stay the course and live my life your way. Amen.

"Lord, Help Me!"

O LORD, hear my plea for justice. Listen to my cry for help. Pay attention to my prayer, for it comes from honest lips. Psalm 17:1 NLT

The psalmist cries out to God for help in this Psalm; and if you read the rest of it, you will see that he is basing it on his behavior and God's character. It is a comforting emotion to pray and know that there is nothing between you and God.

It's a wonderful Psalm, and I would recommend you read all the verses. We find the heart of his petitions in verses 7-9. After asking God to bend down and hear his prayer, he proceeds:

Show me your unfailing love in wonderful ways...

Guard me as you would guard your own eyes...

Hide me in the shadow of your wings...

Protect me from wicked people who attack me...

He felt threatened as we all may at some point in our life. The threats may or may not come from individuals or other people; but they are real, and we long for protection. In earnest desperation, the writer cries out these words: "Arise, O Lord! Stand against them, and bring them to their knees!"

Whatever threats you may face today, they are no match for our God. Call out to him and tell him your deepest concerns. He will listen. He will respond. He cares deeply about his children.

PRAYER

Father, I need you today. Please help me overcome my fears and anxieties. Give me the courage I need to face the circumstances and people that threaten me. Amen.

Every One of Us

For we must all stand before Christ to be judged. 2 Corinthians
5:10 NLT

Does this verse scare you? I hope not. I do hope it gives you pause
and a moment to evaluate how you are doing at living your life on
this planet.

There will be a day when we stand before God and give an account of
our lives. We will be judged on several things. Our devotion to God matters. Our management of our time and resources matters. Our attention
to the poor and widows matters. Our relationships matter.

Our lives on this earth are but a fraction of time compared to eter-
nity, and yet what we do while here affects what happens in eternity.
Reviewing one's life and priorities is always a good practice to observe.
It's as simple as asking yourself a couple questions:

Do I love God with all my heart, mind, soul, and strength?

Do I love my neighbor as much as I love myself?

They sound like simple questions, but they are actually the profound
measure God gave us to judge ourselves by. Live your life from this day
forward making sure there is nothing or no one between you and the
God who will someday judge your life. It's a very freeing way to live. Love
him more than anything and you will be surprised how little you have
to worry about.

PRAYER

*Dear Lord, please help me to not live in fear of eternity but to live
in a way that pleases you. Help me in the areas I struggle in, and
give me the strength to always make right choices. Amen.*

I Can't Take it Anymore

Let the day of my birth be erased, and the night I was conceived.
Let that day be turned to darkness. Job 3:3-4a NLT

Job uttered these words at the beginning of a terrible siege of events that included the loss of his entire family and fortune. He was covered with terrible boils and endured the accusations of three of his friends while suffering the worst.

No wonder he was wanting to erase the day and remembrance of his conception and birth. Recently, I interacted with an individual that suffers from depression. In the midst of changes brought on by government mandates and quarantine orders, he blurted out that he just couldn't take it anymore. A couple of days ago, I sat in a trauma room at the local hospital and watched the nineteen-year-old mother of a six month old baby rock back and forth with grief while holding the lifeless body of this precious little girl.

Life can be beyond hard to take sometimes.

What do you do when there seems to be no hope? Where do you turn when it seems impossible to move forward? How do you manage your sanity, your emotional health, and the pain that comes with circumstances that are out of your control? The better question is: whom do you trust? Who loves you more than you love yourself? When Job spoke these words, remember he was still talking to God.

Never quit talking to God. You don't have to always pray spiritual or flowery words. You can be honest with God. Tell him what you think and feel. Don't hold back; but once you are done, be quiet and listen. Let him speak. Let him lead you, because he will. Once you've finished expressing your fears, anger, and discouragement, you will find him waiting to lead you and love you. Job heard from God. Job 38-41 is God's response to Job's questions.

God has not left you or deserted you. He is not against you. Celebrate that he made you and knows you and has promised to never leave you or forsake you.

Dear Lord, I am full of questions sometimes because life is such a mystery. Help me to never take my eyes off you. Keep my focus on things that matter in eternity. May your will be done on earth as it is in heaven. Amen.

And God Knew

And God saw the people of Israel – and God knew. Genesis 2:25
ESV

Israel had been enslaved to the Egyptians for a long time. We read that the people were groaning under the bondage and they began to get serious about crying out to God for help. Their cry came up before God; he heard their groaning and he remembered his covenant with Abraham, Isaac, and Jacob.

Moses then writes these words, "And God saw the people of Israel – and God knew." The New Living Translation puts it this way, "He looked down on the people of Israel and knew it was time to act."

God knew!

You want God to know. You want God to know everything about you, and he does. Jesus taught that he knows the count of the hairs of your head and he knows when sparrows fall. Jesus also said that we are way more important to God then a flock of sparrows. If he knows about every sparrow, he certainly knows all about you.

In 1905, Civilla Martin penned these words,

Why should I feel discouraged, why should the shadows come,
Why should my heart be lonely, and long for heaven and home,
When Jesus is my portion? My constant friend is he:
His eye is on the sparrow, and I know he watches me;
His eye is on the sparrow, and I know he watches me.
I sing because I'm happy, I sing because I'm free,
For his eye is on the sparrow, And I know he watches me.

He knows. He is watching over you. He knows when it is time to send help.

PRAYER

Heavenly Father, I know that you see and know everything about me today. Help me to believe this and find comfort in it. Please know that I need your help. When you "know it," I can rest in the fact that you are acting on my behalf. Amen.

A Prayer Worth Praying Every Day

May the words of my mouth and the meditation of my heart be pleasing to you, O LORD, my rock and my redeemer. Psalm 19:14 NLT

In my opinion, this is one of the most powerful prayers in the Bible. I know of a pastor who prays this prayer with his congregation at the end of every service. Psalm 19 is known for other classic words and phrases as well. Here are a few:

"The heavens proclaim the glory of God. The skies display his craftsmanship" (verse 1).

"The instructions of the Lord are perfect, reviving the soul. The decrees of the Lord are trustworthy, making wise the simple" (verse 7).

"The commandments of the Lord are right, bringing joy to the heart. The commands of the Lord are clear, giving insight for living" (verse 8).

"They are more desirable than gold, even the finest gold. They are sweeter than honey, even honey dripping from the comb" (verse 10).

And then the psalmist David ends with this wonderful prayer of asking and adoration. He asks that his words and thoughts be pleasing to God. What an awesome way to live! What could happen in your life if every word and every thought were surrendered and given to God? Why would you want to do this? You wouldn't unless like the psalmist you adored him as your Rock and Redeemer.

When you know the forgiveness of God and enjoy the protection of his mighty strength and power, he becomes your Rock and Redeemer. If you were meeting a president of the United States, you would weigh every word and make sure your head and heart were in the moment. How much more and how appealing is it to honor the Lord with our attention to what comes out of our mouths and inhabits our hearts?

It's a prayer. Make it your prayer today and believe that God will answer and turn your heart completely toward him.

PRAYER

May the words of my mouth and the meditation of my heart be pleasing to you, O LORD, my rock and my redeemer. Amen.

Nothing Is Ever Hidden from God.

Fear God and obey his commands, for this is everyone's duty. God will judge us for everything we do, including every secret thing, whether good or bad. Ecclesiastes 12:13b-14 NLT

These are the last words written by Solomon in the book of Ecclesiastes. After writing about life and how we should approach everything from relationships to talking to God, he sums up his thoughts with these words: "Fear God and obey his commands, for this is everyone's duty."

Could it be that our living should be reduced down to these two things? What would things look like in your life right now if you were fearing God and obeying his commands?

Martin Luther likened fearing God to that of a child that has tremendous love and respect for their earthly father or mother and who dearly wants to please them. The child's fear is not because of threatened punishment or abuse but they are afraid they will displease their parents who represent their source of security and love. This is the heart of fearing God. We should operate our lives, choices, attitudes, and affections based on displeasing God.

The easiest way to do this is to just simply know what he wants and to obey him. Even God who instituted the sacrificial systems of atonement in the Old Testament also spoke through the prophet Samuel with these words, "What is more pleasing to the LORD: your burnt offerings and sacrifices or your obedience to his voice? Listen! Obedience is better than sacrifice, and submission is better than offering the fat of rams."

God still just wants us to follow him and obey.

Do whatever you have to do to obey. Make whatever adjustments you need to make, but align yourself with God's will and ways. He is coming back someday, and when he comes as Solomon has written, "God will judge us for everything we do, including every secret thing, whether good or bad."

This is not a negative message but a life-changing message. Let God help you move away from anything displeasing or contrary to his will. Walk in the confidence and love of a child in compliance with their parents. There is no better feeling.

Dear God, I often forget or ignore this truth, and I pray that you will help me to always remember. You are God! You do see and know everything about me. Please give me the strength to fear and obey you. Amen.

The Joyful Sound

Blessed are the people who know the joyful sound! They walk, O Lord, in the light of your countenance. Psalm 89:15 NKJV

The joyful sound? What could that possibly be referencing? There is nothing in the verses before or after that would suggest what this joyful sound might be. With a little bit of research, it becomes clear that it is a reference to people from all time periods who know the sound of the gospel. The sound of redemption. The sound of God's grace and salvation.

In the Old Testament, this could have been the sound of the Israeli army in battle shouting the name of God or the same army returning from battle singing songs of victory in God's strength. It could have been the sound of sacrifices being made at the temple—the animals that would shed their blood and give their lives to atone for the sins of the people. It could have been the wind in the mulberry bushes or the still small voice. It could have been the trumpets blown to announce Jubilee and the releasing of debtors and servants, giving them freedom from their burdens.

In the New Testament it is the sound of an angel declaring to shepherds, "Don't be afraid, for behold, I bring you good tidings of great joy which shall be to all people."

The joyful sound is the sound of the gospel. The sound of salvation for you and I. This is the sound that allows us to walk in the light of his presence.

"Blessed are the people that know..." It's not just hearing about it or even hearing it but it is about knowing this joyful sound. Because you have received Jesus Christ you know this sound. It is the sweetest sound on earth.

Over 100 years ago, Priscilla Jane Owens penned these words,

We have heard the joyful sound: Jesus saves! Jesus saves!
Spread the tidings all around: Jesus saves! Jesus saves!
Bear the news to every land, Climb the steeps and cross the waves;
Onward!—'tis our Lord's command; Jesus saves! Jesus saves!

Give the winds a mighty voice, Jesus saves, Jesus saves;
Let the nations now rejoice. Jesus saves, Jesus saves;
Shout salvation full and free, Highest hills and deepest caves,
This our song of victory, Jesus saves, Jesus saves.

It is a sound worth sharing. Have you heard the joyful sound?

PRAYER

Dear Jesus, the sound of the gospel must be the sweetest sound one could hear. It is the sound of hope and salvation. I thank you that I have heard this sound and chosen to follow you. Amen.

Learning to Stand Strong

In 1 Peter 5:8-9 we read these words of caution: *Stay alert! Watch out for your great enemy, the devil. He prowls around like a roaring lion, looking for someone to devour. Stand firm against him, and be strong in your faith.*

We share a common adversary of our faith. In fact, in the rest of verse 9 Peter reminds us to "Remember that your family of believers all over the world is going through the same kind of suffering you are."

How do we overcome this destroyer and great enemy? This roaring lion?

Stay alert!

Watch out!

Stand firm!

Be strong in your faith!

Yes, he prowls like a roaring lion, but we have God on our side. Don't be afraid, but do the things necessary to maintain your faith and keep your eyes open. Keep your eyes on Jesus always. If you falter or fail, don't stay down. He is your healer and restorer and he can rescue from the clutches of this enemy.

Today press in close to Jesus. He is our great protector and provider. Jesus overcame this enemy and will help us do the same.

PRAYER

Dear Jesus, my hope is in you! I have no hope against this foe that seeks my destruction, but with you on my side I can overcome. Help me stay strong in the faith and keep you on my side. Amen.

Trifling with God

By this time the whole church and, in fact, everyone who heard of these things had a healthy respect for God. They knew God was not to be trifled with. Acts 5:11 MSG

These words were written at the end of a story about the early church and found in the book of Acts. A man and his wife conspired together to hide some money they received for a piece of property. They both lied about it and the consequences were startling. They both dropped dead for lying to the Holy Spirit!

This caused quite a stir within the church community as you might imagine. The writer says everyone that heard about it developed a healthy respect for God as a result of this story.

I am fascinated by that result and wonder if we have that level of respect for God in our lives.

Respecting God means that we don't presume on his grace by doing things we know to be wrong. The Bible says, "Remember, it is sin to know what you ought to do and then not do it" (James 4:17 NLT).

With knowledge comes responsibility. What the early church found out through this graphic demonstration was simply stated in the Message Bible. "They knew God was not to be trifled with." This story should serve as a warning for all of us. People don't automatically die from sinning against the Spirit of God, but ultimately the wages of sin is death.

Don't allow yourself to be caught up in the cares of this life to the detriment of following Jesus one hundred percent. When you center your life and integrity around Jesus and your relationship with him, you stand much less of a chance of trifling with God.

The psalmist prayed a prayer that all of us should pray every day. It is found in Psalm 19:13: "Keep back your servant also from presumptuous sins; let them not have dominion over me."

What a great prayer! Pray it today. Pray it every day, and let God keep you and lead you to an even closer walk with him. To trifle with God is a fatal exercise. Don't trifle, but turn to him with all your heart, mind, and soul and live!

Dear God, please don't let me presume on your grace and fall into a sinful pattern or habit. Help me today to take this seriously and to know that what I do or don't do matters. Amen.

Life Fades, but God's Word Is Forever

As the Scriptures say, "People are like grass; their beauty is like a flower in the field. The grass withers and the flower fades. But the word of the Lord remains forever." And that word is the Good News that was preached to you. 1 Peter 1:24-25 NLT

If you are over forty years of age, you are aware that change happens in your bodies. Outward beauty is sometimes retained by people, but we do fade and wither with age. It is life. Inward beauty does not need to fade or wither. When our hearts are right and aligned with Jesus Christ, everything we do and say will be life-giving and generous toward those around us.

The good news is, as Peter writes, "The word of the Lord remains forever." One Scripture says, "Let the word of Christ dwell in you richly." Hide God's Word in your heart. Consume it like it is a love letter—because it is! It is God's Word to you, and it is new each morning.

His Word is Good News because it proclaims Christ, and it changes us from the inside out. Be beautiful today! You may be having a bad hair day or struggling to feel good about your outward appearance, but you can be beautiful every day from the inside. Radiate God's love to those around you. Share his kindness, mercy, and compassion today and people will think you are beautiful. Let his never-fading Word show through you today. Those around you will feel your beauty, and in response you will come to not worry so much about fading and withering. You are loved today!

PRAYER

Dear Jesus, I am filled with gratefulness today for your Word and the promises you have given me today. As life passes by, I pray that I will always love and embrace the good news of salvation that you provide for all people. Amen.

Better Food

But Jesus replied, "I have a kind of food you know nothing about."
John 4:32 NLT

Jesus had just finished sharing the good news of salvation with a very broken and scorned woman that had been married five times and was with yet another man. He purposefully went out of his way for this encounter, and it was epic in its results. Her life was changed, and for two days she brought others to see and hear the one that had told her everything she had ever done.

Many of her friends and the people of her town came to faith in Christ!

As the disciples returned from a search for something to eat they off Jesus some food and He responds with these words: "I have a kind of food you know nothing about."

This story is a revelation of the heart of our Lord. He came that we might have life and have it abundantly. He came to seek and save those who were lost. He came to do the will of his Father, and that will was to offer salvation to the lost, broken, and hurting. He explained it this way to his disciples: "Then Jesus explained: 'My nourishment comes from doing the will of God, who sent me, and from finishing his work.'"

He goes on to explain the joy of the harvest of souls. Nothing brings greater joy than to be about God's business. Your encounter today might not be as dramatic, but rest assured God will use you if you are willing to bring the good news to others. We forget this sometimes, and we get so bogged down in our lives that we forget we hold in our possession the words of life.

Pray today that God will let someone intersect with you that needs to know him. Allow God to do his work through you. It may be better than a home-cooked meal!

PRAYER

Dear Lord, if you would like to use me today to share the message of salvation, I am willing. Lead me to the right person and I will be faithful to testify about you. I would even be willing to miss a meal! Amen.

Delighting God!

For the Lord delights in his people; he crowns the humble with victory. Psalm 149:3 NLT

God could be delighting in you today! If you are following him and not ashamed to be named as one of "his people," he is finding joy in you. The notion that you and I could bring delight to God seems impossible, but that's what the psalmist wrote.

What about our lives brings God delight? Based on other Scriptures, we can be sure that our obedience to God's Word brings him delight. We know that putting him first is high on his list. When we put him first we will also love our neighbors as ourselves.

When we allow God's Spirit to inhabit our lives, we begin to exhibit the fruit of the Spirit. God finds it delightful when we are full of love, joy, peace, patience, kindness, goodness, faithfulness, gentleness, and self-control (Galatians 5:22-23).

He is delighted when we anticipate and look forward to his return. Stay humble before God. Seek to do his will and to love others as he would love them. Do what is right, always. More than anything, put him first in your life. Be the delight of God today. Live in the victory of a surrendered and godly life.

PRAYER

Dear Lord, I don't know how I can bring delight to you today, but I want to please you with all of my heart. I give myself to you today. Fill me with your presence. Amen.

Do You Observe a Sabbath Day?

On the seventh day, God had finished his work of creation, so he rested from all his work. And God blessed the seventh day and declared it holy because it was the day when he rested from all his work of creation. Genesis 2:2 NLT

Do you observe a Sabbath in your life? On the seventh day of creation, God rested; but he did more than that. He blessed the day and declared it holy. Later he went on to reinforce the concept by making it one of the Ten Commandments. This principle and commandment was so serious in the Old Testament that Moses declared this about it: "You have six days each week for your ordinary work, but the seventh day must be a Sabbath day of complete rest, a holy day dedicated to the Lord. Anyone who works on that day must be put to death" (Exodus 35:2 NTL).

Why?

God made us. He knows what we need for physical, emotional, and spiritual renewal. He wasn't joking about it. We were built for a day of rest every seven days! How different would your life look if you actually observed a day of rest? How much better would you be spiritually and physically? This should be one of the easiest commandments to keep and observe, and yet it is probably one of the most ignored and broken commandments.

This is a reminder from our Creator. Take care of yourself. The world can get along without you for a day. Take a day and rest, worship, and relax. It's more spiritual than you may think.

PRAYER

Dear God, to be completely honest, I hardly ever really observe a day of rest. Other than going to church, my Sabbath often feels like every other day. Please help me to take this seriously and to obey your commandments. Amen.

Who Knows What's in Your Heart?

The human heart is the most deceitful of all things and desperately wicked. Who really knows how bad it is? But I, the LORD, search all hearts and examine secret motives. Jeremiah 17:9-10 NLT

These may not necessarily be the verses you want to read in a devotional setting, but oh how important they are. They serve to remind us that we must guard our hearts at all times. Our emotions and feelings should be the least trusted of all that makes up a human being.

Our emotions or "heart" can cause us to think unclearly about life, relationships, things that matter most, and most importantly about God. When we allow our hearts to lead us, we are probably headed for trouble.

We are told that God searches our hearts and examines our motives. The psalmist cried out, "Search me, O God, and know my heart; test me and know my anxious thoughts. Point out anything in me that offends you, and lead me along the path of everlasting life" (Psalm 139:23-24 NLT).

Take a few minutes to sit quietly before God today and let him search your heart. Let him examine your motives, your direction, and your dedication. Let him test you, and then allow him to lead you to the right path, the path of everlasting life. His way is always the best way.

PRAYER

Dear God, I will sit quietly before you today. Please search my heart. Show me where I may be headed in the wrong direction, and give me enough strength and grace to make the corrections needed. I am listening for your voice. Amen.

What Is Holding You Back?

"Unwrap him and let him go!" John 11:44 NLT

These words spoken by Jesus were said outside the tomb of his friend Lazarus. Jesus showed up several days after Lazarus's death and raised him from the dead and called him to come out of his grave. It must have been a startling moment for those weeping and wailing outside of his tomb. Not only did he call Lazarus to life but he ordered the things that were bound around him to be taken off.

I wonder today what circumstances in your life may have you bound. You may even feel as though a part of you has died that can never be resurrected. No matter what it may be, Jesus is the resurrection and life. He has the power over everything that threatens to chain us and destroy our freedom in him.

As you pursue God in prayer today, try to put yourself in Lazarus's place in those moments between walking out of a grave and still being bound but hearing Jesus say, "Unwrap him and let him go!"

Could he be speaking those words into your life today? Could this not be the day you come out of your "grave" and move into the light and love of Jesus Christ?

It is my prayer for you today that you hear these words deep in your heart and mind today. Allow Jesus to unbind you from whatever has you bound. Allow him to give you new life and a new start today. Allow him and his power to do what you cannot do for yourself. If not today, then perhaps tomorrow; but don't give up your faith and belief. He is your hope. He has the power to break every chain that binds us.

PRAYER

Dear Jesus, you know the things that bind me today and keep me from being the person I really need to be. Please free me and show me the way to walk so that nothing will hinder me from truly serving you. Amen.

Where Are You?

Then the Lord God called to the man, "Where are you?" Genesis 3:9 NLT

The first two people created by God were given so much. They not only were given much, but they had so much to lose. They were given one rule to live by; and if they could refrain from eating the fruit of the tree of the knowledge of good and evil, they apparently would have lived forever.

God originally gave this command to not eat the fruit to Adam prior to Eve being created. Eventually she discovered the tree and the fruit and was taken in her senses. The Bible says,

"She saw that the tree was beautiful and its fruit looked delicious, and she wanted the wisdom it would give her. So she took some of the fruit and ate it" (Genesis 3:6 NLT).

They partook together and directly disobeyed the only rule that God had given them. It is so hard to understand why and how that could happen until we put the spotlight on ourselves. Honestly put it on ourselves. Not the Sunday morning show up at church us but the real us when no one is looking. It might be that you are always good. It may be that you never wrestle with or struggle with temptation. But the reality is that most people face it daily.

I don't believe we have to fail or fall, but sometimes it happens to good people. Adam and Eve were not bad people, but they succumbed to temptation and lost so much for themselves and everyone that came after them. It was the fall of the human race. It was really big!

When we fail or fall, like this first couple we want to run and hide. We don't want anyone to know, so we try to keep our heads up and move forward as though nothing happened. It is into this moment that God comes looking for us. He asked them a simple question.

"Where are you?"

Could it be that God is asking that same question to you today? Maybe it's not about a major sin of some kind, but you have not been as connected to God as you need to be. You know, and he certainly knows it.

He is asking today, "Where are you?" How will you respond?

Dear God, thanks for asking this question. Even though you know exactly where I am, it feels good to know that you care enough to ask. I am here. Please lead me to where I need to be. Amen.

Raise Your Affections

Think about the things of heaven, not the things of earth. Colossians 3:2 NLT

In times of great challenge, our perspective will often change. Things most familiar are no longer an option. When life changes, we may be challenged emotionally, physically, and spiritually.

How are you doing? If you could talk to Jesus face to face today, what would you tell him?

The apostle Paul was writing to a church that was experiencing persecution and other difficulties brought on by Roman oppression. They hardly had any rights. They were meeting from house to house because there were no buildings for the church to meet in. (This may have been a blessing.)

Into this church came these words: "Since you have been raised to new life with Christ, set your sights/affections on the realities of heaven, where Christ sits in honor at God's right hand" (Col. 3:1 NLT).

The best thing that can happen to us in times like these is that we change or adjust our minds and hearts to think more like Jesus wanted us to think in the first place. Moments of uncertainty should drive us to our knees and the Word of God.

When we focus our attention on the things of heaven, everything around us takes on far less importance. Our time on this earth is truly a vapor. Many of us wonder where time goes and how it goes so fast. I encourage you to spend some quality time with God today. Let the hope of heaven be a reality in your life and not something you will think about when and if you know you are dying. Heaven and God's eternal presence is the hope that will give you peace when everything around you is not very peaceful.

PRAYER

Dear God, fill my mind and heart with the hope of heaven today. Help my attitude to be pleasing to you. Let your love fill my soul, and let me share that love with those around me today. Amen.

The Most Important Workout

Strengthen the weak hands and make firm the feeble knees. Isaiah 35:3 ESV

During this time of quarantine and social distancing, I have been reading a lot of Scripture. I have been searching the Scriptures, in fact. I am not blaming God or even suggesting that he is responsible for the virus that everyone is fighting, but you need to know that he will go to great lengths to get our attention.

This verse was uttered and written after a long siege of God's judgment and attempt to get Israel to look his way. People died, food was scarce, water sources dried up, animals perished, fires raged, nations were decimated, and even populous cities were destroyed. Here's just one example of a descriptive verse: "The highways lie waste; the traveler ceases" (Isaiah 33:8).

We are indeed living in uncertain times. Our lives have been rerouted, rearranged, and forced to change in ways we never imagined, and yet this is not at the level of biblical proportions. It could be far worse!

So what are you doing spiritually different during these days? Have you prayed more? Are you reading the Bible to search for answers? Have you evaluated your own life and relationship with God? I hope so! When Isaiah said to strengthen the weak hands and make firm the feeble knees, it was a reference to God's mercy being poured out and the devastation being over.

This is a great time to work on your relationship with God. You may feel the effects and frustrations of these days, even as a Christian; but let it cause you to build up your faith and trust in God. Work on it! Spend time in God's Word. Pray earnestly and build an authentic, life-altering relationship with God.

The verse that follows Isaiah 35:3 says, "Say to those that have an anxious heart, be strong, fear not!" Look to the Lord and let him cast out the fear, worry, and anxiety. He is still God.

PRAYER

Lord, you alone know the fears I have. You alone know what is happening around me that causes me to be afraid and worry. Please strengthen my hands and my feeble knees. Help me to be strong in you! Amen.

The Lord's Arm

Listen! The LORD's arm is not too weak to save you, nor is his ear too deaf to hear you call. Isaiah 59:1 NLT

No matter what may be happening in your life today, it doesn't affect God's availability or strength. When we face trials or great challenges we must keep verses like this in mind. Isaiah was the voice of God for Israel at the time this was written.

He was continually calling people to evaluate their relationship with God. Our relationship is critical when it comes to enjoying God's ability to help us in time of trouble.

The key to God's presence in our lives is obedience. While you may or may not get it right all the time, your desire must be to please God with your life daily. We obey him with our attitudes, our allegiances, our time, our talents, and our resources. The desired life is one where all is surrendered to God—a life where we surrender both the blessings and burdens of life and trust in his sovereign will.

I have watched people suffer unimaginable loss of family or possessions. Those not connected with God are often left to battle bitterness for years. Those who were surrendered to his will certainly felt the pain and hurt but moved on and allowed it to make them better instead of bitter.

"Listen!" the writer says, "the Lord's arm is not too weak to save you, nor is his ear too deaf to hear you call." Believe this. Draw close to God until you know that no matter what, you can trust him with your life. He is strong. He is listening. He is for you. Are you for him?

PRAYER

Dear God, thank you for being strong on my behalf. You know that there are times when I can't walk through things on my own. I am weak but you are strong. Thanks for listening and hearing my prayer. Amen.

The Lord Hears His People

The Lord hears his people when they call to him for help. Psalm 34:17 NLT

Do you ever wonder if God can hear you? Do you ever struggle with the one-sided conversations we call prayer?

It is difficult sometimes to stay the course when praying for something because we may lose sight of the fact that God is listening. The Psalmist points out that if we are "his people," the Lord will hear our calls for help.

Since there is a condition attached to this promise, I would encourage you to make sure you are one of God's people. You know what that means, right? It means that you love him enough to follow him and obey his Word. It means you live like Jesus would want you to live.

I once had a conversation with a man that absolutely was not following Jesus in any way, shape, or form with his life but he told me with a straight face that he was a believer. For some reason, I didn't let it pass and reminded him that the devil was a believer but that Jesus was looking for followers.

When you are one of God's people, you will know it. You will live like it and love those around you like it. Your dealing in business and at work will show it. Your attitude toward the marginalized of society will show it. Your priorities and motives will show it.

I would encourage you to always be moving closer to God instead of away from him. Always choose to believe that his way is the best way to go and live your life in the center of his will. Then know that he hears your call. He is tuned in to your tears and your cry for help. Even if you fall always, fall reaching in his direction. God loves you and longs to be in a genuine relationship with you so that he can speak into your life!

PRAYER

Dear God, I may not have always made the right choices. I may not have put you first in my life, but I want that to change. Show me how to live for you and how to serve you with my life. I want to be one of your people. Amen.

What Happened to Your Freedom?

You were running the race so well. Who has held you back from following the truth? It certainly isn't God, for he is the one who called you to freedom. Galatians 5:7-8 NLT

If you are going to run a race you want to be wearing clothes that allow you to feel free and not encumbered or bound up.

The apostle Paul compares our spiritual life to running a race. Of course, when running a race, great thought and even scientific theory goes into making sure resistance is not a factor.

The question for us to consider today is rooted in false teaching and the fact that it is easy to get sidetracked in our faith if we are not very careful. Staying close to God and working on that very personal relationship is one way to avoid being distracted or delayed by false teaching.

Consistent prayer is also a way to secure and protect our faith. Make sure you are tuned in to the subtle nuances and nudges of the Holy Spirit. By praying, we stay connected with our head and hearts to God's truth.

Don't allow anyone or anything to slow you down. Keep running the race that God has laid out for you.

"Therefore, since we are surrounded by such a huge crowd of witnesses to the life of faith, let us strip off every weight that slows us down, especially the sin that so easily trips us up. And let us run with endurance the race God has set before us" (Hebrews 12:1 NLT).

PRAYER

Dear God, please help me understand and recognize false teaching and even the people around me that are not helpful for my faith. Give me the endurance to run all the way with you. Amen.

Don't Hold Anything Back

*So fear the L*ORD *and serve him wholeheartedly.* Joshua 24:14 NLT

Joshua was about to pass from this life at the age of 110, and he issued a big challenge to the people of Israel. These were God's people, but they struggled to follow him at times. Joshua asked them to choose between following God or the idols and gods of the people around them. In a now-classic statement, he declares, "As for me and my family, we will serve the Lord."

After reminding them of all that God had done for them historically, he issues this admonition: "So fear the Lord and serve him wholeheartedly."

This is a good word for us to follow. The word "fear" is referring to a sense of respect, awe, and submission to God. What he has always longed for is to find a people or person that will follow him wholeheartedly. For the Christian serving God, following him should be a natural instinct. He should be the first thought we have in the morning and the last thought we have at night.

When you are serving him wholeheartedly, everything that happens in your life will be filtered and processed by seeking his counsel and wisdom. Because we fear and trust him, we can experience peace when things aren't going our way. We can know joy when our hearts are filled with grief. Why? Because we serve him with our whole heart. Hold nothing back. Be all in, every day and in every way.

PRAYER

Dear Lord, please know that I don't want anything to keep me from serving you with my whole heart. Help me today to surrender anything that would hinder me from being all-in in my walk of faith and following you.

Delight and Desires

Take delight in the Lord, and he will give you your heart's desires.
Psalm 37:4 NLT

Reading this verse pushed me to reflect on what must it mean to take "delight in the Lord." Many of us have read this verse before, and it is easy to focus our attention on the last part. The idea that God will give you your heart's desires is appealing for most people.

Let's focus on the first part of the verse and identify some practical ways we might delight in the Lord. For those of us that are parents, this should be easy to understand. We take delight in our children (most of the time). When we delight in our kids we spend time with them. We watch the things they do. We notice who they are and are becoming. We may laugh at the funny things they do. We hold them close and talk to them. We listen to them talk and enjoy their uniqueness. If they are adults, we delight in them when they make good choices with their lives. We delight in opportunities to be in their presence, especially if they don't live close by. We long to see them. We desire to hear their voice on the other end of a phone call. We remember their words, and sometimes those words reduce us to joyful tears. Why? Because we delight in them.

When we delight in God we learn as much about him as we are able. We study his every move and look for ways to express our love and loyalty. We take his words to heart. We want the things he wants, and we refuse to do anything that would grieve our heavenly Father. We live in his presence and delight ourselves in his promises. At some point our desires become aligned with his desires, and he gives us the desires of our heart.

- Focus your full attention on God this week.
- Allow him to make some adjustments in your life.
- Believe that God cares about the smallest details of your life.
- Express your love to God with total abandon.
- Open the Word of God and let him speak to you.

Develop a conversational relationship with God. Take moments throughout your day to speak to him as you would to someone in the room. Remind him that you love him or whisper your need for his help in the moment.

God never wanted anything from us more than he wants a relationship with us. Delight yourself in him today.

Dear God, today I will focus my thoughts and thanksgiving on the delight it is to walk with you. You do give me the desires of my heart when they fall within your will for my life. I delight in you today! Amen.

Search Me, O God

The faithful love of the Lord never ends! His mercies never cease. Great is his faithfulness; his mercies begin afresh each morning. Lamentations 3:22-23 NLT

Instead, let us test and examine our ways. Let us turn back to the LORD. Lamentations 3:40 NLT

Lamentations 3:22-40 contains some amazing, encouraging, and thought-provoking words. I encourage you to read the whole section. There is in verse 40 a clear call and invitation to test and examine our life, our walk, and our relationship with God. This is a much-needed exercise for even the most mature Christian. The psalmist wrote: "Search me, O God, and know my heart; test me and know my anxious thoughts. Point out anything in me that offends you, and lead me along the path of everlasting life" (Psalm 139:23-24 NLT).

Below are some questions you might want to consider using for spiritual inventory. Find a quiet place. Reflect and review your life today. Recognize any places of weakness or distraction. Repent of any sin or failure. Retrace your steps back to the center of God's will and his presence.

- Am I reading the Bible enough to allow the Word of God to work in my life?
- Do I seek to honor God in my thoughts, actions, and habits?
- What kind of person am I when no one is looking?
- Do I need to "clean-up" my thoughts, behaviors, language, and actions?
- Are there "compartments" of my life that are off limits to God?
- Is worship a habit in my life?
- Do I worship God with my life?
- Do I have a heart and commitment to reach spiritually lost people? How do I serve God?
- Do I seek to forgive others first before expecting others to forgive me?
- Am I holding grudges or harboring resentment towards other people?

- Do I need to ask forgiveness?
- Do I need to make Jesus first once again in my life, relationships, and worship?

You may have your own way of self-examination, but don't be afraid to be honest with God. He longs to help you walk in his ways and to grow in your faith and trust. You may feel the sting of failure, but know that God wants to lead you back. He always is searching for people that may have lost their way. God is always about redemption and mercy when we turn toward him.

Here is one last selection of verses from this classic chapter in Lamentations: "For no one is abandoned by the Lord forever. Though he brings grief, he also shows compassion because of the greatness of his unfailing love. For he does not enjoy hurting people or causing them sorrow" (Lamentations 3:31-33 NLT).

PRAYER

Dear God, I know that even if I stray from your path that you will look for me and find me. I want to always do my part to examine my heart and life and make sure that I am following you. Amen.

How Hungry Are You?

Jesus replied, "I am the bread of life. Whoever comes to me will never be hungry again. Whoever believes in me will never be thirsty.
John 6:35 NLT

Ever notice that no matter what you eat at breakfast or lunch, eventually your body gets around to reminding you that you are hungry again. It's the way it's supposed to work. We need food and water to survive.

Jesus is not speaking of food and water that we consume for our daily physical strength but something much more important. He is of course saying that if we come to him and partake of what he offers, our spiritual hunger and thirst will be satisfied and quenched.

A recently-written worship song includes these words:
Christ is enough for me
Christ is enough for me
Everything I need is in you
Everything I need
Jesus is and always has been enough.

In 1744 William Williams was being accused of various misdemeanors against the Church of England. He left the church and devoted himself to Methodism, which was a newly-formed faith community. During his faith journey, he felt the need for this Bread that satisfies and penned these words:

Guide me, O my great Redeemer,
Pilgrim through this barren land;
I am weak, but you are mighty;
Hold me with your powerful hand.
Bread of heaven, bread of heaven,
Feed me now and evermore,
Feed me now and evermore.

Can you hear his invitation to you today? Allow Jesus to truly be your source of soul satisfaction. Want what he wants and let him live in you.

PRAYER

Dear God, I am so hungry for more of you. You are the Bread of Life, and I need you now more than ever. Feed me, Lord, with more of your presence. Amen.

God's Benefits are Outstanding

Bless the Lord, O my soul; And all that is within me, bless his holy name! Bless the Lord, O my soul, And forget not all his benefits: who forgives all your iniquities, who heals all your diseases, who redeems your life from destruction, who crowns you with loving-kindness and tender mercies, who satisfies your mouth with good things, So that your youth is renewed like the eagle's. Psalm 103:1-5 NKJV

What kind of benefits do you receive? It's a question that people ask each other regarding everything from their employment to insurance.

The psalmist is in a mode of praise and worship and it is centered around the benefits he is receiving from God on a daily basis. In case you missed them when you read the verses, let me put them in a list for you.

- Who forgives all your iniquities,
- Who heals all your diseases,
- Who redeems your life from destruction,
- Who crowns you with lovingkindness and tender mercies,
- Who satisfies your mouth with good things.

What a great list! God forgives our sins! I guess if you don't think you have any, that won't be as impressive to you; but he will forgive you both for what you do and what you left undone. He heals our diseases. Not everyone gets a miraculous healing on this earth, but we know that there is the promise of eternity where there will be no more sickness, suffering, or pain.

He will redeem your life from destructive behavior and circumstances that you find yourself in. Don't believe it? Ask Adam and Eve, the prophet Elijah, Samson, King David, or the disciple named Peter. They felt his redemption firsthand.

He will crown you with love and mercy! Who doesn't need a lot of that? He will satisfy the desires of your heart and the appetites we have with good things and not harmful things.

Rejoice today in your benefits! Make sure you stay connected to the source of all these blessings and respond with the psalmist, "Bless the Lord, O my soul; And all that is within me, bless His holy name! Bless the Lord, O my soul, And forget not all His benefits!"

Dear God, how many times have you blessed me with these benefits in my life? I'm afraid I can't even count the times. Thank you for being so good to me and for your love and mercy that is pointed my direction all day long. Amen.

Who Told You that You Were Naked?

"Who told you that you were naked?" the Lord God asked. Genesis 3:11 NLT

It may seem like a strange question at first, but God knew that Adam and Eve had disobeyed. With that disobedience had come knowledge they didn't previously possess. It was his way of questioning their actions and the fact that they thought they could hide.

If we ever cross a line with God, or when we cross a line that we know is not within his will, there is something that happens deep in our consciousness. We know almost immediately that we have sinned or failed. God has built an active conscience into every human being. Over time you can learn to ignore it or even deaden it. At the extreme this leads to unlawful and tragic behavior. It could lead to sinful or disobedient behavior.

We should be thankful for an active conscience that leads us to a godly sorrow when we fail or do something we know is against the Word of God or godliness. That still small voice that speaks deep in our inner being is none other than the Holy Spirit of God.

Is there something you carry with you that you have never dealt with? Is there anything in your past or present that you don't know what to do with? Like Adam and Eve you may even try to cover it up, but God knows; and yet you still don't know what to do.

When they covered themselves with fig leaves sewn together it was not the best choice. One of the first recorded acts of God's mercy was his willingness to make them new clothes even while punishing them for their sinfulness. Fig leaves would not be good long term clothing, but animal skins were perfect to cover their nakedness.

God loves you; and no matter what your "nakedness" is, he already knows about it and is ready to forgive you and mercifully lead you to a better place. Trust him with your failures. Trust him with your future. Follow him no matter what; and if you fall or fail, don't give up but get back up and keep pursuing God. You will find that he is not very far away.

Dear God, before you I will always be naked. There is nothing that is hidden to you. You know everything about me. You know my strengths and weaknesses. Please help me in my walk with you today. Amen.

Sleep and Safety through God

In peace I will lie down and sleep, for you alone, O LORD, will keep me safe. Psalm 4:8 NLT

During times of uncertainty, we very often struggle with healthy sleep patterns. Sometimes people may even deal with moments of high anxiety that leads them to sleeplessness and emotional stress.

The psalmist paints a beautiful picture of peace and serenity. Most of us only long for this kind of sleep. When I am at home I sleep very lightly because somehow in my mind I need to hear if anything happens that might threaten my family. Other nights might be interrupted by concerns that roll over and over in my mind and rob me of peace and sleep.

What's keeping you up at night?

How can you and I overcome sleepless nights and a lack of inner peace?

We must find and reinstate our trust in the Lord. Ultimately, our lives, our safety, our health and security must be trusted to God because he and he alone controls the ebb and flow of our lives. The only way to trust him at this level is to be in a daily relationship that builds trust and communication.

Reach out to the Lord today and let Him be your source of peace, sleep, and safety.

PRAYER

Dear God, I welcome you into my life. Let me draw close to you so that when my mind and heart begin to fear I will find my peace in you. Amen.

Three Crosses

I passed a field a few days ago and there were three crosses on the top of a rise and very visible to anyone driving down the highway. As I pondered them for the few seconds they were in my view, I wondered why all three crosses were displayed in this manner. Why not just one? The middle one is where all the attention should focus, right? The three crosses tell our story.

We are told in Scripture that the two thieves on either side of Jesus spoke to him shortly before he died.

One of the criminals hanging beside him scoffed, "So you're the Messiah, are you? Prove it by saving yourself—and us, too, while you're at it!" But the other criminal protested, "Don't you fear God even when you have been sentenced to die? We deserve to die for our crimes, but this man hasn't done anything wrong." Then he said, "Jesus, remember me when you come into your kingdom." And Jesus replied, "I assure you, today you will be with me in paradise." Luke 23:39-43 NLT

There were three crosses, and this is why I think they are all important to remember.

Hateful and Rejecting: The first man that spoke was sarcastic and challenging. Bitterness is evident in his words to Jesus. You don't want to be the person that rejects Jesus, especially in your dying moments. His anger kept him from reaching out to the only hope this world has ever known.

Helpless but Accepting: The second criminal to speak understood his helplessness but was accepting of the notion that Jesus was a man that had done nothing wrong. I am sure he knew who Jesus claimed to be and the religious politics of why he was hanging on a cross between two common criminals. I am not the first to wonder if he might not have worked a crowd where Jesus was preaching and healing the sick. Maybe he had heard just enough to give him faith to believe and accept Christ as the Savior of the world.

Hopeful and Protecting: The third cross is the focus. Jesus gives us hope. He provides a protection from the sentence of death that comes with sin. The Bible says that the wages of sin is death, and no one wants that, especially death and eternal separation from God.

On this day, allow yourself to engage these three crosses. Place yourself at the foot of the center cross and allow this Jesus, the Son of God, to forgive you where needed, to heal your hurts, to give you hope, and to strengthen your faith.

PRAYER

Dear Jesus, I love the fact that you died so that we can have forgiveness and eternal life. May I always look to your cross and to your face for the forgiveness and redemption I so desperately need. Amen.

It's in My Heart

Don't let me wander from your commands. I have hidden your word in my heart, that I might not sin against you. Psalm 119:10b-11 NLT

Growing up in church, memorizing Scripture was a part of my young life. Listening to hundreds of sermons, Sunday school lessons, and other exposure to the Scripture tended to put lots of it in my mind and heart.

The psalmist hits on something here that we all should pay attention to as we walk through this life. There is something very powerful about the Word of God. In fact, Jesus told his first disciples that the Holy Spirit would remind them of the things he had taught them (John 14:26).

I have found this to be true many times when a verse of Scripture I hadn't thought of in a long time comes back to my mind at just the right time. Of course, this wouldn't happen at all if I hadn't first read it and hidden it in my heart. The Word hidden in our hearts becomes a powerful ally in our efforts to obey the commands of God.

What Scriptures can you begin to hide in your heart today? Open up your Bible or Bible app and make sure you are adding God's truth into your daily life. This world is absolutely no friend to following God's commands. It is a daily struggle to navigate temptations, self-centeredness, ungodly attitudes, or even to love everyone as we've been commanded. Hide the Word in your heart today!

PRAYER

Dear God, please don't let me wander from you, especially to follow my own desires when they conflict with your will. Let your Word live in me and keep me from disobeying your will. Amen.

Do You Really Understand What Jesus is Trying to Do?

Jesus replied, "You don't understand now what I am doing, but someday you will." John 13:7 NLT

Jesus was speaking to one of his disciples who protested when Jesus stooped down to wash his feet. Peter was very vocal and even declared, "You will never wash my feet." It seemed very awkward for this Rabbi, this teacher, this prophet and Son of God to be doing a servant's job.

How many times do we find ourselves in situations that seem hard to understand? We see what we see and know what we know but our eyesight is limited and our knowledge many times excludes the big picture.

Can you hear the voice of Jesus saying these words to you today?

It is true you don't understand. It is true that life seems upside down at the present. Because you trust Jesus, you have to believe that he is working. Like Peter who protested but finally sat back down and surrendered his feet to a kneeling Savior and allowed him to wash his feet, we must submit to the unseen will of God. It is hard to do, but at times we have to live by faith.

Today sit back and take a deep breath. Allow Jesus to work on your behalf. You may not understand now, but as he said to Peter, "Someday you will." You can always trust Jesus to be on your side.

PRAYER

Dear Jesus, I am so lost at times and make decisions based on what I think instead of what you think. Help me to learn how to hear your Word in my head and heart. Help me to follow you with everything I am every day. Amen.

Can You Hear Me Now?

"Come to me with your ears wide open. Listen, and you will find life. Isaiah 55:3 NLT

God really does want to communicate with us. He longs to be in a relationship with his human creation. So what are you going to do about that?

To find God and hear God is a challenge. I'm not talking about an audible voice, but to communicate with him and feel as though it is a two-way conversation is a challenge. The good news is that he gives us instructions.

- Come to me
- Open your ears
- Listen

To come to him means you set aside time and dedicate it and guard it. Don't allow the distractions of the day to push you out of your time to "come to God." Opening your ears means that you will put down the devices and turn off the TV or radio. Clear your head and take some deep breaths. More than likely you will hear God through reading his Word, a sermon, a song, or even through the words of a friend. And then he says, "Listen."

To listen means you hear with your heart. Allow the Holy Spirit to speak to you by allowing him to live in you. For the Spirit of God to dwell in you, all things offensive to God must be removed from your life. This is a challenge in the ungodly culture we live in. Close to 100 percent of the movies prepared for our entertainment are offensive to the life God calls us to live and to the standard of his Word. Television is hardly worth turning on. Our smartphones control so much of what we do and what we do with our time. Social media calls to us from our waking moments to our last thoughts at night.

Where is God in all of that? Make time for him. Open your ears and listen for him. His words and his presence will bring you comfort and peace. Or as he says it in this verse, "you will find life."

Dear God, help me to value the opportunity I have to spend time with you. Give me the ability to connect with you in such a way that you become way more important than the distractions that rob me on a daily basis. Amen.

Coming to God with Boldness

This High Priest of ours understands our weaknesses, for he faced all of the same testings we do, yet he did not sin. So let us come boldly to the throne of our gracious God. There we will receive his mercy, and we will find grace to help us when we need it most.
Hebrews 4:15-16 NLT

Always turn toward God. The Hebrews writer identifies Jesus Christ as our High Priest. Usually high priests would be set apart or not as available as we might want. A high priest would be inaccessible by virtue of his office and duties. But not Jesus.

He is a High Priest that understands our weakness we are told. He walked this earth as a human being and faced the testings and temptations that we all face. No, he didn't sin, but he knows the pressure and pull. "So let us come boldly to the throne of our gracious God."

You might want to read those words multiple times. Let them fill your mind and heart. Don't be timid about it ... come boldly to the throne of our gracious God. When you really know who God is, you will be more inclined to rely on his mercy and grace. When you come boldly, this is what you will find: "There we will receive his mercy, and we will find grace to help us when we need it most."

Today is a good day to move boldly into his presence! Receive and find mercy and grace. Allow him to be God in your life. Allow him to touch you with his power and peace.

PRAYER

Dear Jesus, I come to you today, and I am so thankful to be able to come boldly. I bow before your throne and wait on your grace and mercy to help me today. Amen.

Let Christ Rehab Your Life

And I am certain that God, who began the good work within you, will continue his work until it is finally finished on the day when Christ Jesus returns. Philippians 1:5 NLT

When we come to Christ and allow him access to our lives, he will make many changes. One might think of it this way. When someone buys a house to rehab it, they assess where all of the needs are and then prepare to change some things. They look for damage to repair, walls to break down, junk to remove, and they think about how different things will look when the work is completed.

Some of the work is internal and will not be seen by most people. Wires and old pipes are replaced, and sometimes things are changed in the basement or in the attic. Fresh paint, new flooring, and other adjustments and improvements will make the house valuable once again. The point is that when you begin the work of rehabbing a house, you see it through to completion. Maybe to sell or maybe to live in.

Christ does this rehab in our lives if we let him. He does both internal and external work. He does work that no one else will ever see and he does work that will make those around us wonder why we are so different. He supports us. He strengthens us when we are weak. He builds into our lives a faith that will not be swayed by storms and threats. He prepares us for eternity!

Our lives on this planet are but a vapor of time, but eternity is forever. The writer of this verse reminds us that this work of Christ will be completed on the day Jesus returns. He is coming back! Allow him access to every part of your life. Allow him to lovingly restore you from the inside out. He is the master builder and you won't believe the changes when he is done.

PRAYER

Dear Jesus, there is not one room of my heart that I want to keep you out of. Make them all new; tear out the things that don't belong, and replace them with things that do. Do your work in my life today. Amen.

Anything Is Possible?

What do you mean, "If I can"? Jesus asked. "Anything is possible if a person believes." Mark 9:23 NLT

This response by Jesus was given to the father of a very troubled son. The parents had dealt with it since the boy was very young. In desperation, this father was trying to muster his faith and believe that Jesus could help them.

There are events in all of our lives that will call for us to have faith that may extend beyond our personal strength or ability. In those times, we may be tempted to question the ability or even willingness of God to meet our needs.

Here is what the dad said to Jesus, "Have mercy on us and help us, if you can."

I'm not sure I've ever said "if you can" to the Lord, but I am sure that there have been times when I have wavered in my confidence. Most of us don't doubt the Lord's ability, but we may find it hard to believe for our situations. If you are there today, try to focus on his words to this desperate father: "Anything is possible if a person believes."

God knows everything about you today. He knows your fears and struggles, and he knows how to help you through them. Press in close to him today. He loves you and is waiting to help you. When you live a trusting and Christ-following life you will take things as they come and overcome them with his help and power.

PRAYER

Dear Jesus, you certainly do know everything about me. You know what I need today in my life. Please help me to accept your guidance and grace in every area and relationship I have. Amen.

Because He First Loved Me

Those who accept my commandments and obey them are the ones who love me. And because they love me, my Father will love them. And I will love them and reveal myself to each of them." John 14:21 NLT

Our love for God has always been the true test of our allegiance and discipleship. When we love him as we should, we accept his Word, his commandments, and we live by the principles found throughout the Bible.

Jesus speaks these words as he is preparing his first disciples for his death on the cross and his eventual ascension back to heaven. He would be leaving them alone to carry on the work of sharing the message of salvation to the world. It was a big task, and he promised to send the Holy Spirit to help guide them as they carried out his mission.

The promise we find today in this verse is that if we truly love and serve God, he will love us back and reveal himself to us. His presence in our lives will provide comfort in the face of adversity, faith when the path ahead seems unsure, and guidance when we reach the end of our own resources. The key is, you have to love him every day.

Jesus said the greatest commandment is to "love the Lord your God with all your heart, all your soul, and all your mind." Today, find ways to show and tell him how much you love him. Maybe today you would like to pray with the psalmist:

PRAYER

Make me walk along the path of your commands, for that is where my happiness is found. Psalm 119:35 NLT

The Door Is Always Open

For the grace of God has been revealed, bringing salvation to all people. Titus 2:11 NLT

Every year there is a time referred to as open enrollment. We hear about it, we see commercials about it, and sometimes we may even take advantage of it. The most significant open enrollment of all time happened with the advent of Jesus Christ to this earth.

We are about to enter what retailers refer to as the holiday sales season. It is busy, stressful and pushes us to our limits sometimes with crowds, traffic, and financial pressure.

I have some good news.

Open enrollment happened once and for all when Jesus came to this earth. When he opened enrollment it was an invitation to become part of his kingdom. It was an invitation to spiritual health. It was an invitation to be forgiven and to walk in spirit and in truth. It was an invitation to emotional, mental, relational, and physical healing.

It is an invitation to grace. God's grace.
It is an invitation worth singing about.
It is an invitation to join God's family, no questions asked.
It is a personal invitation.
It is for everyone, no matter what.
It is for you.

Don't go through another day without enrolling and accepting God's salvation to and for all people

PRAYER

Dear Jesus, thank you for this universal invitation for everyone. This is the good news of the gospel and I am so thankful to have heard it. I always want to be enrolled. Amen.

Living the New Life

My old self has been crucified with Christ. It is no longer I who live, but Christ lives in me. So I live in this earthly body by trusting in the Son of God, who loved me and gave himself for me. Galatians 2:20 NLT

The most effective or most godly leaders historically are men and women who have surrendered their loves and lives to Christ completely. This act enables us to lead from a very different perspective. When we are surrendered to Christ, we care about and concern ourselves with different priorities than what might be considered conventional wisdom. While solid leadership principles are still important, so are the needs of those we lead. Love, joy, peace, patience, kindness, goodness, faithfulness, gentleness, and self-control become the characteristics that others identify about us. What a great call and challenge to live the surrendered life as leaders! My prayer for us today is that we lead and love like Jesus.

This is the call to the extinguished life.
  "It is no longer I who live, but Christ lives in me."
This is a call to a relinquished life.
  "So I live ... by trusting in the Son of God."
This is the call to the distinguished life.
  "So I live in this earthly body by trusting in the Son of God, who loved me and gave himself for me."

PRAYER

Dear Jesus, may I always live a surrendered life. May you always live in me and give me the everlasting life I need so desperately. You make me new every day. Amen.

A Prayer List

Psalm 86 is attributed to David. In many ways it seems to be a typical psalm or what you would expect to find when you read the Psalms. The difference for me is that this prayer or song is very direct and personal. Below I have pulled out the direct requests found in Psalm 86 and David's rationale for asking. In my mind they may serve as a guide for prayer today.

Bend down, O LORD, and hear my prayer; answer me, for I need your help.

Protect me, for I am devoted to you.

Save me, for I serve you and trust you. You are my God.

Be merciful to me, O Lord, for I am calling on you constantly.

Give me happiness, O Lord, for I give myself to you.

Teach me your ways, O LORD, that I may live according to your truth!

Grant me purity of heart, so that I may honor you.

Look down and have mercy on me.

Give your strength to your servant.

Send me a sign of your favor.

Interspersed in this Psalm are words of praise and honor to God; here are a few of them that you may want to end with today.

O Lord, you are so good, so ready to forgive, so full of unfailing love for all who ask for your help. I will call to you whenever I'm in trouble, and you will answer me.

No pagan god is like you, O Lord. None can do what you do!

All the nations you made will come and bow before you, Lord; they will praise your holy name.

For you are great and perform wonderful deeds. You alone are God (Psalm 86:5, 7-10 NLT).

PRAYER

Dear God, please hear my prayer. Bend down my direction, please. I so need you right now. There is no god like you. Amen.

Building Trust

Bestselling author Stephen Covey wrote the now classic *Seven Habits of Highly Effective People*. His son wrote the book entitled, *The Speed of Trust*. While his dad's book has sold more copies, the book on trust is also a bestseller. Without trust as leaders or individual Christians, we really have nothing. Those around us will cease to follow, and those we are trying to influence will have little respect or desire to be led. There is a fascinating Scripture in Isaiah in which Isaiah identifies some key trust characteristics for godly leaders.

The world is on fire, so to speak, and Isaiah lists the traits that are most needed to withstand the fire and to build trust.

The sinners in Jerusalem shake with fear. Terror seizes the godless. "Who can live with this devouring fire?" they cry. "Who can survive this all-consuming fire?" Those who are honest and fair, who refuse to profit by fraud, who stay far away from bribes, who refuse to listen to those who plot murder, who shut their eyes to all enticement to do wrong, these are the ones who will dwell on high. The rocks of the mountains will be their fortress. Food will be supplied to them, and they will have water in abundance. Isaiah 33:14-16 NKJV

Integrity: Our life and words must be consistent (verse 15).

Justice: We must never accept dishonest gain (verse 15b).

Convictions: We won't accept bribes and can't be bought off (verse 15c).

Positive Focus: We won't listen or participate in evil plans (verse 15d).

Pure: We will possess a disciplined mind that stays away from vulgarity and impurity (verse 15e).

Secure: We will make others feel secure because of their own personal spiritual foundation (verse 16).

These godly characteristics will build trust and allow the godly leader or individual to lead effectively and righteously. Godly leaders who possess these traits will develop others and not destroy them. They will build hope and a strong sense of security in those they lead.

PRAYER

Dear God, give me the courage to live out my life with no shortcuts. Enable me to keep my integrity and stay true to you no matter what is happening around me. Amen.

Finding Rest

The apostles returned to Jesus from their ministry tour and told him all they had done and taught. Then Jesus said, "Let's go off by ourselves to a quiet place and rest awhile." He said this because there were so many people coming and going that Jesus and his apostles didn't even have time to eat. Mark 6:30-31 NLT

The setting for this story is in the heart of Jesus' three-year ministry. Just prior, he had sent the twelve disciples out to do ministry on their own. John the Baptist, Jesus' cousin, was beheaded; and the crowds were swarming around Jesus, drawn by the sensationalism of people being healed. The blind saw, the deaf heard, the lame walked, and it was attracting huge crowds of people.

When life is at its busiest we must do whatever it takes to find rest. Jesus knew this, and in fact the Sabbath was established for rest and recovery physically, mentally, and spiritually. There were four intentions in this one sentence Jesus spoke:

- Go someplace different: "Let us go off."
- Get away from the crowd: "by ourselves"
- Make it a quiet place "to a quiet place"
- Rest: "and rest awhile."

This is so hard to do, but I would encourage you to make sure you find time to allow God to speak into your life and work. Don't press on in your own strength, because eventually you will be empty and not have the ability to go on. The lesson here is that even our best intentions are sometimes taken away from us. Look at the following verses:

"So they left by boat for a quiet place, where they could be alone. But many people recognized them and saw them leaving, and people from many towns ran ahead along the shore and got there ahead of them. Jesus saw the huge crowd as he stepped from the boat, and he had compassion on them because they were like sheep without a shepherd. So he began teaching them many things" (Mark 6: 32-34 NLT).

Shortly after this, he fed this group of five thousand people he was teaching. It was exhausting for him and the twelve disciples. The rest was not to be just yet, but in Mark 6:45 we read: "Immediately after this, Jesus insisted that his disciples get back into the boat and head across the lake to Bethsaida, while he sent the people home."

Do what you can today to make sure you are resting in the Lord. Follow his lead and take the time you need for quiet, peaceful rest.

PRAYER

Dear Lord, help me to understand my need for rest. Make me more diligent about Sabbath observance so that my body will stay healthy and be at its best for you. Amen

He Is My Strength

My health may fail, and my spirit may grow weak, but God re-mains the strength of my heart; he is mine forever. Psalm 73:26 NLT

Life happens. Our bodies and minds are fragile entities with unknown expiration dates attached. We may enjoy the energy of our youth and feel empowered through middle age; but as our age advances and the days add into months and years, we begin to feel the effects of time. Of course one's health failing is not limited to just older adults. All across our nation there are children's hospitals filled with sick, ailing, and even dying kids.

The psalmist makes a big statement in a few words. No matter what happens to us, as long as God is the center of our daily life we will find him available to strengthen us for the experience. Life is very short and eternity is without end. Placing Christ at the center of our lives seems like it should be an easy choice, but often people neglect to do it until something is really wrong. When a crisis happens we often rush to find Christ and figure out how to have a relationship with him because now we need him.

The psalmist's words are preemptive. He suggests that negative things may happen but God *remains* the strength of his heart. Put Christ first in your life today. Work at accepting his love for you daily and returning the favor by living for him and making sure he is the most important voice and power in your life.

PRAYER

Dear God, you know every detail of my life. You know the good, the bad, and the ugly. Please give me the courage to draw close to you. Give me the strength to surrender every area of my life to you. Be the strength of my life. Amen.

Don't Give Up Your Freedom

Christ has set us free to live a free life. So take your stand! Never again let anyone put a harness of slavery on you. Galatians 5:1 MSG

Freedom isn't free! We've all heard that before. In the case of our spiritual walk, our freedom came at the cost of Jesus' life. If you have Christ in your life and are following him, you have been given a life of freedom. Somewhere, at some point in your life, you realized your absolute need for Jesus. Life happens around us and circumstances change, but God never changes. There are times in our life when for the sake of our freedom and our spiritual journey we should take an extended time to reflect on where we are and what is happening in our lives. You only get one chance at this life, and in a blink of the eye our lives approach the end—or more accurately the beginning of eternity. This is not a negative devotional thought but an encouragement to not let go of the most important decision any one ever makes and that is the decision to follow Christ. Here are some suggestions as you work through your freedom evaluation:

- Acknowledge that Christ has set you free.
- Affirm your commitment to stand firm.
- Avoid the things or people that might fracture your faith.

Freedom is the liberty to function in the kingdom of God daily. That is not about church attendance, but it does mean that every day will be God-honoring. You've seen these verses before, but here is a great reminder of what God wants to do through us and in us:

"So here's what I want you to do, God helping you: Take your everyday, ordinary life—your sleeping, eating, going-to-work, and walking-around life—and place it before God as an offering. Embracing what God does for you is the best thing you can do for him. Don't become so well-adjusted to your culture that you fit into it without even thinking. Instead, fix your attention on God. You'll be changed from the inside out. Readily recognize what he wants from you, and quickly respond to it. Unlike the culture around you, always dragging you down to its level

168

of immaturity, God brings the best out of you, develops well-formed maturity in you" (Romans 12:1-2 MSG).

Dear Lord, thank you for setting me free! Please help me never to go back to a life of bondage to anything or anyone. I want to always embrace what you do for me. I want to live in your freedom. Amen.

You Can Make a Difference

Can one person make a difference in our world? It is an awfully big place with billions of people that most of us never encounter or think about. Somewhere inside all of us is a feeling and desire that our lives ought to count for something.

A most amazing thought is that every one of us has the potential to make a difference to God. Think about that for moment. Here are a couple of examples of God looking for one person to make a difference.

"Run up and down every street in Jerusalem," says the Lord. *"Look high and low; search throughout the city! If you can find even one just and honest person, I will not destroy the city."* Jeremiah 5:1 NLT

"I looked for someone who might rebuild the wall of righteousness that guards the land. I searched for someone to stand in the gap in the wall so I wouldn't have to destroy the land, but I found no one" (Ezekiel 22:30 NLT).

God is all powerful but there are times when our omnipotent God looks for and needs a man or woman to carry out his will on earth. In times of crisis he looks for men and women to carry out his plan and to step up and lead. Remember that sometimes God's leadership plans look very different than this world's ideas of leadership. It is not uncommon for God to call a person to do something outside the norm so that in the end people will know that only God could have done it.

1. **We are called to intervene in this world on behalf of God.**
2. **We are called to be involved in God's story on the earth.**
3. **We are called to intercede with God for people in our spheres of influence.**

Be listening for God's call in you today. Allow yourself to be part of God's story. Don't spend all your time asking for him to bless what you are doing, but find out what his will is and step into it. It is always right to care deeply for those you work and live around. Praying for them is one way to deepen your level of leadership and usability to God. He wants to use you if you will let Him. Be the one...

Lord, I know that you are looking for men and women that will serve with their whole hearts. May I always be available and on your call list. I want to be involved in my world. Amen.

Guard Your Heart Above All Else

Guard your heart above all else, for it determines the course of your life. Proverbs 4:23 NLT

This admonition is found surrounded by verses about wisdom. Phrases like, "Pay attention and learn good judgment," or "Get wisdom; develop good judgment." "Don't turn your back on wisdom, for she will protect you," and "Getting wisdom is the wisest thing you can do."

Wisdom would say to guard your heart. Be careful what you let into your heart and soul. If we are to love God with our heart, mind, soul, and strength, what we allow into our heart is critical to attaining wisdom and guarding our hearts.

Guarding includes: protecting, standing guard over, patrolling, defending, shielding, preserving, sheltering. It could also include defending, fortifying, and saving.

Guard your heart above all else, for it determines the course of your life.

Things to remember:

Above all else. Nothing is more important than this. You and I control our hearts, and God says it is more important than anything else; and here's the reason.

It determines the course of your life. Where we let our hearts go is where we go. What we give our hearts to is what we love and embrace. The course of our life is determined by us.

Maybe it is what the apostle Paul was thinking when he encouraged us to put on the whole amour of God. We should do everything the Bible tells us to do to protect our hearts and souls.

PRAYER

Dear God, you remind us in your Word that our hearts our desperately wicked and naturally turn from you. Please give me your presence and grace in my life that will guard my heart daily and always give me the strength to go your way. Amen.

You Are So Valuable to God!

But not a single sparrow can fall to the ground without your Father knowing it. And the very hairs on your head are all numbered. So don't be afraid; you are more valuable to God than a whole flock of sparrows. Matthew 10:29-31 NTL

God knows exactly where you are! I find myself reminding people of this often. We can sometimes get so lost and caught up in the drama surrounding our lives that we forget about who God really is. He knows everything!

We pray to him with an understanding that his answer may not fit our plans and wishes. This requires a constant and steady trust in the one who sees the big picture of our lives. I once heard a man thank God for his dad's survival of a procedure at the local hospital. He remarked, "God was faithful." In reality, God was faithful even if the procedure was a complete failure. I doubt that he would have acknowledged that if the news was not what he wanted.

God is good! He is faithful in every situation, and he will be faithful to you. Trust him and remind yourself of his unfailing love for you. I don't know why it is important for him to know the number of hairs on your head, but the writer says that he does. He knows sparrows and he knows you. Let his love and care envelop you today as you remain faithful and true. You are of great value to the Lord.

PRAYER

Lord, I know how well you take care of even the littlest sparrow. Thanks for reminding me today of how much more you care about me. Amen.

Sometimes Only God Can Help Stop the Tears

My tears flow endlessly; they will not stop until the Lord *looks down from heaven and sees.* Lamentations 3:49-50 NLT

This past week I've talked with people dealing with life and death issues. Life all of a sudden got very real for them. Priorities are shifted, relationships are tended, and hope is sought after. Some are facing illness, and at least one close friend lost a precious grandson in a terrible accident.

The tears flow as an expression of our fear, grief, and sometimes despair. The prophet Jeremiah wrote the book of Lamentations and he was known as the weeping prophet. He was no stranger to tears. In these verses we are reminded how important God's presence is to us when we are facing troubles and sorrows. The tears showed no sign of stopping, and he expresses his only hope as being found in the knowledge that the Lord is aware of the situation.

"They will not stop until the Lord looks down from heaven and sees."

No matter what you may be facing or will face in the future, I encourage you to put your complete trust in our Lord. He does know. He does see. He is aware. He is with you wherever you go if you are in a relationship with him. We are reminded in Scripture that if we draw close to him, he will draw close to us. When all around us seems to be shifting out of our control, God is the one constant that will not change, wither, or leave you alone. He knows. He sees it all and he knows right where to find you.

PRAYER

Dear Lord, when I can't seem to stop crying or I feel overwhelmed, I will remember that you are looking down at me. It is you that knows and cares for me. I will find joy in this today. Amen.

Adopted and Loved

No, I will not abandon you as orphans—I will come to you. John 14:18 NLT

No one wants to be an orphan. To be orphaned means that you are without parents and that probably there has been deaths or a traumatic event. Studies have shown that orphans may struggle with emotional and behavioral problems. They may experience abuse, exploitation, neglect, lack of love and care of parents. Of course, many avoid these issues thanks to people that are willing to adopt.

Adoption is a biblical theme. It is God's word. It is His promise.

"God sent him (Jesus) to buy freedom for us who were slaves to the law, so that he could adopt us as his very own children" (Galatians 4:5 NLT).

"God decided in advance to adopt us into his own family by bringing us to himself through Jesus Christ. This is what he wanted to do, and it gave him great pleasure" (Ephesians 1:5 NLT).

God loves you more than you probably love yourself. He longs to adopt you through salvation into his family. When you are in his family, you experience unconditional love, security, support, guidance, trust, peace, joy, and most of all grace. He will lead you and love you. He will be unlike any Father you have ever known. All of us need this adoption.

PRAYER

Dear God, I am so thankful today that you were willing to adopt me into your family. I am at home with you. You are my heavenly Father, and I could ask for no better. Amen.

You and One Other Is All You May Need

For where two or three gather together as my followers, I am there among them. Matthew 18:20 NLT

Jesus made this promise to his first disciples, but it covers all believers for all time. If you are a follower of Christ, it is important to experience his presence. Jesus says if you and one or two other people get together, I will be there among you.

There is one stipulation. You have to be followers. Other translations say, when you gather "in my name." This is so important. To be a follower of Jesus Christ or to invoke his name in prayer means that you are in a relationship with him. He is not just someone you think about when the wheels fall off of your life; but you worship and thank him every morning when you wake up, and he is your last thought when you go to sleep, and you live for him all day, every day.

Find other people who are followers of Jesus and make sure you share this powerful bond. Pray for one another. Support each other. Find those people at work, in your community, and at church. I know there are groups of you that gather at work each morning or maybe when a need arises.

Want to be successful at navigating this life? Be a true follower of Christ who can reach out and call others to prayer. Be a person who is known for living in his presence. Gather as his followers (in his name) and he will be there. He will "be among you."

PRAYER

Dear Jesus, I have experienced your presence while praying and worshiping with others. I don't want to ever forsake the community of believers I am surrounded with. Thank you for this promise. Amen.

Confession Is Good for the Soul

Confess your sins to each other and pray for each other so that you may be healed. The earnest prayer of a righteous person has great power and produces wonderful results. James 5:16 NLT

This verse seems to be filled with different subjects at first glance, but in reality they all tie together. The subject is about healing, but when you are praying about this James suggests that you might have unconfessed sin in your life that also may need to be dealt with. In previous verses he writes about calling for the elders and being anointed with oil, and he says that not only may you be healed but that God will forgive your sins as well.

Confession may seem to be a negative action, but it is quite the opposite. Confessing and coming clean in your life with God and people is purifying to the soul. It is like a new start or a do over. Sometimes we all need a new beginning.

Healing is much more than physical healing. The healing that Jesus offers includes physical, emotional, spiritual health, and even the healing of memories and relationships. Don't let anything stand between you and God. Don't let there be any actions or issues that you carry like baggage because you've been unwilling to confess or be completely honest. Nothing will bring healing to your life like knowing that your life is clean before God.

When your soul is clear, then pray and remember, "The earnest prayer of a righteous person has great power and produces wonderful results." Trust him. Believe in him, and allow him to tune your heart to full devotion.

PRAYER

Dear Jesus, I am so thankful you allow us to confess our sins, mistakes, and failures. There is something so wonderful about knowing there is nothing to hide. Always show me my failures, and I will confess them you to you. Amen.

When Your Plans Fall Through

The heart of man plans his way, but the Lord establishes his steps.
Proverbs 16:9 ESV

So often, we make our plans as though there is nothing that might interrupt them. In reality, life sometime has a way of messing with our best made plans. If we trust the Lord with our days on this earth, we can know that even in the interruptions, he still has a plan for our steps.

Usually our best vision of God's establishing steps in our lives is seen when we look back on things that did or didn't happen like we thought they would.

Are you questioning something that fell apart that you so wanted to happen? Is there some plan you thought was going to be perfect but it didn't happen because of circumstances beyond your control?

If the Lord is establishing your steps, you are going to be just fine no matter where these steps may take you. Remember, following Jesus is not always safe; but we are walking toward eternity, and someday we will be safe forever and with our Lord. In days of uncertainty, know that the Lord is not only walking with you but that he is guiding you as well.

PRAYER

Dear Lord, to be honest, there are times when I question where you seem to be leading me. When pain and suffering are happening or I experience loss, help me to not question my steps and to trust that you are leading me. Amen.

Plow Up Your Heart!

Israel is like a trained heifer treading out the grain—an easy job she loves. But I will put a heavy yoke on her tender neck. I will force Judah to pull the plow and Israel to break up the hard ground. I said, "Plant the good seeds of righteousness, and you will harvest a crop of love. Plow up the hard ground of your hearts, for now is the time to seek the Lord, that he may come and shower righteousness upon you." Hosea 10:11-12 NLT

Spiritual renewal is something we all need from time to time. Our culture and daily surroundings along with "life" that sometimes comes in challenging ways is distracting and can cause us to move away from God. The good news is that God loves when his people turn and repent. He is always there to receive them back to the close walk he desires from us. In these verses Hosea is quoting God himself as he addresses Israel and Judah.

We all like to take the easy way at times. Ver. 11a

The heifers treading out the grain had the best job ever. The load wasn't heavy and they had a lot to eat as they worked. All of us enjoy these kinds of moments in our lives. The sad thing is that prosperity often moves our hearts and attention away from God. A former university president I worked closely with once told me the only way America would ever turn back toward God would be a famine or a war. This is true for the churched and the unchurched because often the need to return is about the same.

We all learn from the hard work and yoke. Ver. 11b

Notice that God recognized their tender necks but put the yokes on them to force them to break up the hard ground and prepare it for planning seeds and the rains that would come. In this case it was Judah and Israel as he called them back to himself.

I don't personally believe that God causes pain, but I do believe he will use the circumstances that happen in our lives to draw us to himself. It was Jesus that said, "My yoke is easy and my burden is light." The point is that it is still a yoke and a burden. (For further study: the word yoke in Hosea is obviously a reference to a piece of wood put on the necks of oxen. In Jesus day it also meant allowing yourself to be assigned to a rabbi or teacher. The yoke was your connection to that person.)

We all love the blessing of being in the will of God. Ver. 12

It's all about cause and effect. Here are some action steps:

- "Plant the good seeds ... and you will harvest a crop of love."
- "Plow up the hard ground of your hearts, for now is the time to seek the Lord."

We plow and plant, and the promise is that he will come and shower righteousness upon us.

PRAYER

God help me to take seriously my personal walk with you. Deliver me from the influences around me that threaten to turn my head and heart away from you. Break up any hardness, and plant your seeds of righteousness in me. Allow me to reap a crop of love. Let your rain and righteousness fall on me. Amen.

What's on Your Mind?

And now, dear brothers and sisters, one final thing. Fix your thoughts on what is true, and honorable, and right, and pure, and lovely, and admirable. Think about things that are excellent and worthy of praise. Philippians 4:8 NLT

We are inundated on a daily basis with messages and many of them are not positive. World events, daily news reports, television, movies, and even social media can cause us to feel overwhelmed by negative messages and discouraging images. As the writer of Philippians is wrapping up writing this letter to an early first century church, he reminds them to control what they allow into their minds.

This used to be a normal part of living a Christ-following life; however, in our effort to be connected and part of the society we live in, many people practice no self-discipline in this area. What would happen to your attitude if you truly practiced this admonition? How much closer would you feel to Jesus Christ if you paid attention to what you were feeding your thoughts?

Many of the negative things we see and encounter are not even based on truth. I know people that beat themselves up because of things they see on other people's Facebook pages. The reality is that only part of a person's life is typically on Facebook or social media. Most of us only post the good stuff. Very few people show the reality of life and the heartaches that come from time to time or the unrest, frustrations, and challenges that are a normal part of the human story.

So what should we do with this? Let me outline it for you and maybe you can start working on this list today:

Fix your thoughts: (what a great phrase)
On what is true and honorable
And right
And pure
And lovely
And admirable

Think about things:
> That are excellent
> And worthy of praise

The Christ-following life is always about putting God first. It's not always easy to do, but it should be what we strive for daily. Let me share the two verses before our devotional Scripture for today. Let God's peace guard your hearts and minds.

"Don't worry about anything; instead, pray about everything. Tell God what you need, and thank him for all he has done. Then you will experience God's peace, which exceeds anything we can understand. His peace will guard your hearts and minds as you live in Christ Jesus" (Philippians 4:6-7 NLT).

PRAYER

Dear Jesus, fix my heart, mind, and thoughts on you. Please help me overcome the distractions of this life and all the noise that competes for my attention. Let your peace guard my heart and mind. Amen.

Sentence of Death

For we do not want you to be ignorant, brethren, of our trouble which came to us in Asia: that we were burdened beyond measure, above strength, so that we despaired even of life. Yes, we had the sentence of death in ourselves, that we should not trust in ourselves but in God who raises the dead, who delivered us from so great a death, and does deliver us; in whom we trust that he will still deliver us, you also helping together in prayer for us, that thanks may be given by many persons on our behalf for the gift granted to us through many. 1 Corinthians 1:8-11 NLT

The apostle Paul wrote this to a church that supported his ministry. He was writing from a rugged ministry commitment and one where he often suffered because of his faith in Christ. His reference to a sentence of death was not a metaphor, it was real. For most of us, that is not the case; but we have to have that attitude toward things that may arise in our lives. Having the "sentence of death" in ourselves is simply being totally surrendered to God. Our faith is so strong in God that we don't come undone when our lives take an unexpected and even tragic turn.

- A sentence of death is often appealed, but as Christians we embrace it.
- A sentence of death is thought to be the worst sentence one can receive, but for Christ-followers it is the ultimate achievement.
- A sentence of death is given for taking someone else's life, but in our case it is for being willing to lose our own.

Think of the man or woman who is on death row. The time is now at hand. Only a few hours and they will be put to death. The moment is coming when they will take their last breath and they know exactly when that is going to happen. For the Christian on death row there is an incredible hope that they will transfer from this world to the arms of him who raises the dead. Karla Faye Tucker was executed in 1998 for committing murder. While in prison, she became an outspoken follower of Christ. Many struggled with her death because of her dynamic change, but she faced it head on with great faith. Her last words included this sentence: "I'm going to be face to face with Jesus now."

No matter what happens in our life, we can be so trusting of our Savior that we are willing to die if needs be to fulfill his will. Don't trust in yourself, because you are very limited, but trust in God. Remember, he raises the dead and he promises life eternal. Being a Christian is about a vibrant relationship with Christ that transcends the church, a pastor, or anything else. It is a daily attitude and walk that will sustain us from life to death.

PRAYER

Dear Lord, as you know, I sometimes fear death. Help me to live my life with a healthy view of dying daily to you. May I embrace the surrendered life as my life. Amen.

Help my Unbelief

The father instantly cried out, "I do believe, but help me overcome my unbelief!" Mark 9:24 NLT

It was in the middle of a large crowd of people that a man spoke these words to Jesus. He had brought his demon-possessed son to Christ for healing. Jesus said it was possible if he only believed and then the dad uttered these words.

I must tell you that I find great hope in them.

I do believe. I believe that God is God, that Jesus is the Son of God, and that the Holy Spirit has been given us for daily support and guidance. I believe in the creation story as recorded in the Bible. I believe in all of the miracles that fill the pages of God's Word. I have no trouble believing that God can do what no other entity or god can do. I believe he knows all, is all-powerful, and is present everywhere.

If I am honest, sometimes I have trouble believing for myself. Like this father, whose son was rolling around in the dirt and foaming at the mouth, sometimes my circumstances challenge my ability to believe that God is working on my behalf. I think he wants to. I think he promised to, but I still need help with my unbelief.

What is it that you are struggling with today? What obstacle, what circumstance? What is looming in the future that has raised your anxiety to a new high level? It's okay to pray this prayer and be honest with God. Tell him that you are struggling to believe. Ask him to increase your faith and to give you peace.

PRAYER

Dear Lord, I really do believe in you and I don't want to say the word "but" in this prayer ... but I need your help. Please help me with my unbelief. Help me overcome and trust you with my life. Amen.

Great Is His Faithfulness

Yet I still dare to hope when I remember this: The faithful love of the Lord never ends! His mercies never cease. Great is his faithfulness; his mercies begin afresh each morning. Lamentations 3:21-23 NLT

These words were written during a horrific time of punishment on Israel for their disobedience against God. They experienced complete devastation and even death because of their waywardness and willful sinful behaviors. But then comes this moment. The writer musters up the strength and hopefulness to remember what it was like to be in a healthy relationship with God. This is a turning point in Israel's years of judgment and captivity. Things are about to get better. A lot better.

There are four things we should always remember and never let go of. No matter how tough life is or how discouraging our present circumstances, these four things are true about God. They were true, they are true, and they will always be true. Here are your reminders today:

- The faithful love of the Lord never ends.
- His mercies never cease.
- Great is his faithfulness.
- His mercies begin afresh each morning.

As you are reading this today, chances are you can testify to God's faithfulness in your life. All people on this planet receive his mercy in one form or the other. Even God's judgments are merciful if they bring us back to him.

Hymn writer Thomas Obadiah Chisholm picked up this theme from the book of Lamentations and penned a now classic hymn. Why not make this your prayer of worship today:

PRAYER

"Great is thy faithfulness," O God my Father,
There is no shadow of turning with thee;
Thou changest not, thy compassions they fail not.
As thou hast been thou forever wilt be.

"Great is thy faithfulness!" "Great is thy faithfulness!"
Morning by morning new mercies I see;
All I have needed thy hand hath provided—
"Great is thy faithfulness," Lord, unto me!

Loyalty and Kindness for the Win

Never let loyalty and kindness leave you! Tie them around your neck as a reminder. Write them deep within your heart. Then you will find favor with both God and people, and you will earn a good reputation. Proverbs 3:3-4 NLT

The actions of loyalty and kindness are here intertwined by the writer. We are all called to loyalty. We are called to be loyal spiritually, emotionally, vocationally, and even corporately. When we really believe in what we are doing and who we are, being loyal is not hard. This passage suggests that we never let them leave us. Tie them around your neck and write them deep in your heart.

When we are loyal to an organization, a family, or a person, kindness is a given. We have no reason for anger or mistreatment when our hearts are in the right place. Resentment can lead to unkindness; but when loyalty is in the mix, resentment is replaced with kindness.

The promise connected to living with loyalty and kindness is pretty amazing. We will find favor with God and people. We will earn a reputation for living well. You can't ever be too kind. People love kind people.

PRAYER

Lord, help me understand the depth of loyalty you want from me. Let the fruit of your Spirit flow through me in the form of kindness to others. Let me have the strength to live my life for you and in you. Amen.

God's Powerful Hand

At the same time, God's hand was on the people in the land of Judah, giving them all one heart to obey the orders of the king and his officials, who were following the word of the LORD. 2 Chronicles 30:12 NLT

God's hand was moving. Anytime you read that God's hand or hands are active, something big is happening. In this context, Judah was trying to realign themselves with God's Word and wishes. They were being invited by the king to obey God's rules for worship and Passover. In the invitation sent out across Israel and Judah they were encouraged to submit themselves to the Lord and to worship him. Unlike their ancestors, who time after time rejected God's call, something happened to bring them together with one heart and mind to obey.

It was God's powerful hand!

I wonder what God's hand could do for you or in you today. I wonder how much many of us really want his hands mixed into our lives. His hand requires obedience on our part. The people of Judah set out to destroy all the pagan altars erected to false gods. The priests and the people purified themselves in preparation for a new day and a new start.

When God's hand moves near you it will be a call to follow; and when you do, things that have been out of kilter will begin to fall into place. Joy will return even in the midst of sorrow. Peace will come back because you are following the giver of all peace. Be open to God's hand moving you along in the right direction.

The people of Judah were so moved by God's presence that they came together for seven days and enjoyed it so much they extended their time together another seven days. God heard their prayers and blessed them over and over. Let his hands be a blessing to you today.

PRAYER

Dear Lord, I welcome your hands into my life. I realize that when your hands are working on my behalf I will have protection, guidance, security, and faith. Amen.

Decisions

"Thousands upon thousands are waiting in the valley of decision. There the day of the Lord will arrive soon. Joel 3:14 NLT

This Scripture is part of a much larger Old Testament story of the relationship between Israel and God. As I read these words, I am made to think of millions upon millions around the world that are standing today in some valley of decision.

Maybe you are faced with decisions that are overwhelming to you. They come to all of us at one time or the other. These decisions may affect our relationships, our finances, our health, and even our safety; but all of us wind up in the "valley of decision."

Sometimes we only see the high mountains when we are walking through a valley. Our view can be limited when compared to the view from the top of a mountain, but it is in these valleys that we make decisions that allow us to have the mountaintop experiences along the way. We choose paths and directions that lead and guide our future.

There is always hope! This verse reminds us that the day of the Lord will arrive soon. Be encouraged and don't give up. It is in the valley that God arrives to meet us and lead us. He is leading you today even in this current valley you may be walking through. Keep your eyes on him and listen for his voice as you read his Word. He will guide you and help you make your decisions.

PRAYER

Dear God, you know the decisions I am trying to make in my life today. I ask that you would arrive to show me the way. I will wait until your will is clear. Amen.

I Will Follow the Light

I am the light of the world. If you follow me, you won't have to walk in darkness, because you will have the light that leads to life. John 8:12 NLT

There are certain key words in the New Testament that are very important to our Christian journey. Two of them are in this verse. Jesus was teaching, as he often did, and he offered these words of wisdom. He referenced himself as the "light of the world" and suggested that we would be following him.

"Light" and "follow" are two key words for disciples of Jesus.

Light is what expels the darkness from our walk. Light is what guides us as we trek toward eternity. Sometimes it is hard to find his way in a sea of voices all speaking at once through the media, social media, and even in our own churches. We are tempted to just believe what everyone else believes or to look around us and gauge our devotion by those that we see and hear. I would encourage you and implore you to keep your eyes on Jesus.

Following is what Jesus asks us to do. He asked us to pick up our crosses and follow him. He asks us to leave things behind and follow him. He promises to make us fishers of men if we follow him. He will reveal the path we are to walk if we are following.

It's a good day to evaluate your involvement with the light and following the light. Let his light dispel the darkness that brings fear and hopelessness. Follow Jesus with fervency and purpose. This light and this following will, in his words, "lead to life."

PRAYER

Dear Jesus, you are the only light I want to follow. I am walking and following you to avoid the darkness. Let your light lead me to everlasting life. Amen.

I Will Be Faithful to Your Word

Jesus said to the people who believed in him, "You are truly my disciples if you remain faithful to my teachings. And you will know the truth, and the truth will set you free." John 8:31-32 NLT

This is a direct quote from Jesus. Another translation says it this way, "If you abide in my word." Why is it so easy for us to neglect the Word of God? Why do we often get distracted by the things and people around us to the point of ignoring God's Word?

I wonder what it will be like for current generations when we face the evaluation of our lives someday as we stand before God. I wonder how lopsided our time will be when it flashes in front of us and compares our time spent with God and time spend with the ever-present media that constantly calls and tempts us into hours of wasted time?

These verses call for evaluation. They call for us to examine our hearts and lives. They call for us to consider if we are abiding in his Word. Are we remaining faithful to his teachings? It is very easy to adapt our lives to the culture and our own desires instead of consistently being faithful to Jesus.

The good news is that we can move back toward him and press into his Word. He welcomes us back even when we may have wandered off in our own direction. Ultimately, you and I are responsible for our spiritual maturity and strength. Know the truth and let it set you free!

PRAYER

Dear Jesus, more than anything I want to always be your disciple. To do this I know I must stay connected to your Word. Open your truth in my life like never before. Amen.

Never, Ever Give Up!

That is why we never give up. Though our bodies are dying, our spirits are being renewed every day. 1 Corinthians 4:16 NLT

Subconsciously we all know it. We don't want to think about it or even talk about it, but the fact is, even if we are not currently sick, we are all terminal. For human beings the death rate is at 100%. All of us will face death at some point in our lives. One translation of this verses says: "Though the outward man is perishing, our inward man is being renewed day by day."

We can only do so much about our bodies. We can try to eat right, live right, exercise right, and still age will creep ever so slowly into our bones and bodies. So what are we to do?

Allow your "inward man" or spirit to be renewed daily. Let God feed you with spiritual food and presence that will sustain you when you are fighting the physical assaults that happen to our bodies. Hide the Word of God in your heart and the Holy Spirit will bring it to your mind when you most need it.

Our greatest investment of our time and focus should be spent in the renewing of our inward spirits. Here are some suggestions for how to do this:

Rejoice always.
Pray without ceasing.
In everything, give thanks.
Do not quench the Spirit.
Do not despise prophecies.
Test all things; hold fast what is good.
Abstain from every form of evil.
— Taken from 1 Thessalonians 5:16-22 NKJV

The most influential Christians I have ever known are those that have maintained their inward spirits as they age gracefully. They are loving, kindhearted, and encouraging to those around them even though they may be struggling physically. Let God work in your heart every day.

PRAYER

Dear Lord, every day I live I am getting older; but I pray that while my body may someday expire, my soul will grow stronger in you. Renew my inward spirit, I pray. Amen.

No Fear

Then Jesus came over and touched them. "Get up," he said. "Don't be afraid." Matthew 17:7 NLT

What knocks you off your feet? Peter, James, and John were the three disciples Jesus chose to go up the mountain with him as he prayed and struggled about his upcoming trip to the cross. First they fell asleep and then woke up to see two prophets that had been dead for a long time talking with Jesus. When God's voice came out of the heavens it was too much for them and they fell on their faces and were terrified.

Jesus then spoke these words to the men shaking on the ground: "Get up, Don't be afraid."

Ever been overcome with fear of the unknown? Maybe even today you are fighting thoughts of fear, or the current realities in your life are threatening your peace and keeping you up at night. This same Jesus that compassionately spoke to his disciples speaks these same words to us in our fearful times. Maybe today you can envision Jesus bending over you and placing his hand on your shoulder. Maybe you can hear him speak these words in your soul, "Get up and don't be afraid."

Jesus loves you and knows all about your struggles. If you feel like you are down, let Jesus give you the courage to get up. If you are afraid, trust him with your fear and doubts. He loves you and he cares deeply about you.

PRAYER

Dear Jesus, I pray today for my friends and family that may be really struggling with fear and anxiety. Whatever it is, Jesus, I am asking you to help them and comfort them today. Amen.

Conviction for the Win

Fools make fun of guilt, but the godly acknowledge it and seek reconciliation. Proverbs 14:9 NLT

The word is conviction. Conviction doesn't conjure up joy and happiness, but it is necessary that we engage and understand our need for conviction in our lives. God's Holy Spirit abides in us to provide a sensitivity to right and wrong and enables us to reject actions or sins that produce guilt. If we find ourselves straying then we have an Advocate with the Father who will pray for us and help us back to reconciliation.

There is nothing better than knowing and living in the knowledge that there is nothing between your soul and the Savior. Keep your heart open and soft to the conviction the Holy Spirit may bring to your life.

An ancient song written by Charles Wesley and long ago cut from the hymnbooks includes the following words that could be used as a prayer today for us today. (If you feel the desire to sing it and don't know the original tune you can sing it to the tune of Amazing Grace.)

PRAYER

I want a principle within of jealous, godly fear,
A sensibility of sin, a pain to feel it near.
I want the first approach to feel of pride or fond desire,
To catch the wand'ring of my will, and quench the kindling fire.
From thee that I no more may part, no more thy goodness grieve,
The filial awe, the fleshly heart, the tender conscience, give.
Quick as the apple of an eye, O God, my conscience make;
Awake my soul when sin is nigh, and keep it still awake.
Almighty God of truth and love, to me thy pow'r impart;
The mountain from my soul remove, the hardness from my heart.
Oh, may the least omission pain my reawakened soul,
And drive me to that blood again, which makes the wounded whole.
— Charles Wesley (1749)

Obey, Listen, and Hold On

Serve only the LORD your God and fear him alone. Obey his commands, listen to his voice, and cling to him. Deuteronomy 13:4 NLT

It is an oft-repeated theme throughout Scripture. Although it's expressed many different ways in both the Old and New Testaments, the message is simply this: put God first. In this Scripture, Moses outlines for us a way to do this. Follow his logic as he spells it out.

"Obey his commands, listen to his voice, and cling to him."

Obey his commands: Sounds simple, but to keep them you have to know them. Don't ever forsake the reading of the Bible. Contained in God's Word you will find his laws for living. You will find out how to be a reflection of our heavenly Father in word, thought, and deed.

Listen to his voice: God speaks to us though the quiet impressions of the Holy Spirit, and to hear or feel his presence you need to be walking with him. He may speak through a sermon, a song, a book, or even a friend. His impressions are always gentle and don't come with a rushed or hurried spirit.

Cling to him: No matter what may happen in your life, make sure you never let go of God. Embrace and love him with all of your heart, soul, mind, and strength. He wants your attention and affection, and you show it best by serving with diligence and with fervor.

Put God first in your life today. Arrange whatever you have to do to be able to do this. Make sure no person, material things, or anything else takes his place on the throne of your heart.

PRAYER

Dear God, it is my desire every day to serve you with all of my heart, soul, mind, and strength. I will obey you, listen to you, and when necessary cling to you. Amen.

God's Favor

*But Noah found favor with the **LORD**.* Genesis 6:5-8 NLT

It was by faith that Noah built a large boat to save his family from the flood. He obeyed God, who warned him about things that had never happened before. By his faith Noah condemned the rest of the world, and he received the righteousness that comes by faith. Hebrews 11:7 NLT

Why did Noah find favor with God? What was it about him that caught God's attention?

What is God's favor?

I think based on this story we can safely conclude that God's favor is always stirred by obedience. I know this cuts crossways with some theologies; but in reality, God has always called his people to obey. We are even reminded that in God's eyes obedience is better than sacrifice, which was a big statement in the Old Testament world. Noah wasn't a perfect man, but he was willing to listen and obey. He was deemed a righteous man. Christian leaders, of all people, should hunger for this endorsement from God on our lives and actions.

We can draw some conclusions from what Noah did with his life after hearing the call of God.

He walked with God.
Noah was a righteous man, the only blameless person living on earth at the time, and he walked in close fellowship with God. Genesis 6:9b NLT

He worked with God.
So Noah did everything exactly as God had commanded him. Genesis 6:22 NLT

He worshipped God with his life.
So Noah, his wife, and his sons, and their wives left the boat. And all of the large and small animals and birds came out of the boat, pair by pair. Then Noah built an altar to the Lord, and there he sacrificed as burnt offerings the animals and birds that had been approved for that purpose. Genesis 8:18-20 NLT

What an awesome opportunity we have to walk, work, and worship today! Serve him with your whole life!

Dear God, may I always walk with you, work with you, and worship you with my life. Amen.

We Are His Ambassadors

So we are Christ's ambassadors; God is making his appeal through us. We speak for Christ when we plead, "Come back to God!" For God made Christ, who never sinned, to be the offering for our sin, so that we could be made right with God through Christ. 2 Corinthians 5:20-21 NLT

Can you imagine receiving a call from a president of the United States asking you or appointing you to be an ambassador to another country? The official definition says, "an accredited diplomat sent by a country as its official representative to a foreign country."

This is the consistent call of God to Christ followers from the time of Christ until now. We are called to represent him as his ambassadors on this planet. The above Scripture says, "God is making his appeal through us." Startling words actually when you think about them. What an appointment. What an opportunity. We are disciples and ambassadors.

Here are some things Christ's ambassadors will do and be:
- You will love him with all your heart, mind, and soul.
- You will love your neighbors as much as you love yourself.
- You will be a neighbor.
- You will go and make disciples. You will teach them and baptize them.
- You will be a light.
- You will be salt.
- You will love your enemies and those that persecute you.
- You will forgive.
- You will not serve two masters.
- You will pray.
- You will produce fruit.
- You will share with the least of these.
- You will pick up your cross and follow Christ.
- You will give a cup of cold water in Jesus' name.
- You will plant and you will harvest.
- You will be his witnesses in Jerusalem, Judea, Samaria, and to the ends of the earth.

Let him make his appeal through you today! Live and love like Jesus. Follow his ways. Represent the kingdom of God, for there is coming a day when we will be rewarded for our faithfulness to the call. We are his ambassadors!

PRAYER

Dear Jesus, thank you for the opportunity to represent you on this earth. May I always be true to follow your example as provided in your word. Amen.

Wrestling With God

For we are God's masterpiece. He has created us anew in Christ Jesus, so we can do the good things he planned for us long ago.
Ephesians 2:10 NLT

Every one of you reading this is a masterpiece created uniquely by God himself. You are not only unique but you were created to do some things that only you can do! Your gifts, strengths, and personality allow for you to have opportunities to enter in to God's story and struggle on this earth.

Until we get to heaven, life can be a struggle at times. We struggle in our families; we struggle at work or in other relationships. Sometimes finances can be a challenge. We can struggle with our health, both physically and even emotionally.

How can God use us when life seems to be one struggle after another?

The God who seems at times to be a sadist in your struggles has loved you in spite of what it may feel like. I am reminded of Jacob, who wrestled with God all night in a titanic struggle (Genesis 32:22). Like Jacob, wrestling that night, God allows you:

1. To struggle *against* him
2. Then to struggle *with* him
3. Then, at last, to struggle *for* him.

Why? So that as you surrender, you become more like the one who prayed in Gethsemane, "Not my will, but yours be done." You become all he created you to be. Your struggle and story become part of his story, and there is nothing more exciting than that. Don't be discouraged! Let God be in the struggle. Let God finish his masterpiece in your life.

PRAYER

Dear God, I know there are days that I struggle and maybe even with you. I don't want to wrestle with you, but I long to wrestle through this life for you. Give me strength, I pray. Amen.

I Will Be Satisfied

For he satisfies the thirsty and fills the hungry with good things.
Psalm 107:9 NLT

God often is blamed for things that happen to us. People who haven't thought about God in years or attempted any kind of relationship will quickly talk about God when life takes a bad turn. Serving God and being in an authentic relationship with him doesn't shield anyone from troubles and sorrows.

As long as we live on this broken planet we will all face times of turmoil and great challenge. We all eventually deal with circumstances that are out of our control. Who do we turn to in those moments? Who is reliable and powerful enough to give us the strength we need to endure? Some turn to other people. Some practice self-medication in a search to help bear the pain and survive the struggle.

There is only one hope. There is only one that can sustain us when life seems uncertain, and that is Jesus. He is a friend that sticks closer than a brother, the Bible reminds us. He is our intercessor, and he is sitting at the right hand of God praying for us daily. He longs to be in a relationship with us so that he can help us not only to receive salvation but to live every day in his presence while on this earth.

We are all created with a need for God. Unless and until we recognize it and acknowledge it, we will spend our lives searching for other things to satisfy our needs. Nothing but Jesus will ever bring true satisfaction.

The psalmist says when you are thirsty enough and hungry enough God will fill you with good things. Are you hungry for change in your life? For any reason do you need to rediscover this eternal source in the form of Jesus our Savior?

Jesus said, "Blessed are those who hunger and thirst for righteousness, for they shall be filled" (Matthew 5:6 NKJV).

Whatever you are thirsting for or hungering for today, the answer is Jesus. Don't be afraid to let him into the corners and margins of your life. Let him fill your life with good things that can only come from him.

PRAYER

Dear Lord, I know that you have promised to satisfy the hungers of my life. Please help me to always look to you for this satisfaction and not in the wrong places or with the wrong people. Amen

Can These Bones Live?

Then he asked me, "Son of man, can these bones become living people again?" "O Sovereign LORD," I replied, "you alone know the answer to that." Ezekiel 37:3 NLT

Ezekiel stumbled into a field of dead and dry bones. God directed him there to make a point. The point was to be found in the answer to this question: "Can these bones live?" As long as God is in it and on it, the answer is a resounding "Yes!"

I wonder if you have ever been in a "bone yard." I've been in some pretty dead places and seasons in my life. I remember so well the first church I was privileged to pastor. There were about twelve people when I arrived in a church that would seat 150 to 200. Light bulbs were burnt out in the high ceiling of the sanctuary. Basement Sunday school rooms were filled with clutter and dust from years of inactivity. I remember reading this chapter in Ezekiel and wondering if this "dry bone" church could live again.

With youthful naiveté and blind trust, I pushed forward; and with God's help the bones did come back to life. I was only there three years but today it is a thriving church in the community and doing a healthy ministry. Dry bones can live again!

Whatever it is in your life that feels dead, ask God to make it come alive. Take him to your bone yard and allow him to breathe life back into your situations.

PRAYER

Breathe on me, Breath of God,
Fill me with life anew,
That I may love what Thou dost love,
And do what Thou wouldst do.

Breathe on me, Breath of God,
Until my heart is pure,
Until with Thee I will one will,
To do and to endure.

Breathe on me, Breath of God,
Till I am wholly Thine,
Until this earthly part of me
Glows with Thy fire divine.
    —Edwin Hatch

Great News!

The Spirit of the Lord is upon me, for he has anointed me to bring Good News to the poor. He has sent me to proclaim that captives will be released, that the blind will see, that the oppressed will be set free, and that the time of the Lord's favor has come. Luke 4:18-19 NLT

The good news of Jesus Christ never gets old. It may get old in the context of how it is shared, but the news itself never changes. Denominations and churches may water it down or even totally disregard it, but the message never changes. It is the message from Jesus himself. Quoting from the ancient prophet Isaiah, he stood in the temple and read the words declaring his ministry and message. Let me break it down.

- To bring good news to the poor
- To proclaim that captives will be released
- To proclaim that the blind will see
- To proclaim that the oppressed will be set free
- To proclaim that the time of the Lord's favor has come.

Whatever may be going on in your life, at home, at work, or in your family, you should be able to find good news in this proclamation. Jesus came to enable the human race to find life, abundant life in him. That doesn't mean you will be rich, but it does mean that you will find satisfaction in him. Be rich in your relationship with Jesus. Don't let anything or anyone bind you. Find freedom in Christ. He came to this earth that you might be free and find your wholeness in him.

PRAYER

Dear Jesus, I know that you came to set the captive free. You preach good news! May I remember this all day today and live in the freedom you have given me. Amen.

Why Are You So Angry?

"Why are you so angry?" the Lord asked Cain. "Why do you look so dejected?" Genesis 4:6 NLT

Someone once said, "Don't let it make you bitter but let it make you better." Circumstances happen in our lives that can test us to our core. On this earth we may be treated unfairly by friends or even family. Someone might die before we think it was his or her time. Tragic incidents that shake up our normal routines and possibly finances can cause us to struggle with the new reality of our lives.

Cain felt rejected by God because he didn't offer the right sacrifice. He missed the point of his own disobedience and became angry and bitter at God and his brother. This anger drove him to the point of murder.

We must do whatever we can to avoid allowing our emotions and responses to our circumstances, relationships; illnesses or deaths put us in a place of opposition to God. Sometimes disobedience on our part can take us to a place that threatens to do us and those around us spiritual harm.

- Evaluate your spiritual condition based on the word of God.
- Pray daily prayers of surrender so that your priorities stay in focus.
- Ask God to heal your heart, soul, emotions and put your trust in Him.
- Write down the things you struggle with and keep them in front of God.

PRAYER

Dear Lord, I don't want to be angry at you or anybody else. Please help me guard my heart against selfish thinking and bitterness. Let me learn from Cain's experience. Amen.

God Is Always Searching

The eyes of the LORD search the whole earth in order to strengthen those whose hearts are fully committed to him. 2 Chronicles 16:9a NLT

For the eyes of the LORD run to and fro throughout the whole earth, to show Himself strong on behalf of those whose heart is loyal to Him. 2 Chronicles 16:9a NKJV

God is always looking for people and leaders that will be completely his. You can't fake this because it is God you are dealing with. What a promise and comfort to know that God's eyes are searching for men and women with loyal and committed hearts so that he can provide strength to do what he has called us to do.

Think of all the great exploits that were accomplished by men and women in the Bible that were done in the power of our strong God. For Esther it was "such a time as this," for Moses it was operating in the power of the great I Am, and for Nehemiah it was rebuilding a wall and the gates of Jerusalem. God saw them and strengthened their hearts for the task at hand. God's eyes are on you today if your heart is fully committed to him. I wonder if you know what he is strengthening your heart to do today? If you are fully invested and committed to God, he will be there for you.

"Be of good courage, and He shall strengthen your heart, all you who hope in the Lord" (Psalm 31:24 NKJV).

PRAYER

Dear God, more than anything else I want my heart to be fully yours. Give me the strength today to serve with my whole heart and to be found with nothing between my soul and my Savior. Amen.

I Will Praise Him

All praise to God, the Father of our Lord Jesus Christ. It is by his great mercy that we have been born again, because God raised Jesus Christ from the dead. Now we live with great expectation, and we have a priceless inheritance—an inheritance that is kept in heaven for you, pure and undefiled, beyond the reach of change and decay. And through your faith, God is protecting you by his power until you receive this salvation, which is ready to be revealed on the last day for all to see. 1 Peter 1:3-5 NLT

If you are a follower of Jesus Christ, you are a recipient of a Bible full of promises. No promise is greater than the hope of our salvation. From being born again to a promised inheritance kept in heaven for us, the blessings are immeasurable. In this passage, we find several things to praise him for:

We have been given salvation!
 "By His mercy we have been born again."
We are strong!
 "We live with great expectation!"
We are shareholders!
 "We have a priceless inheritance reserved in heaven."
 (beyond the reach of change and decay)
We have been given security!
 God is protecting us by his power.

Whatever is before you today can be accomplished through the strength and hope found in your relationship with Christ. When he is at the center of your life, everything else is filtered through him. Salvation through Jesus Christ the Son of God should not be ignored or taken lightly. It is more than a free ticket to heaven. It is a relationship full of daily grace, wisdom, mercy, power, compassion, and hope. Like the old song says, "When all around my soul gives way, he then is all my hope and stay."

Prayer

Thank you, God, for you great mercy daily that works in our lives! Thanks for making me a part of your kingdom even on this earth. It is all by your mercy. Help me to never lose the expectation you have given. Amen.

Master of the Sea

Jesus was sleeping at the back of the boat with his head on a cushion. The disciples woke him up, shouting, "Teacher, don't you care that we're going to drown?" When Jesus woke up, he rebuked the wind and said to the waves, "Silence! Be still!" Suddenly the wind stopped, and there was a great calm. Then he asked them, "Why are you afraid? Do you still have no faith?" The disciples were absolutely terrified. "Who is this man?" they asked each other. "Even the wind and waves obey him!" Mark 4:38-41 NLT

If you are going to be in a storm you can't do better than having Jesus in your boat. You would think after all the miracles and ministry that the disciples had watched Jesus do that they might have been a bit more confident.

When the storm hit it was furious and they feared for their lives, yet there was Jesus asleep right in front of them. Here are some lessons to learn from this story:

- It may be okay to "yell at Jesus" when the crisis merits it. Crying out to God is a better way to say it.
- Even when Jesus is in your boat, the storms of life can still be scary.
- You may think he's sleeping, but he is still in charge of everything.
- Jesus is still baffled by our lack of faith.
- Keep Jesus in your boat.

All of us experience terrifying moments in our lifetimes of living. We fear the unknown. We wrestle with our circumstances. We are afraid of the future and sometimes even the present. Make sure your relationship with Christ is sure. When storms come, do everything you can to rest in him. Call out to him. Focus on Jesus. Even when our prayers aren't answered the way we would like, we can still rest in him. Keep him in your boat and trust him with your life.

When he reaches out his hand,
Billows cease at his command;
Winds and waves obey his will
When he says to them, "Be still."
"What man is this?" they all did say,
"That the winds and sea obey?"
He's the one who sails with me,
Oh, he's still the Master of the sea.

PRAYER

Dear Lord Jesus, I have faced some storms in my life. I don't always do well trusting that you are in control. Forgive me for this, please. I pray that my faith will grow steady and strong. Amen.

Can You Watch With Him?

Couldn't you watch with me even one hour? Matthew 26:40b NLT

These words, spoken by Jesus, were no doubt filled with pain and disappointment. Even reading them now one can feel the emotions. Jesus was praying with some of His disciples in the garden just prior to being led away to face the torture of the crucifixion. His disciples were overwhelmed with the teaching He had just given them. I believe they were probably scared and for the first time beginning to realize that He wasn't going to be a conquering King who would overthrow the Roman rule. He wasn't going to be one to lead the Jews out of the Roman captivity they lived with daily.

They couldn't watch with him. They couldn't even stay awake.

How are you doing in your relationship with Jesus? If you are like me you are full of good intentions, maybe even great intentions. Sometimes life just smacks us down and we are at a loss to know how to deal with it. Sometimes sleep feels like the best option.

When you face a garden of difficulty just know that Jesus will not fall asleep. He will stay with you. He doesn't slumber or sleep. Even today, He is waiting to hear from you and to walk with you throughout this day. Stay awake. Stay alert. Know that He will watch with you day and night.

PRAYER

Dear Jesus, I need you every hour. Thank you for going to the cross. Thank you for praying and showing your vulnerability in the garden when you prayed. I find great comfort in knowing you will watch with me. Amen.

Dying for Your Faith...

About that time King Herod Agrippa began to persecute some believers in the church. He had the apostle James (John's brother) killed with a sword. When Herod saw how much this pleased the Jewish people, he also arrested Peter. Acts 12:1-3 NLT

I like to try to immerse myself in the context of Scripture as I read it. As I read this Scripture, I couldn't help but remember what was going on around the first Christians in the first century. It was not safe. Jesus came back from the dead, but then he went to heaven. They were left to face persecution, loss of vocations, shortage of food, loss of homes, and the loss of their lives.

In the book of Acts, we usually think about Stephen, who was the first one to be killed for his faith; but here is this man, James. This event shattered the illusion that somehow the twelve enjoyed a unique divine protection.

Remember what Jesus said to these men when He called them. It was not very appealing. He included these words:

- I am sending you out as sheep among wolves.
- For you will be handed over to the courts and will be flogged with whips in the synagogues.
- You will stand trial before governors and kings because you are my followers.
- When you are arrested, don't worry about how to respond or what to say. God will give you the right words at the right time.
- A brother will betray his brother to death, a father will betray his own child, and children will rebel against their parents and cause them to be killed.
- And all nations will hate you because you are my followers. But everyone who endures to the end will be saved.
- Students are not greater than their teacher, and slaves are not greater than their master.
- But don't be afraid of those who threaten you.

- Don't be afraid of those who want to kill your body; they cannot touch your soul.
- Fear only God, who can destroy both soul and body in hell
- And the very hairs on your head are all numbered. So don't be afraid; you are more valuable to God than a whole flock of sparrows.
- Everyone who acknowledges me publicly here on earth, I will also acknowledge before my Father in heaven. But everyone who denies me here on earth, I will also deny before my Father in heaven.

When we lose control of our lives, freedoms, and the ability to do what we want, it is but a small taste of what the early Christ followers endured. What does it mean for us? What can you do to endure whatever may come?

Stay connected to Jesus.

Stay committed to Jesus.

Stay confident in Jesus.

PRAYER

Dear Jesus, I realize now that the world around me can be turned upside down by the actions of others. I am not completely in control, but I know that you are. Give me courage and determination to never give up on you no matter what may or may not happen around me. Amen.

Daily Faithfulness

When you've done everything expected of you, be matter-of-fact and say, "The work is done. What we were told to do, we did." Luke 17:10b NLT

If you are a follower of Jesus Christ, you will be aware that the Bible and especially the New Testament is full of guidance on how we should live out our lives daily.

We know we are to love God with our heart, soul, mind, and strength.
We know we are to love our neighbors as ourselves.
We know we are to make disciples, baptize and teach them to obey what he has commanded.
We know we are to practice forgiveness.
We know we are to be kind.
We know we are to be gracious.
We know we are to be compassionate.
We know we are to pray often.
We know we are to be thankful every day.
We know we are to be patient.
We know we are to practice self-control.
We know we are to avoid seeking revenge.
We know we are called to live honest lives.
We know we are called to love our enemies.

These things and many more are the assignments Jesus gave us to do as we walk the journey of our lives on this earth. These things will make a difference in the lives of people around us.

PRAYER

Lord, please give me the desire to follow you every day and to be faithful in my spiritual walk with you. Allow your Spirit to live in me and guide me daily as I interact with others around me. Amen.

Qualifications

In the book of Acts there came a time in the history of the early church that the administrative responsibilities became too much for the disciples to handle. What has always fascinated me with this story is the qualifications listed for the seven that would be chosen to serve food to widows and carry out this program. It might seem like a mundane task, but God's leadership standards were high.

So the Twelve called a meeting of all the believers. They said, "We apostles should spend our time teaching the word of God, not running a food program. And so, brothers, select seven men who are well respected and are full of the Spirit and wisdom. We will give them this responsibility. Then we apostles can spend our time in prayer and teaching the word." Acts 6:2-4 NLT

Three qualifications:

- **Well respected**
- **Full of the Holy Spirit**
- **Full of wisdom**

Whatever you are called to do in life or in leadership, making these three part of what and who we are is not a bad idea. You can't buy respect—it is earned by treating others kindly no matter who they are or what position they may hold. Being full of God's Spirit comes with the surrendering of ourselves, our wishes and wants. When we abandon ourselves to him and trust him with our lives, his Spirit lives in us and functions on our behalf.

The Proverb writer said, "Joyful is the person who finds wisdom, the one who gains understanding. For wisdom is more profitable than silver, and her wages are better than gold" (Proverbs 3:13-14 NLT).

Whatever your title or position, you will never go wrong putting God first. You may be called to do mundane things, but if God is in your life you will flourish through him.

Dear God, because of you in my life I hope that I am always well-respected, full of the Holy Spirit, and full of wisdom. May it be so even today. Amen.

What God Requires

No, O people, the LORD has told you what is good, and this is what he requires of you: to do what is right, to love mercy, and to walk humbly with your God. Micah 6:8 NLT

When the prophet Micah asked the questions preceding this verse he was writing on behalf of an Israel who had the hardest time obeying God and keeping all his rules. In previous verses, they were inquiring what they needed to do to bring the Lord back to their side and to bring forgiveness for their sins.

The prophet answers no to their suggestions and gives them a simple formula for following God and doing his will. It is still practical today and may provide you with a way to prioritize your life around what God requires from us.

Have you ever wondered exactly what God wants from you and how you can live in a way that daily responds correctly to him?

Here are the three requirements:

Do what is right:

Do the right thing. Our only hope of doing this is to allow the Holy Spirit to guide us in all of our actions, reactions and relationships. It is his sweet Spirit that will guide us into all truth and allow us to be a reflection of Jesus every day of the week. Is there anything wrong that you need to make right?

Love mercy:

This is hard. We would all like to think we are merciful but at our core we are tested in this. It is hard to show mercy to people we know take advantage of others. It is hard to show mercy to those that hurt other people physically, emotionally, or both. And yet here it is for us to follow: "love mercy." It is hard to show mercy or love mercy for our enemies, but Jesus instructed us to love our enemies. Is there anyone that you need help loving and showing mercy to?

Walk humbly with your God:

To walk with God at all should produce a humbleness in us daily. Andrew Murry said, "Pride must die in you, or nothing of heaven can live in you." Walking humbly with your God is to acknowledge daily that you are nothing without him. He is your life, your breath, your health, and everything about you. His blessings are what allow us to function. Maybe we should practice mentally pausing throughout our days to whisper to God, "I am nothing without you." Rick Warren reminds us, "You cannot exalt God and yourself at the same time."

PRAYER

Dear Lord, with your help and grace, I will do these three things.
I will do right by God's strength and grace.
I will love mercy by God's strength and grace.
I will walk humbly with you, God, by your strength and grace.
Let it be so. Amen.

Imitating God

Imitate God, therefore, in everything you do, because you are his dear children. Live a life filled with love, following the example of Christ. He loved us and offered himself as a sacrifice for us, a pleasing aroma to God. Ephesians 5:1-2 NLT

"Imitation is the sincerest form of flattery," someone said. How do you imitate God? We've all seen children imitate one another and in fact we probably did that ourselves. What does it look like to imitate God?

You will follow him.

That's all he asks of us. He wants us to follow him in all of our circumstances and life experiences. Do life his way. Follow with intention.

You will forgive like him.

Jesus forgave us. He offers to forgive all people everywhere. We are instructed to forgive others as he forgave us. It's a profound concept when you think about it.

You will be faithful like him.

Jesus said to the people who believed in him, "You are truly my disciples if you remain faithful to my teachings" (John 8:31 NLT).

You will be fruitful like him.

"You didn't choose me. I chose you. I appointed you to go and produce lasting fruit, so that the Father will give you whatever you ask for, using my name" (John 15:16 NLT).

Be like him today. Love God with your life. Imitate God in word, thought, and deed.

PRAYER

Dear Jesus, you left me such a great example to follow in every area of my life. Help me to be willing to love sacrificially as I respond to others today. Amen.

Permission Granted

Then the people hired masons and carpenters and bought cedar logs from the people of Tyre and Sidon, paying them with food, wine, and olive oil. The logs were brought down from the Lebanon mountains and floated along the coast of the Mediterranean Sea to Joppa, for King Cyrus had given permission for this. Ezra 3:7 NLT

Taking risk is often part of our lives. Sometimes we are called on to make decisions for others. This is especially true if you are a leader. You will make decisions for people you work with and may even implement new pathways and directions. This often comes with risk and even the possibility of failure.

When the Jews received a decree from Cyrus the king that they could return to their homeland and begin life there again, most didn't jump at the opportunity. Out of a population of hundreds of thousands of Jews in 538 B.C. only about 49,000 responded to the offer. To respond meant giving up comforts and things familiar for the chance to rebuild.

Christian leaders at times must give those around them permission to take risks and to lead even into unknown territory. This takes courage and wisdom. It takes patience and prayer.

Whatever God is calling you to in ministry, I pray often that you will have the wisdom and courage to do it his way. He offers us both wisdom and courage if we but ask for it. They rebuilt the house of God as a priority. Putting God first is still a priority. Trusting God with our days, decisions, and direction is a must if we are truly followers of Christ.

PRAYER

God, I pray for your protection and guidance. Help me to not be fearful but to follow you at home, at work, and as I navigate the culture I live in. Lead me, Lord, and I will follow even to places that aren't comfortable. Increase my faith. Amen.

How Great Is Our God

Oh, how great are God's riches and wisdom and knowledge! How impossible it is for us to understand his decisions and his ways! Romans 11:33 NLT

One of the first prayers many children learn opens with these words, "*God is great, God is good.*" Indeed, he is both great and good! Remind yourself today of our God's goodness and his greatness.

The psalmist says that he is a God of great riches, wisdom, and knowledge. In fact, we know that he is a God who shares with us the richness of his grace and mercy. He is a God who almost begs us to pray for wisdom because he wants to share it with us. When it comes to knowledge, our God would make all the most common search engines pale in comparison because of what he knows. He knows the hairs of your head, he knows when sparrows fall, and he knows every tear that flows down your cheek. The Bible even suggests that he bottles our tears.

It is impossible to process who God is and what he really is, but we can sing with the psalmist and have great confidence that our God knows and that his ways are beyond our ways. Trust him today that he has your best interest in mind. When we follow him we do so in all seasons of our lives. We trust him with the good, the bad, and even the ugly. How great is our God!

PRAYER

Lord, today we sing and speak of your greatness and goodness. Help us to walk and work in confidence today believing that you rule and reign in this world. Allow us to hear your call and walk in your ways. Amen.

Help Me to See

Turn my eyes from worthless things, and give me life through your word. Psalm 119:37 NLT

We live in a world filled with worthless things. Some people feel constantly bombarded by schedules, time-consuming activities, and the many things they pack into their lives daily. For others, time seems to drag on and they wrestle with boredom and in many cases loneliness. It is easy to lose sight of the things that matter most no matter what stage of life you may be in currently.

The psalmist is suggesting that our eyes may sometimes lose focus and perspective. We may fail to remember the things that should matter most for followers of Jesus Christ. Here are some things God's Word says we should focus our eyes on. His life-giving Word says:

- Love God with all your heart, mind, soul, and strength.
- Love your neighbors as yourself.
- Make disciples.
- Love one another.
- Be kind, tenderhearted, forgiving one another.
- Imitate God in everything you do.
- Take no part in worthless deeds of evil.
- Make the most of every opportunity.
- Be filled with the Spirit.
- Give thanks for everything.
- Sing psalms, hymns, and spiritual songs.
- Put on the whole armor of God.
- Pray in the Spirit.
- Do everything without complaining and arguing.
- Don't worry about anything.
- Fix your thoughts on what is true, honorable, right, pure, and lovely.
- Let the peace that comes from God rule in your hearts.

This is a partial list taken right from God's Word. Focus your eyes on the things that matter the most. Train your heart to desire God's Word more than anything or anyone else. Dive deep into God with your life—after all, he wrote the best manual for living.

PRAYER

Dear God, I pray that the eyes of my heart will be focused on you daily. May I always desire your will and way in my life. Give me eyes to see. Amen.

Firm Footing Ahead

Teach me to do your will, for you are my God. May your gracious
Spirit lead me forward on a firm footing. Psalm 143:10 NLT

Life can be messy. This journey we call life can take us down roads that
we never thought we would walk. You might feel like the psalmist.
Apparently, for whatever reason, he felt as though his walk was unstable.
Something about the path he was on felt dangerous and unsafe.

So he prays.

He calls out to God, affirming his faith in God, and asks him to
teach him how to do his will. How long has it been since you prayed that
prayer? Have you ever prayed and asked God to teach you how to do his
will? There is something so appealing about this.

It suggests humility, self-awareness, and godly desire. No matter
what has happened or is happening, the writer is quick to turn toward
God and ask for specific help. He wants to learn how to follow on his
own, not just a quick rescue.

May you find a firm footing today. May the gracious Spirit of God
be your teacher and guide. May you learn things today that could only
come from the Teacher himself.

PRAYER

Dear God, thank you for the chance to follow you another day.
Please teach me to do your will every day that I live on this planet.
Lead me forward and I will follow. Amen.

Can You Be Quiet?

I wait quietly before God, for my victory comes from him. Psalm 62:1 NLT

Waiting quietly?

How hard is that? Even the psalmist had a hard time with this one based on all the Psalms written where he expresses everything from great joy to discouragement and maybe even depression.

Often we are quick to speak, especially if we are in some kind of trouble. We like to share our troubles. We like to look for help from our family and friends. None of that is wrong, but there may come a time when we need to be quiet and let God work.

Ultimately, all of our victories come from God.

A few verses later this same psalmist writes, "Let all that I am wait quietly before God, for my hope is in him." Our victory and our hope comes when we are quiet before God. Let him speak. Let him strengthen your heart and give you courage.

The writer of Lamentations says it this way: "The Lord is good to those who depend on him, to those who search for him. So it is good to wait quietly for salvation from the Lord" (Lamentations 3:25-26 NLT).

Be still and wait. Let God see your quiet trust and submission to his powers. He knows right where you are. Sometimes there can be great comfort to be found in the silence.

PRAYER

Dear God, help me to understand the importance of silence in my life. There are so many distractions that call for my attention. Let me be quiet today and listen for your voice in my life. Amen.

Unfailing Love

"So the Word became human and made his home among us. He was full of unfailing love and faithfulness." John 1:14 NLT

In this opening chapter of the Gospel of John, we find this profound acknowledgment of the incarnation of Jesus Christ on this earth. He is the Word. He existed in the beginning of time. He was with God and was God and he is still God.

John highlights two characteristics that are worth pondering today. He is "full of unfailing love and faithfulness." There will be times in our lives when we need one or both of these working on our behalf.

Maybe you have felt the sting of failure and struggled to accept the forgiveness and restoration that Jesus offers. You want to believe that he still loves you but the doubt is real, based on your own insecurities. Be assured today, he is full of unfailing love for you! No matter what, he wants you to return and know his love.

Perhaps life has thrown you an unexpected challenge and you have no idea how it is going to work out. I encourage you to remember that he is full of unfailing faithfulness. It will require trust, but he will be faithful. Don't give up. Accept his unfailing love and faithfulness. He is for you today.

PRAYER

Dear Jesus, you are unfailing in your love and faithfulness. Thank you, Lord, for these daily gifts to me. I receive them today with gratitude. Amen.

His Plans Are Always Best

"For I know the plans I have for you," says the LORD. *"They are plans for good and not for disaster, to give you a future and a hope."*
Jeremiah 29:11 NLT

These were God's words to Israel, and they were spoken to the Jewish people that God sent into captivity for their disobedience. They were now living in strange cities, and they had lost most of the freedoms they once enjoyed.

We all go through seasons like that; maybe not because of disobedience, but something happens and the familiar changes and life looks very different. What do you do in those times? Do you give up hope? Do you allow the pressures of change and life to distract you? Sometimes we do.

Let these words spoken by the Lord give you hope and confidence. While contextually they were spoken for a nation in exile, they also give us a solid indicator of the nature of God. He is for his followers. Even when they might not be as strong as they need to be, as long as they are turning toward him, he will be there.

On top of that, he has plans for you! They are good. They include a future and a hope! God knows where you are today. Don't give up. Keep looking up and you will find him.

PRAYER

Dear God, I can think of no one I would want making plans for me other than you. Help me to believe this even when I am not prospering or hopeful. Amen.

Christ Is All That Matters

In this new life, it doesn't matter if you are a Jew or a Gentile, circumcised or uncircumcised, barbaric, uncivilized, slave, or free. Christ is all that matters, and he lives in all of us. Colossians 3:11 NLT

Ever since Christ came to this planet, things have never been the same. He broke down all the walls that separated the Jews from the rest of the world. The gospel message of redemption and hope was now for "whosoever will."

In this verse, we are reminded that "Christ is all that matters."

No matter what circumstance you find yourself in today. No matter the challenges, the discouragement, the temptations, the joy, or the sorrow, Christ is all that matters. When you are walking with Jesus daily, you are an overcomer because Christ is all that matters. Does this mean you will avoid sorrow, heartache, and disappointments? Not at all. Life happens; and it contains the good, the bad, and sometimes even the ugly, but we walk through it and endure.

Make sure that he is first in your life today. It is a constant struggle to keep others, things, or circumstances from climbing up on the throne of our hearts and taking over. Make sure Jesus is there above anyone and anything else. Make sure that Christ is all that matters.

He loves you so much and wants to be all that matters in your life. He longs for that kind of relationship with you. Open up your heart and let him in. Your life will never be the same.

PRAYER

Dear Jesus, I long for you to be my all in all. Don't let me make anything in my life more important than you. Don't let me put anybody ahead of you. Amen.

Real Love

We know what real love is because Jesus gave up his life for us. So we also ought to give up our lives for our brothers and sisters. 1 John 3:16 NLT

The first part of this verse is a great reminder of Jesus' great love for us. We find comfort, love, mercy, and grace in his real love for us. He gave up his life so that we might be saved. We are absolutely fine with his sacrifice. We are even thankful most of the time.

Then comes the rest of the verse: "so we also ought to give up our lives for our brothers and sisters."

How are we going to accomplish that? What do you imagine that John had in mind when he wrote these words of admonition? Jesus often said, "Pick up your cross and follow me." He was consistent in inviting us to share in his death.

So how can we lay down our lives for our friends? Let me give you a few words and you make the associations as His Spirit leads you.

Sacrifice
Unselfish
Last
Humble
Forgiveness
Helpless
Silent
Suffering
Poverty
Servant
Patient

May God help us as we endeavor to lay down our rights and our lives in an effort to love our brothers and sisters.

PRAYER

Dear Lord, please help me to be less selfish and self-centered. Give me the ability to love with abandon as you love me. Fill me with your presence today. Amen.

Who Are You (or I) to Judge?

Recently I was reading during my personal devotional time and came across this Scripture. I had read it before and know it is part of Luke's account of the Sermon on the Mount, but for some reason these verses really stuck out to me.

Do not judge others, and you will not be judged. Do not condemn others, or it will all come back against you. Forgive others, and you will be forgiven. Give, and you will receive. Your gift will return to you in full—pressed down, shaken together to make room for more, running over, and poured into your lap. The amount you give will determine the amount you get back. Luke 6:37-38 NLT

We are commanded to subtract two things and add two things to our lives. These commands come with promises. Here they are:

✓ *Don't* judge and you won't be judged.

✓ *Don't* condemn and you won't be condemned.

✓ *Do* forgive others and you will be forgiven.

✓ *Do* give and you will receive.

Many times our human nature is quick to judge others for one thing or another. This judgment can take place in the grocery store, at a restaurant, at work, at home, and even at church. When faced with a person or situation we have a choice to make. If we react with judgment followed by condemnation it will return to us as judgment and condemnation; but if we forgive quickly, we become givers of life, peace, grace, compassion, and mercy. One choice takes us to a place of censoring, shunning, strife, and even hatred, while the other produces the fruit of the Spirit, which includes love, joy, kindness, forbearance, goodness, gentleness, and self-control.

Make the right choice and Jesus says, "Your gift will return to you in full—pressed down, shaken together to make room for more, running over, and poured into your lap. The amount you give will determine the amount you get back."

Be a giver. Let Jesus love others through you.

PRAYER

Dear Jesus, Give me the grace I need to not judge anyone today or any other day for that matter. Please help me practice forgiveness for others and to love like You love me. Amen

Finding God

If only I knew where to find God, I would go to his court. Job 23:3
NLT

Most of us know the story of Job. Scattered throughout the book of
Job we find his desire to speak with God, to tell God what is going
on, and to attempt to plead for mercy. He was truly suffering.

The fact is, Job did nothing to deserve the devastation that was happening in his life. We are always quick to point to some kind of cause and
effect when bad things happen. We think we need some kind of explanation. That is not how God works.

God is God. He is everywhere and in every situation. That doesn't
mean he is causing things to happen as much as he may be allowing life
to play out. If we don't really know God or know how he works, we can
find ourselves traveling down what turns out to be a road of bitterness
and questioning.

Whatever is happening in your life today, know that God is well
aware of it. Our lives on this planet are far less than perfect. We face
great obstacles in our families, our health, our relationships, and even in
death. Troubles never come at the right time, but you can rest assured
they will come. No one is exempt from troubles.

Know where to find God. You don't have to go to his court to plead
your cause, but you can go before him wherever you are and speak with
him. You may be surprised what you can learn when you allow him to
walk with you through your pain. God has not walked away from you.
He has not turned his back on you. He wants to hear your voice, and he
will listen. He will provide for you.

PRAYER

*Dear God, I am guilty of thinking that you don't care. I may have
even blamed you for causing my pain. Please forgive me and draw
me close to you. Even if nothing changes let me find satisfaction in
your presence. Amen.*

Send the Rain

I lift my hands to you in prayer. I thirst for you as parched land thirsts for rain. Psalm 143:6 NLT

I woke up to the sound of a steady summer shower. It has been raining now for a couple of hours. No lightning. No thunder. As I lay in bed for a bit longer than usual, I was listening and thinking about what I was hearing. It's still raining; and as I sit and watch the woods outside my window, I can see the movement of the rain on the leaves.

Flowers are drinking, gardens are soaking this up, and the ground is receiving a much-needed bath. When it is done, there will be a little less pollen to choke on and things will appear a little cleaner. Creeks may even have a little more water flowing in them.

I long for a soaking rain in my soul. The kind of God encounter that is prolonged and that makes a big difference. An encounter that brings life-sustaining water like Jesus offered the woman he talked to at a well one day. He said, "Anyone who drinks this water will soon become thirsty again. But those who drink the water I give will never be thirsty again. It becomes a fresh, bubbling spring within them, giving them eternal life."

She needed a renewed life for sure. The psalmist said he thirsted for God like parched ground for rain. Let the rain come! Let his rain come into my soul and wash away the dust, dirt, and grime of life. Cleanse my heart and mind and renew a right spirit within me. I pray that his rain will produce the fruits of his Spirit in my life on a more consistent basis. Let it rain. I am thirsty for you.

PRAYER

Lord, send your rain into my soul today. Send a prolonged shower of your presence. I need you now more than ever. I thought life would get easier, but the older I get the harder it seems. Let your rain bring new life in me. Amen.

What Does God Want From You?

"Give to God what belongs to God." Luke 20:25b NLT

These words were spoken in answer to a question about paying taxes to Caesar. Of course, the question was designed by the Jewish leaders to trap Jesus by forcing him to say the wrong thing. After responding to their question about taxes, he followed up with these classic words:

"Give to God what belongs to God."

They should give us pause as we consider what we possess that really belongs to God. I think most of us know it down deep inside of us. God created us to do his work on this earth and for companionship. He didn't create us to follow our own way or follow the culture around us. We are repeatedly warned in the Bible that to follow the world around us is to follow a pathway of destruction.

God simply wants you! He wants to hear from you every day. He wants to work through you to bring love, hope, compassion, and grace to this world. He also may choose to use you to bring the truth of his Word to those around you. Being a truth teller may be dangerous depending on how far the culture has drifted away from his Word. Sometimes the most loving thing we can do is to stand up for what Jesus taught even if it threatens our very lives. This becomes much more of a threat in an environment of unrest and lawlessness. When there is no respect for the law, society becomes very dangerous and unstable. No matter though to the Christian, because we are called to keep on giving him our lives both in life and death situations.

Today, make every effort to surrender your actions to Christ. Let the words of your mouth and the mediations of your heart be pleasing to God first before you speak them to others. Let your actions be reflective of what Jesus would do and not what you would do. Be attentive to the Word of God. Let it live in you as you give back to God what belongs to God.

Dear God, help me today to realign my life to allow me to give it back to you. You gave me life in the beginning and allowed me to be born, the least I can do is give my life back to you. Help me to understand what this means today and in the days ahead. Amen.

God Directs and Delights

The Lord directs the steps of the godly. He delights in every detail of their lives. Though they stumble, they will never fall, for the Lord holds them by the hand. Psalm 37:23-24 NLT

There are two things in these verses that God promises to do for those who are godly. He promises to guide us and guard us. Fifteen times in this Psalm it states that God is sovereign in the lives of those he blesses. In other words, he is first.

"The Lord directs the steps of the godly."

Perhaps today you are seeking guidance from God or perhaps you feel that you really need his protection. The promise for us today is that God will direct our steps if we are godly or leaning hard toward him and his ways.

"The Lord delights in every detail of our lives."

It is hard to grasp that God could be this big; but the more you know about God, the more you discover his powerful sovereignty. He is everywhere and in all things. He is aware of every detail of our lives today and delights in being a part of them.

"The Lord delivers us from danger and destruction."

In the letter written to Timothy, the apostle Paul gives this clear testimony of God's deliverance.

"But the Lord stood with me and gave me strength so that I might preach the Good News in its entirety for all the Gentiles to hear. And he rescued me from certain death. Yes, and the Lord will deliver me from every evil attack and will bring me safely into his heavenly Kingdom. All glory to God forever and ever! Amen" (2 Timothy 4:17-19 NLT).

The mature follower will tell you the Christ has never been a disappointment. He is never early and he is never late. His timing is perfect when he comes to help. It may not be our timing, but he will show up and he will hold us by the hand. The longer we serve him, the more we come to see him as he is and understand how mighty he is on our behalf.

This is what happened to Lucy in C. S. Lewis's *Chronicles of Narnia*. When she gazed into the Lion's face (Aslan the lion represented Christ in the story), this dialogue followed:

"Welcome, child," he said.

"Aslan," said Lucy, "you're bigger."

"That is because you are older, little one," answered he.

"Not because you are?"

"I am not. But every year you grow, you will find me bigger."

God is on your side today directing, delighting and delivering you. Serve Him boldly.

PRAYER

Dear Lord, your willingness to guide and guard me brings great comfort to me today. May my steps always be in your path. Amen.

The Place of Grace

For the grace of God has been revealed, bringing salvation to all people. And we are instructed to turn from godless living and sinful pleasures. We should live in this evil world with wisdom, righteousness, and devotion to God, while we look forward with hope to that wonderful day when the glory of our great God and Savior, Jesus Christ, will be revealed. Titus 2:11-12 NLT

The grace of God is a much-used phrase, but what does it mean for us on a daily basis? This grace brings us three areas of consideration for our lives on a daily basis.

The Message: "For the grace of God has been revealed, bringing salvation to all people."

The message of grace and salvation is something every man and woman should engage personally. We are to receive this undeserved gift of salvation based on the merits of Jesus Christ as our Savior.

The Mission: "And we are instructed to turn from godless living and sinful pleasures. We should live in this evil world with wisdom, righteousness, and devotion to God."

Those of us who access this salvation and grace are tasked with our own mission. That mission is to turn from the things we once were to become a reflection of things that matter to God. We are to live with his offered wisdom, his righteousness, and sincere devotion to God. That simply means that our mission is to put God first no matter what circumstances we are facing in our lives.

The Meditation: "While we look forward with hope to that wonderful day when the glory of our great God and Savior, Jesus Christ, will be revealed."

As we walk through this world and live out our lives we face challenges, disappointments, and even failures. Through it all we have a hope that should never go away. We should do everything we can to hold onto the hope of Christ's returning. We should meditate on that day and long for the time when all of our devotion to God will pay off. Eternity with God is our goal. Anything less is to miss the opportunity of a lifetime and beyond.

For his grace has been revealed to you...

PRAYER

Dear Jesus, thank you for the grace extended to me daily. It is only your mercy and grace that allow me to make this earthly journey. My hope is in you. Amen.

Put God's Purpose First

Get all the advice and instruction you can, so you will be wise the rest of your life. You can make many plans, but the LORD's purpose will prevail. Proverbs 19:20-21 NLT

What a timely reminder that all of us probably need on this day. I have lived my life believing that leaders are readers. Thanks to parents that chose to raise their children without a television, I was given a constant supply of books to read. Those books fueled my mind and imagination. In adulthood that thirst to read continues. Through reading and listening to others, we can fill our hearts and minds with wisdom and knowledge. Of course, God's Word remains the book that we should give the most priority to in our thirst for knowledge.

We make our plans, we utilize what we know and have learned, but it is important to remember that God's ways are higher than our ways. His wisdom far exceeds our own. His purposes will trump our purposes every time. So stay in God's Word. Hunger to know more about him. Push your way through the crowds and noise that surround us every day and stay close to him.

His purpose will prevail and you want that. Even though you might not think you want it, you do. Learn what you can, but ultimately trust God with your life, your loves, and your daily walk. Always turn to him first. Make sure your plans are aligning with his plans and purpose.

PRAYER

Dear God, ultimately, everything that happens in my life needs to be surrendered to you. Please help me do this with people, plans, my job, and even my family. You know what I think I need, and you also know what is best for me. Amen.

For Such a Time as This

Who knows if perhaps you were made queen for just such a time as this? Esther 4:14 NLT

It's a great story full of drama and intrigue. Esther is a Jew and should not be the queen, but now she has a chance to reveal her heritage. This calculated reveal may save her people from annihilation, or it may mean her immediate death.

Most of us are never faced with such life and death drama, but there are definitely moments when God calls on us to move in uncomfortable spaces. It is in these moments that we should pray and ask God for the wisdom he promised to give us. In these moments, we should also take much time for prayer and reflection.

God's Spirit never pushes us to do something with an over the top urgency. He will make his will plain to us if we are patient enough to wait on him. Someone once said God opens and shuts doors. They also made the point that sometimes the long wait between one door shutting and another opening is a "long hallway."

What is God wanting to do through you that may be your "for such a time as this" moment? Don't be afraid; if he is calling you to do something, he will supply you with the grace, strength, and power to do it.

PRAYER

Dear God, please give me the confidence to respond to your call on my life. May I always be willing to say yes when you call. Amen.

What Is in Your Hand?

Then the Lord asked him, "What is that in your hand?" "A shepherd's staff," Moses replied. Exodus 4:2 NLT

What is God asking you to do? Most of the time when God asks us to do something it will be something that we cannot do without Him. For many of us, our first response might be to offer excuses as to why we are not the right person for the job.

Moses was 80 years old. He was a fugitive from Egypt and had been for forty years. He lives with his father-in-law Jethro and keeps his sheep. When God calls him to lead the people of Israel out of Egyptian bondage and to freedom and the promise land, he offers lots of excuses as to why he is not the right person to do the job.

God asks him a simple question, "What is that in your hand?" As far as Moses is concerned it was just a simple common shepherd's staff but it was much more than that. It represented his perception of himself and his problem but it also represented his potential with God's help. Eventually that staff played some major roles in the job God called him to do.

We love to focus on our weaknesses or at least they beg for our attention but with God all things are possible. With God, there is nothing that you can't do if He ask it of you. When you follow God you will more than likely go down paths that you could never imagine. The faithful followers will always be asked to do things that call for His assistance, the Spirit's power and great faith on our part.

What is that in your hand? Are you willing to use it for God? The very thing you think is a weakness may be what God wants to use the most. Let God use you today to do the unthinkable.

And He said to me, "My grace is sufficient for you, for My strength is made perfect in weakness" (2 Corinthians 12:9 NLT).

PRAYER

Dear Lord, I have a lot in my hands. You have given me so much and so many opportunities. Help me to always make myself available to You even if I don't feel adequate. With You all things are possible. Amen

Sometimes You Just Fall to Your Knees

At the time of the sacrifice, I stood up from where I had sat in mourning with my clothes torn. I fell to my knees and lifted my hands to the LORD my God. Ezra 9:5 NLT

Ezra was mourning the departure of God's people from following God's ways. This was a huge burden for the prophet, and he was spending time before God in remorse, deep sadness, prayer, and intercession.

Chances are, there will be moments in the life of all Christ followers when we will drop to our knees in pain, cry out to God for help, and maybe even find a reason to repent. The point is, we can come to God with everything. We can come and not even talk if the pain is too much. We can place ourselves in his presence and seek his face and blessing. In the moments that touch your life with sorrow or grief, don't be afraid to place yourself before God as a little child would come to his or her father when help is needed or fear is all consuming.

Sometimes I think God allows us to shoulder some things we wish would go away or not be part of our lives, but if we handle it correctly by trusting God even in the darkness we will grow from the experience.

Ezra was beyond burdened, and something amazing happened in his quest for God's help. In Ezra 10 we read, "While Ezra prayed and made this confession, weeping and lying face down on the ground in front of the Temple of God, a very large crowd of people from Israel—men, women, and children—gathered and wept bitterly with him."

Stay close to God and he will be close to you. It may be that he will even bring others into your life to help you bear your burdens.

PRAYER

Dear God, you alone know the burdens that I carry in my heart. You alone know how to help me stay strong. I may stand, I may kneel, or I may fall on my face before you; but I know you alone are my help. Amen.

The Benefits of God's Presence

The LORD replied, "I will personally go with you, Moses, and I will give you rest—everything will be fine for you." Exodus 33:14 NLT

Moses received promises from God for rest and that everything would be fine for him. Wouldn't it be great to wake up to that assurance? Wouldn't it be amazing if we could muster up the faith to believe that for ourselves?

The reality is that most of us are desperately in need of rest, and many of us have lived long enough to know that everything is not always fine for us. We face uncertainties, we fight health related battles, we walk through the valley of the shadow of death, we mourn and grieve, we wish we had more money, and so many more things.

The reality is, Moses didn't have a perfect life either; but because of his faithfulness and relationship with God, he was given the help he needed to endure and face life's challenges. He still had a long way to go when God promised these things. He was a faithful leader but had his share of emotional difficulties, bouts of self-doubt, and even organizational struggle.

God was with him all the way. He led him and gave him encouragement as well as other leaders to help him. When it came down to the end of his mission (leading Israel to the promised land), he saw it from a distance and knew that his journey was over. God allowed him to see it and then fulfilled his promise for rest and for everything to be okay.

"So Moses, the servant of the Lord, died there in the land of Moab, just as the Lord had said. The Lord buried him in a valley near Beth-peor in Moab, but to this day no one knows the exact place. Moses was 120 years old when he died, yet his eyesight was clear, and he was as strong as ever" (Deuteronomy 34:5-7 NLT).

Don't miss the fact that "The Lord buried him." There is something about this that I love. God took care of him to the end. Follow God with all your heart, soul, mind, and strength. Love him first. You will find rest, and everything will be just fine for you.

Dear God, as you were with Moses, will you be with me? Let me find the faith to follow you even when rest is illusive and things don't feel fine. I trust you and will place all my hope in you. Amen.

A New Vision

It was in the year King Uzziah died that I saw the Lord. He was sitting on a lofty throne, and the train of his robe filled the Temple. Attending him were mighty seraphim, each having six wings. With two wings they covered their faces, with two they covered their feet, and with two they flew. They were calling out to each other, "Holy, holy, holy is the Lord of Heaven's Armies! The whole earth is filled with his glory!" Their voices shook the Temple to its foundations, and the entire building was filled with smoke. Then I said, "It's all over! I am doomed, for I am a sinful man. I have filthy lips, and I live among a people with filthy lips. Yet I have seen the King, the Lord of Heaven's Armies." Then one of the seraphim flew to me with a burning coal he had taken from the altar with a pair of tongs. He touched my lips with it and said, "See, this coal has touched your lips. Now your guilt is removed, and your sins are forgiven." Then I heard the Lord asking, "Whom should I send as a messenger to this people? Who will go for us?" I said, "Here I am. Send me." Isaiah 6:1-8 NLT

Isaiah was already a prophet, but something happened in Isaiah 6. He encountered God and it was life changing. Left behind in this classic story is a pattern that has been repeated millions of times in others' lives. When you encounter God, it will affect you in a way that changes your priorities and focus. When you see Christ, you will see yourself and others differently. Here is what happened to Isaiah.

- **He saw the Lord. It was an upward vision.**
  "I saw the Lord. He was sitting on a lofty throne, and the train of his robe filled the Temple"
- **He saw himself. It was an inward vision.**
  "Then I said, 'It's all over! I am doomed, for I am a sinful man. I have filthy lips, and I live among a people with filthy lips.'"
- **He saw others. It was an outward vision.**
  "Then I heard the Lord asking, 'Whom should I send as a messenger to this people? Who will go for us?' I said, 'Here I am. Send me.'"

This is consistent with the call of Christ for our lives and our period in history. The call has always been the same for all Christ followers: "Go and make disciples." But it has also been a consistent message that we shouldn't go until we have had an encounter with God. It was Jesus that said this to his disciples: "Do not leave Jerusalem until the Father sends you the gift he promised, as I told you before. John baptized with water, but in just a few days you will be baptized with the Holy Spirit."

PRAYER

Dear Jesus, I pray for this fresh vision daily. Help me to see you and the needs of others around me. Please help me to see myself as you see me. Touch my heart with your live coal. Amen.

Leading in Crisis

Messengers came and told Jehoshaphat, "A vast army from Edom is marching against you from beyond the Dead Sea. They are already at Hazazon-tamar." Jehoshaphat was terrified by this news and begged the Lord for guidance. He also ordered everyone in Judah to begin fasting. So people from all the towns of Judah came to Jerusalem to seek the Lord's help. 2 Chronicles 20:3-4 NLT

Sometimes in leadership we are called to make major decisions and respond to threats that are real and measurable. Jehoshaphat was the king of Judah, and in this position he was called to serve the people of Judah by offering protection and the management of the country's resources. Now with three armies coming against his small nation he had to act and act immediately. He did the right thing in consulting with God fast and first.

It's an amazing story of God's deliverance, and I would encourage you to read the whole chapter. You will find that because Jehoshaphat acted, God intervened on their behalf in a very positive way. In fact, here is another part of the passage describing the result of his leadership:

"When all the surrounding kingdoms heard that the Lord himself had fought against the enemies of Israel, the fear of God came over them. So Jehoshaphat's kingdom was at peace, for his God had given him rest on every side" (2 Chronicles 20: 29-30 NLT).

He was not perfect in all his decisions as we read later: "Jehoshaphat was a good king, following the ways of his father, Asa. He did what was pleasing in the Lord's sight. During his reign, however, he failed to remove all the pagan shrines, and the people never fully committed themselves to follow the God of their ancestors" (2 Chronicles 20:32-33 NLT).

The Maxwell Leadership Bible described four styles of leadership regarding this story:

1. Dropouts: leaders who give up and fail to take responsibility.
2. Cop-outs: leaders who make excuses for why they aren't responsible.
3. Hold-outs: leaders who waver too long to take responsibility.
4. All-outs: leaders who own the responsibility and take action—like Jehoshaphat.

Leaders must lead. We must be willing to make the tough calls with the end in mind even when others may not agree with it. When the bad news comes our way, the good news is that we have a God who offers us wisdom and his presence. He will fight on our behalf if we trust in him completely. Never lead alone. Let God lead you as you lead others. You may not be a paid leader, but this works even when leading a family or in the context of ministry.

PRAYER

Dear God, please help me to realize my need for you every day. I know that you are able to guide me and show me the best way to move forward. I am trusting you today. Amen.

No More Fear

"Why are you frightened?" he asked. "Why are your hearts filled with doubt?" Luke 24:38 NLT

Jesus was speaking to his disciples following his resurrection from the grave. They were huddled in a room behind locked doors and filled with fear. I think he questioned their fear because of how much he had tried to tell them about his impending death and resurrection. He had spoken about it often, but when it happened right in front of them they were taken back and didn't know where to turn.

I wonder how many times our hearts are filled with fear and doubt? We may know what the Bible says, and many of the promises that are spoken by God throughout his Word, and yet we doubt and we may even succumb to fear.

Jesus followed up these questions with an invitation to reach out and touch him and to see that he was really there in the flesh. We don't get that privilege, but by faith we can touch him. We can reach out in the midst of our fearful times and know that he is still God. Don't allow fear to get a foothold in your life in light of God's promise to never leave us or forsake us. Don't let doubt grip your mind and soul when Jesus said "I am with you always, even to the end of the world."

A relatively new worship song includes these words:

Oh, fear is a liar with a smooth and velvet tongue
Fear is a tyrant, he's always telling me to run
Oh, love is a resurrection and love is a trumpet sound
Love is my weapon, I'm gonna take my giants down.

We all face fear and doubt at times, but we can overcome them with God's help and love. Accept his love for you today. He knows right where you are!

PRAYER

Dear God, fear is such a powerful force, but not nearly as powerful as you. I give you my fear, and I will depend on you for the power to overcome the lies that get whispered in the ears of my mind and heart. You are God! Amen.

Smart Investments

Don't hoard treasure down here where it gets eaten by moths and corroded by rust or—worse!—stolen by burglars. Stockpile treasure in heaven, where it's safe from moth and rust and burglars. It's obvious, isn't it? The place where your treasure is, is the place you will most want to be, and end up being. Matthew 6:19-20 MSG

Realizing the brevity of life that each of us is given will go a long way in helping us make good investment choices. I have officiated hundreds of funerals and the one thing I can assure you is that no one takes anything with them. Occasionally family members place something meaningful or a picture or trinket in the casket; but more often than not, they are concerned that the expensive jewelry is removed before the lid is shut for the final time.

Being rich here means nothing in death. If that is the case, then how can we invest in heaven? Jesus gave us the key in these two commandments.

- Loving God with all your heart, mind, soul, and strength.
- Loving your neighbors as you love yourself.

Randy Alcorn suggests:

1. **God owns everything. I'm his money manager.** We are the managers of the assets God has entrusted—not given—to us.
2. **My heart always goes where I put God's money.** Watch what happens when you reallocate your money from temporal things to eternal things.
3. **Heaven, not earth, is my home.** We are citizens of a "better country—a heavenly one" (Hebrews 11:16).
4. **I should live not for the dot but for the line.** From the dot—our present life on earth—extends a line that goes on forever, which is eternity in heaven.
5. **Giving is the only antidote to materialism.** Giving is a joyful surrender to a greater person and a greater agenda. It dethrones me and exalts him.

6. **God prospers me not to raise my standard of living, but to raise my standard of giving.** God gives more money than we need so we can give generously.

What does your heavenly investment portfolio look like? What changes can you make today that will enable you to invest in the people around you in the name of Jesus? It may be giving money, but more than likely this heavenly investment will cost you your time, talent, and treasures.

Dear Jesus, I know that I wrestle with this sometimes in my life. Give me the wisdom to look at my life and my stuff in view of eternity. Help me to make a difference now in the lives of those around me. Amen.

Love Your Enemies?

You have heard the law that says, "Love your neighbor" and hate your enemy. But I say, love your enemies! Pray for those who persecute you! In that way, you will be acting as true children of your Father in heaven. Matthew 5:43-45 NLT

Jesus was teaching the first disciples at the top of a mountain. In this sermon, he took many of the Ten Commandments and expanded them with new interpretations.

This is a tough one because most of us believe we must fight for our rights, stand our ground, and basically take on anyone that wants to do us harm. Enemies come into our lives in many different ways so we must be on guard spiritually in dealing with them.

Jesus offers a two-fold solution here. It is a simple yet profound teaching and one that is very hard to practice in some cases.

- Love your enemies.
- Pray for those who persecute you.

Loving your enemies has to be an act of God's grace in your life, but there are many instances from the Bible and recorded history when Christ followers have done this very thing. It is possible and it is commanded by our Lord. It was also modeled for us by Jesus when he was dying on the cross and prayed for those executing him.

Praying for those who persecute us will change much about our attitude, feelings, and even our ability to love.

The goal every day is to act, react, and live out our lives as "true children of your Father in heaven."

Go ahead and try it. Make your heavenly Father proud of you today by the way you treat others. Be loving and pray for everyone you come in contact with today.

PRAYER

Dear Jesus, without doubt this is a hard one to do at times. Give me your strength and grace today as I try to live this out in my own life. Help me to do this not just for enemies but for everyone that is a part of my life. Amen.

He Is Always!

"I am the Alpha and the Omega—the beginning and the end," says the Lord God. "I am the one who is, who always was, and who is still to come—the Almighty One." Revelation 1:8 NLT

The more we know about God, the more we come to trust him with our lives. When we believe in the sovereignty of God, or that he is the supreme power and authority in the world, our lives will be very different from the people that don't believe this or know this.

God says, "I am the beginning and the end."

God says, "I am."

God says, "I was."

God says, "I will be the one still to come."

He is all in all. He is everything including our Creator. He knows everything about us according to the Scripture, including the numbers of hairs on our heads. He sees sparrows when they fall. He knows exactly where you are today and what is going on in your life, and he cares.

Jesus said, "That is why I tell you not to worry about everyday life—whether you have enough food and drink, or enough clothes to wear. Isn't life more than food, and your body more than clothing? Look at the birds. They don't plant or harvest or store food in barns, for your heavenly Father feeds them. And aren't you far more valuable to him than they are?" (Matthew 6:25-26 NLT).

And He said, "Look at the lilies of the field and how they grow. They don't work or make their clothing, yet Solomon in all his glory was not dressed as beautifully as they are. And if God cares so wonderfully for wildflowers that are here today and thrown into the fire tomorrow, he will certainly care for you. Why do you have so little faith?" (Matthew 6:28-30 NLT).

Our God is the same yesterday, today, and forever! He loves you and will give you the grace you need today if you only believe. Linda Evans Shepherd wrote, "What we have to understand is that Jesus is not offering to make our problems disappear; he's offering to give us rest for our souls while he does the heavy lifting." Trust him with your life and trust him with your eternity. Trust him in your journey.

Dear Jesus, I know that you are my Lord and Savior. I know you are with me always. Help me to believe in you, yesterday, today, and forever. Amen.

Growing Through Changing Times

After the death of Moses the Lord's servant, the Lord spoke to Joshua son of Nun, Moses' assistant. He said, "Moses my servant is dead. Therefore, the time has come for you to lead these people, the Israelites, across the Jordan River into the land I am giving them. I promise you what I promised Moses: 'Wherever you set foot, you will be on land I have given you—from the Negev wilderness in the south to the Lebanon mountains in the north, from the Euphrates River in the east to the Mediterranean Sea in the west, including all the land of the Hittites.' No one will be able to stand against you as long as you live. For I will be with you as I was with Moses. I will not fail you or abandon you." Joshua 1:1-5 NLT

All of us go through times when things around us change. This can bring discomfort, fear, and even anger. We generally love what we know and are familiar with most of the time. When the formidable leader Moses died, it became Joshua's turn to lead. I can't image how different things were in his life during this transition. This is an outline of how it played out:

Changing relationships—his friend and mentor Moses dies.
Changing role—taking the place of a popular leader.
Changing responsibility—now in charge of leading an entire nation.
Changing location—relocation and it's BIG!

What are we to do and what can we learn from this great biblical story of transition and change?

1. Lean on God's Provision.
2. Listen to God's Promises.
3. Look for God's Purpose.
4. Live in God's Prosperity.
5. Latch on to God's Power.

Dear God, you know the things in my life that challenge me most. Help me to learn from this story and to never forget what you promised Joshua as he took on this responsibility. I believe that no matter what you call me to do, you will give me the strength to do it. Amen.

Remember Your Faith
Part One

So do not throw away this confident trust in the Lord. Remember the great reward it brings you! Patient endurance is what you need now, so that you will continue to do God's will. Then you will receive all that he has promised. Hebrews 10:35-36 NLT

Just before launching into the great chapter on faith, the writer makes it personal for the readers. In verse 32 he writes, "Think back on the early days when you first learned about Christ." It was so easy then to exercise our faith. Over the years it is easy to become doubtful, jaded, and even cynical. Often our eyes land on people around us instead of Christ. In these verses we are looking at today we are prodded to remember why faith is so important to maintain. Faith is not of works but is a gift from God.

We should: Remember our past — *"So do not throw away this confident trust in the Lord."*

We should: Remember to be patient — *"Patient endurance is what you need now, so that you will continue to do God's will."*

We should: Remember the promises — *"Then you will receive all that he has promised."*

In Habakkuk the writer says, "This vision is for a future time. It described the end and it will be fulfilled. If it seems slow in coming, wait patiently, for it will surely take place. It will not be delayed" (Habakkuk 2:3 NLT).

"Let us hold tightly without wavering to the hope we affirm, for God can be trusted to keep his promise. Let us think of ways to motivate one another to acts of love and good works. And let us not neglect our meeting together, as some people do, but encourage one another, especially now that the day of his return is drawing near" (Hebrews 10:23-25 NLT).

In the Peanuts comic strips, Snoopy often tries to be an author. In one particular strip he's shown on his doghouse typing a novel. He begins his story with, "It was a dark and stormy night." That's the way he always begins his stories. Lucy comes and bluntly shouts, "You stupid dog! That is the dumbest thing I've ever read. Who ever heard of such a silly way to begin a story? Don't you know that all good stories begin, 'Once upon a time'?" So the last frame shows Snoopy starting over. This time he types: "Once upon a time, it was a dark and stormy night."

The dark nights come to everyone on this planet. May God help us to remember our faith and encourage ourselves and each other to stand strong even in the darkest of nights and stormiest moments.

PRAYER

Dear God, I thank you for the reminder to keep my confidence and trust in you. The Bible is full of encouragement, so help me to remember and learn. Amen.

Remember Their Faith
Part Two

Hebrews 11, NLT

In this chapter, the writer names names and calls us to remember the champions of faith in the Bible. Here we find what they did, but please remember that they were not special people in any way except one: they trusted God and did his will. They didn't say "no" but "yes" to God time after time.

They Worshiped by Faith

"It was by faith that Abel brought a more acceptable offering to God than Cain did" (verse 4).

"It was by faith that Abraham offered Isaac as a sacrifice when God was testing him" (verse 17).

"It was by faith that Jacob, when he was old and dying, blessed each of Joseph's sons and bowed in worship as he leaned on his staff" (verse 21).

They Walked by Faith

"It was by faith that Enoch was taken up to heaven without dying.... For before he was taken up, he was known as a person who pleased God" (verse 5). "Enoch lived 365 years, walking in close fellowship with God" (Genesis 5:23 NLT.)

It was by faith that Abraham left home (verse 8).

It was by faith that Moses parents hid him three months (verse 23).

It was by faith that Moses refused to be called the son of Pharaoh's daughter (verse 24).

It was by faith that Moses shared the oppression of God's people instead of ... the fleeting pleasures of sin (verse 25).

It was by faith the people of Israel walked through the Red Sea (verse 29).

They Waited by Faith

It was by faith the people of Israel marched around Jericho for seven days (verse 30).

It was by faith that Noah built the ark while waiting for things to happen that had never happened before (verse 7).

It was by faith that Rahab the prostitute was not destroyed (verse 31). She waited many days.

It was by faith that Sarah had a child in old age (verse 11).

They Witnessed by Faith

"How much more do I need to say? It would take too long to recount the stories of the faith of Gideon, Barak, Samson, Jephthah, David, Samuel, and all the prophets. By faith these people overthrew kingdoms, ruled with justice, and received what God had promised them. They shut the mouths of lions, quenched the flames of fire, and escaped death by the edge of the sword. Their weakness was turned to strength. They became strong in battle and put whole armies to flight. Women received their loved ones back again from death.

But others were tortured, refusing to turn from God in order to be set free. They placed their hope in a better life after the resurrection. Some were jeered at, and their backs were cut open with whips. Others were chained in prisons. Some died by stoning, some were sawed in half, and others were killed with the sword. Some went about wearing skins of sheep and goats, destitute and oppressed and mistreated. They were too good for this world, wandering over deserts and mountains, hiding in caves and holes in the ground" (Hebrews 11:32-39 NLT).

PRAYER

Dear Lord, I hardly know what to say. I know that men and women of faith have done amazing things because they believed in you. Please increase my faith, Lord. Amen.

How Much More. . .

Keep on asking, and you will receive what you ask for. Keep on seeking, and you will find. Keep on knocking, and the door will be opened to you. 8 For everyone who asks, receives. Everyone who seeks, finds. And to everyone who knocks, the door will be opened. You parents—if your children ask for a loaf of bread, do you give them a stone instead? Or if they ask for a fish, do you give them a snake? Of course not! So if you sinful people know how to give good gifts to your children, how much more will your heavenly Father give good gifts to those who ask him. Matthew 7:7-11 NLT

This version of Jesus teaching is from the classic Sermon on the Mount. He talked about praying and asking God for help at other times but most often He always taught about prayer with the hope of answered prayer.

Keep on asking: "Everyone who asks, receives."

Keep on seeking: "Everyone who seeks, finds."

Keep on knocking: "To everyone who knocks, the door will be opened."

Our focus today is on verse 11: "So if you sinful people know how to give good gifts to your children, how much more will your heavenly Father give good gifts to those who ask him."

And out of this verse is one takeaway phrase: "how much more."

How much more will God do for us? How much more can a God do that is sovereign, holy, always present, all-powerful, and all-knowing? He is just. He is faithful. He is full of mercy. There is no entity or power greater than him. He invites us to ask him for what we will. He calls us to believe and exercise our faith. He calls us to believe no matter what may be happening around us. We believe because we believe that he is God and that he never changes. The more you know and learn about God, the more aligned you will be with him in your life and in prayer. Here are some reminders of who he is:

"The LORD is gracious and merciful; slow to anger and great in lovingkindness" (Psalm 145:8).

"Beloved, let us love one another, for love is from God, and whoever loves has been born of God and knows God. Anyone who does not love does not know God, because God is love" (1 John 4:7-8).

"O taste and see that the Lord is good" (Psalm 34:8).

"Know therefore that the LORD your God is God; he is the faithful God, keeping his covenant of love to a thousand generations of those who love him and keep his commands" (Deut. 7:9).

How much more will our God give in answer to our prayers?

On suffering Tim Keller writes: "There is a purpose to it, and if faced rightly, it can drive us like a nail deep into the love of God and into more stability and spiritual power than you can imagine."

PRAYER

Dear Jesus, you taught these words to the first disciples. You want us to realize how much more you can and will do if we but ask. I will keep knocking. I will keep believing. Amen.

Don't Hang Up Your Harp

Beside the rivers of Babylon, we sat and wept as we thought of Jerusalem. We put away our harps, hanging them on the branches of poplar trees. For our captors demanded a song from us. Our tormentors insisted on a joyful hymn: "Sing us one of those songs of Jerusalem!" But how can we sing the songs of the LORD while in a pagan land? Psalm 137:1-4 NLT

The above question is a good one. "How can we sing the songs of the Lord while in a pagan land?" America has become a very pagan land. It might interest you to know that other countries are sending missionaries here by the thousands each year. They view pictures and videos of scenes from American cities and become burdened to come and share the gospel. For those of us that live here, we have to ask: how should we respond?

You can sit or sing.

You can weep or worship.

You can be fruitless or faithful.

Israel was taken into captivity by Babylon and lost all their rights. In this Scripture, we find the singers and most likely Levite priests responded to the captivity with great sorrow and melancholy. They were asked to sing one of the songs of Jerusalem, but they couldn't bring themselves to do it. Was it a missed opportunity? I'll let you be the judge of that.

There were, however, four young men also taken in this same captivity but they reacted much differently; and because of it God used them in a pretty big way. You can read about them in the book of Daniel.

Daniel is a fascinating biblical character because he never compromised his beliefs but kept a great attitude and was able to work directly for four ungodly Babylonian kings. He spent the night in the lion's den but was protected by the angel of God. He stood for what he believed and never felt the need to compromise, and yet God used him in this ungodly kingdom to bring honor to himself and as a light for those around him. Don't hang your harp up just yet. Keep singing the Lord's song.

Be engaged in the culture.

Be faithful in staying true to your convictions.

Be faithful to the Word of God.

Be willing to risk.

Be strong in your faith and trust of God's protection.

Be fierce about your integrity.

Be prepared to watch God work in you and through you.

PRAYER

Dear God, may I possess the courage of Daniel and his three friends. No matter what happens in our culture or how great the threat, may I always stand and tell your story. Amen.

Is This World Wrapping Up?

Everything in the world is about to be wrapped up, so take nothing for granted. Stay wide-awake in prayer. Most of all, love each other as if your life depended on it. Love makes up for practically anything. Be quick to give a meal to the hungry, a bed to the homeless—cheerfully. Be generous with the different things God gave you, passing them around so all get in on it: if words, let it be God's words; if help, let it be God's hearty help. That way, God's bright presence will be evident in everything through Jesus, and he'll get all the credit as the One mighty in everything—encores to the end of time. Oh, yes! 1 Peter 4:8 MSG

I would never attempt to predict when this world will end, but I can predict with much certainty that it will wrap up some day and be over. Some of us were exposed to preaching and teaching that left us convinced that we would never graduate from high school or ever get married when we were growing up. We were sure it was the end of time because of the things that were happening. Now here we are in another century. Not just in a new century, but several years into a new century.

In this passage, Peter gives the early church some sound advice; and if it was good for them two thousand years ago, it is that much more relevant today for us. We are two thousand years closer to the return of Jesus than they were when this was written. Here's an outline to follow as you work through this passage of Scripture.

Everything in the world is about to be wrapped up...
- **Be Aware of your Surroundings**
  Take nothing for granted...
- **Pray and Stay Awake**
  Stay wide-awake in prayer...
- **Be like Christ in Attitude**
  Most of all, love each other as if your life depended on it...
- **Practice Abundant Giving**
  Be quick to give a meal to the hungry, a bed to the homeless—cheerfully. Be generous with the different things God gave you, passing

them around so all get in on it: if words, let it be God's words; if help, let it be God's hearty help.

- **Be God's Ambassador**
  That way, God's bright presence will be evident in everything through Jesus, and he'll get all the credit as the One mighty in everything— encores to the end of time. Oh, yes!

May God help us to stay vigilant and true to our faith as we persevere through the wrap up of this world. We await and much better home.

Dear God, only you know the day and the hour of your return. Help me stay strong and aware of your work in this world. Draw me closer to you than I have ever been. Amen.

Be Careful How You Live

So be careful how you live. Don't live like fools, but like those who are wise. Make the most of every opportunity in these evil days. Don't act thoughtlessly, but understand what the Lord wants you to do. Ephesians 5:15-17 NLT

As I read this, I thought of this outline:
Be careful how you live—Be Sensitive
Be like the wise—Be Smart
Make the most of every opportunity—Be selective
Understand what God wants you to do—Be a seeker

Most of what Jesus taught is totally the opposite of cultural thinking … he taught us these things:

- The way up is down
- The way in is out
- The way to be first is to be last
- The way of success is service
- The way of attainment is relinquishment
- The way of strength is weakness
- The way of security is vulnerability
- The way of protection is forgiveness (even to 7 x 70)
- The way of life is death – death to self, society, family
- Want to be free? Give complete control to God.
- Want to become great? Become least.
- Want to find yourself? Forget yourself.
- Want honor? Honor yourself with humility.
- Want to "get even" with your enemies? Bless, love, and pray for them.

George Muller was born in Prussia on September 27, 1805. His father was a collector of taxes and George seemed to inherit his father's ability with figures. Muller lived out all of the above thoughts.

When Muller was converted to Christ he was impressed by the many recurring statements of Jesus for us "to ask." At this point in Muller's life, he and his wife launched into a daring experiment. First, they gave away all of their household goods. The next step was even more daring: he refused all regular salary from the small mission he had been serving. He then set out to establish an orphan home to care for the homeless children of England.

The first home was dedicated in a rented building on April 21, 1836. Within a matter of days, forty-three orphans were being cared for. Muller and his co-workers decided their experiment would be set up with the following guidelines:

1. No funds would ever be solicited.
2. No debts were ever to be incurred.
3. No money contributed for a specific purpose would ever be used for any other purpose.
4. All accounts would be audited annually.
5. No ego-pandering by the publication of donor's names.
6. No "names" of prominent people would be sought for the board or to advertise the institution.
7. The success of the orphanage would be measured not by the numbers served or by the amount of money taken in, but by God's blessing on the work, which Muller expected to be in direct proportion to the time spent in prayer.

When the first building was constructed, Muller and his friends remained true to their convictions. The public was amazed when a second building was opened six months after the first. They kept concentrating on prayer and eventually there were five new buildings, 110 workers, and 2,050 orphans being cared for.

George Muller not only counted on God to provide, but he believed that God would provide abundantly. For over sixty years Muller recorded every specific prayer request and the results. Muller was responsible for the care of 9,500 orphans during his life. These children never went without a meal. Muller never asked for help from anyone but God. $7,500,000 came to him over the course of his life and he vows it was all in answer to believing prayer. He made the most of every opportunity.

PRAYER

Dear God, sometimes it is really hard to live in this world and remember I am supposed to be living in your kingdom. Somehow give me the ability to live a life closer to you and the things that are important to you. Amen.

Sent By Jesus

As he spoke, he showed them the wounds in his hands and his side.
They were filled with joy when they saw the Lord! Again he said,
"Peace be with you. As the Father has sent me, so I am sending
you." Then he breathed on them and said, "Receive the Holy Spirit."
John 20:21-22 NLT

Jesus was appearing to all of his disciples except Thomas for the first time after the resurrection. They were huddled in fear behind locked doors and he just appeared in the middle of them all. The purpose of this meeting can be summed up by looking at the mission Christ came to fulfill. He came to work himself out of a job. He came to empower others to do the work and be his body on this earth.

Encountering God brings joy! There is no substitute for the joy of the Lord.

Encountering God brings peace! There is no satisfaction like his peace.

Encountering God brings responsibility! There is no service like being God's hands and feet.

Can you imagine being mentored by Jesus Christ? The original twelve disciples received on the job training. It was a rigorous curriculum as they followed Jesus around trying to understand what he was saying and what he wanted them to do. They were all at different levels of faith, and we always need to remember that. Not everyone is at the same place in their relationship with the Lord.

Thomas encountered the disciples soon after they saw Jesus and they told him, "We have seen the Lord!" He quickly responded, "I won't believe he is alive unless I thrust my hands in his wounds from the cross." Eight days later Jesus again appeared and this time offered for Thomas to touch his wounds. (Think about that!) Thomas responded correctly with these words, "My Lord and my God!" He lined up and got on board with the others and the church was born a few weeks later when they burst out of the upper room filled with God's Holy Spirit.

When we encounter Jesus deeply in our lives, we will follow him every day.

We will be encouraged and filled with joy.
We will experience peace flowing like a river in our lives.
We will empower others to be faithful to God.

> A charge to keep I have,
> A God to glorify,
> A never-dying soul to save,
> And fit it for the sky.
> To serve the present age,
> My calling to fulfill:
> Oh, may it all my pow'rs engage
> To do my Master's will!
> —Charles Wesley

Ryan Johnson, from Glen Elder, Kansas, shared this story:

I was heading north out of Salina, Kansas, when I saw him. His name was Charlie.

Charles was sitting in the ditch with large army bags. The cold, misty rain was drenching him and his bags. He wore his Vietnam jacket proudly. It laid over is 400 pound body like a tarp.

I pulled over and asked if I could help. He asked if I would load his bags (and man did he mean bags) on the car and drive them to the gas station that was a hundred yards away, he would appreciate it. I did. He limped along following behind my car. For a few fruitless hours I tried to talk him into going to a rescue mission. I prayed with him and left.

I continued to travel North on HW 81 to my home. That's when Jesus started in. I said, "Jesus, I can't take him home. He could kill me. And Jesus, he really stinks… Jesus there is no way I am letting him stay the night… Now Lord, I prayed with him. I helped him."

I felt the words he said, echoed from Matthew 25, "When you welcome me in ... not if you prayed with me." So, I made a U-turn on Highway 81. I pulled up next to Charlie at the gas station. I said, "Charlie, get in!" Charlie said, "Gitty up!"

For the next hour and a half, I rode with this 400 lb man in my small car. I had to crack the window to be able to breathe through the stench. I heard the story of how a veteran becomes a misfit. It was the common dilemma of needing medicine to get a job and a job to get the medicine.

We got to my place. I laid a sheet on the couch. I washed his clothes and belongings. The next morning I took him to the police station as part of the ministerial alliance agreement to get him a free motel room and a hot meal.

Later that day I received a call from the local hospital's social worker. She said that Charles has been admitted and wouldn't speak to anyone but me. I walked into room 104 and said, "Charlie, what do you want? I've done everything."

He said, "I don't want anything. I just wanted you to know that they told me my heart is bad and I am dying. They want to ship me to Wichita. But I can never hitch a ride out of Wichita, so I want to stay here to die. Last night was the first home I have stayed in in over twenty years. Because of that I felt welcomed. And I know Jesus is asking me to get my real heart right. I just want you to know. I want you to help me accept the Lord."

I am convinced that the devil doesn't care how much we go to church or how awesome we look when we get there, because we aren't doing anything to stir up his domain. But if we could just get serious about our faith like we will wish we would have when we are lying on our deathbed and thinking about answering to God, we would see the lives of those we live around and love change.

PRAYER

Dear Jesus, who is it that you want to love through me today? Give me ears to hear what you want me to hear and eyes to see what you see. Amen.

Leading Is Hard Work

Good planning and hard work lead to prosperity, but hasty short-cuts lead to poverty. Proverbs 21:5 NLT

Planning strategically is a foundational principle of leadership. "Good planning," as stated by the writer, leads to prosperity. Prosperity in this verse really is better defined as success. The Message Bible translates it this way, "Careful planning puts you ahead in the long run."

"Good planning and hard work," are linked together as equally important, and in the ESV it reads this way: "The plans of the diligent lead surely to abundance."

Follow up visionary plans with the hard work that makes it happen. Linking these two together allow us to enjoy the fruit of our labors. Successful people plan well and perform well. They strategize and they sweat to bring things to life. They make a plan and follow it with passion.

When we follow this spiritual advice from the Proverb writer, we are going to benefit in many ways:

We will build strong character.

We will find profit instead of poverty (brought on by "hasty short-cuts").

We will create a path for others to follow.

We will provide for ourselves and those around us.

We will be disciplined leaders.

We will be successful leaders.

Prosperity may be related to money, but we can also be rich in our relationships, our faith, and our community. Work hard and be diligent when God opens the door of opportunity.

PRAYER

Dear Lord, please help me to press onward, forward, and ever upward. Give me the courage to follow the opportunities that you give to me in my life. Amen.

With Mary at the Tomb

Her name was Mary, and she discovered early in the darkness of the morning following Jesus' burial that he was not in the tomb. She had known Jesus. He had changed her life, and then she watched him be tortured and killed. It was an incredible moment that morning at the tomb, and she shared it with two of the disciples who were also on their way to the grave site. The others observed the empty tomb, and the Bible says they simply went "to their own homes." But Mary stayed and encountered a risen Savior!

Mary was standing outside the tomb crying, and as she wept, she stooped and looked in. She saw two white-robed angels sitting at the head and foot of the place where the body of Jesus had been lying. "Why are you crying?" the angels asked her. **"Because they have taken away my Lord,"** *she replied, "and I don't know where they have put him." She glanced over her shoulder and saw someone standing behind her. It was Jesus, but she didn't recognize him. "Why are you crying?" Jesus asked her. "Who are you looking for?" She thought he was the gardener. "Sir," she said, "if you have taken him away, tell me where you have put him, and I will go and get him." "Mary!" Jesus said. She turned toward him and exclaimed, "Teacher!" "Don't cling to me," Jesus said, "for I haven't yet ascended to the Father. But go find my brothers and tell them that I am ascending to my Father and your Father, my God and your God." Mary Magdalene found the disciples and told them, "I have seen the Lord!" Then she gave them his message.* John 20:11

Circumstances, situations, and things happen that cause us to reel in pain. Life can be harsh, cruel, painful, and devastating. You may feel as though life itself has been sucked or drained out of you. If you feel nothing, if you feel dead or you feel like life is not worth living, then I have some really good news. You can be alive again!

We all will endure seasons of weeping.

Mary was so focused on her own loss that while others left to go home she stayed in the cemetery by herself. She stood outside the tomb crying and weeping. She was devastated, but she went from weeping to worship! "Weeping may endure for a night, but joy comes in the morning" (Psalm 30:5).

We must embrace our soul-need to worship.

Every human being on the face of the earth has a built-in internal drive to worship. People worship the craziest things: sports figures, rock bands, and the people in them, weird religious gurus, money, things or possessions, relationships, power, control, titles, sex and pornography, drugs, parents, children, cars, and a whole lot of other crazy things.

To experience our own personal resurrection, we must embrace our soul-need to worship, and the only one that merits our life and worship is Jesus Christ. That is what Mary did. The object of her affection was none other than Jesus Christ the Savior of the world.

PRAYER

Dear Jesus, I love that you came to Mary in her hour of grief and need. You showed yourself to her and brought peace and joy to her heart. I ask that you would do that for people who desperately need you today. Your presence makes all the difference in our lives. Amen.

Let Us Worship and Bow Down

Come, let us worship and bow down. Let us kneel before the LORD our maker, for he is our God. We are the people he watches over, the flock under his care. If only you would listen to his voice today!
Psalm 95:6-7 NLT

I have never heard God speak in an audible voice. It is just not something he does. I've heard him speak in many other ways. I've heard him through a sermon, a song, while reading the Bible and other books, and that strong but silent voice that lets you know when you are about to do something wrong or nudging you to do something right.

The Psalmist encourages us to listen to his voice. Why? Because we are the flock under his care. He is the Great Shepherd and we are his sheep. He offers guidance, protection, and watchful vigilance; but you have to be tuned in to his voice. More than that, you have to be surrendered to his leadership.

How do we do that? With all of the challenges and complexities of life that come our way, we are called to trust him with our lives. The message of the Bible is and always has been surrender to God. Let him live in you and through you. Trust him with your whole life, heart, soul, mind, and strength. Surrender whatever is going on today. The biggest worry and the surprises of our lives should be surrendered to him. How can we do this? Literally, or at least in your mind, accept the invitation of the above verses:

"Come, let us worship and bow down. Let us kneel before the Lord our maker, for he is our God."

PRAYER

Dear God, I bow before you today with thankfulness for all that you do in my life. You are worthy of all the praise and honor you will receive today from around the world. Accept my words of worship and love today. You are my maker. Amen.

Just Obey

If you follow my decrees and are careful to obey my commands.
Leviticus 26:3 NLT

This declaration by God is followed with a list of why obeying his commands is important. While this was written for the Israelites, God has always been about obedience. He wants that from us every day. Look at what God promised to do for them:

I will send you the seasonal rains (verse 4).

I will give you peace in the land and you will sleep with no fear (verse 6).

I will rid the land of wild animals and keep your enemies out (verse 6b).

I will look favorably upon you (verse 9).

I will fulfill my covenant (verse 9b).

I will live among you and not despise you (verse 11).

I will walk among you; I will be your God, and you will be my people (verse 12).

What God is saying to them is crucial for us to hear as well. He was promising to be involved in their livelihood, their families, their protection, and so much more. These are all things we should want and need from God on a daily basis.

It is simple. Just obey what he wants you to do.

Later in the chapter, he talks about what will happen if they don't obey. There certainly are consequences when we don't live God's way. Make sure today you are committed to following God's way with earnestness and prayer. It's the best way to live by far, and he is waiting to lavish you with his presence.

PRAYER

Dear God, without question you always want obedience more than anything else. Please help me today to live my life in a way that pleases you. Give me the strength to love you and live for you in word, thought, and deed. Amen.

Hit the Pause Button

Understand this, my dear brothers and sisters: You must all be quick to listen, slow to speak, and slow to get angry. James 1:19 NLT

What great advice! Do you practice this? It's a triple play of great advice for those who will make it happen in their day to day lives.

Be quick to listen.

Be slow to speak.

Be slow to get angry.

How often most of us do just the opposite? Most human beings struggle to genuinely listen to others and to give them a chance to speak. We are already forming answers in our minds before they have even finished speaking. Too often, we think what we have to say is more important than what is being spoken, and we end up looking foolish because of our interruptions.

Hitting the pause button on our mouth is something to strive to attain. If you and I can learn to listen more and speak less, it will make those around us long for conversations with us. The art of listening, really listening, is very rare.

Of course, if it is a passionate conversation we should also learn to control our anger and not let it control and make fools of us.

These things were so important that James wrote a few verses later, "If anyone thinks he is religious and does not bridle his tongue but deceives his heart, this person's religion is worthless."

Give it a try today. Listen more and speak less. Don't let anger define who you are. Ask God to help you all day long.

PRAYER

God, I really need your help with this one. Allow me to practice listening more and speaking less. Give me a genuine interest in the lives of others today. Amen.

What a Promise!

Praise the LORD! How joyful are those who fear the LORD and delight in obeying his commands. Their children will be successful everywhere; an entire generation of godly people will be blessed.
Psalm 112:1-2 NLT

Remember, fearing God is usually referring to honoring him and respecting him. It is about living in such a way that everything is surrendered to God. When we do this, those around us are greatly affected and influenced to follow God as well.

It is never too late to start living this way. You might be tempted to think the psalmist is referring to parents with young children, but you and I will influence our families as we evolve through the seasons of our lives. We will have unique challenges that will allow us to pledge and demonstrate our commitment to God repeatedly.

There is not much we should pray for or desire more than for our children and families to live with God at the center of their lives. This is not a promise for health and wealth. Some of God's most successful followers have lived lives of great adversity. Respect and following God brings a joy that endures all things. Love him and trust him regardless. You will find great joy!

PRAYER

Dear God, please help me understand and embrace the reality of this promise. I can't think of a greater joy than seeing those I love come to love and follow you. Thank you for this. Amen.

How Long?

How long, O Lord, will you look on and do nothing? Psalm 35:17 NLT

It's a bit shocking to read these words and realize they were written by the psalmist. On the other hand, it is comforting to know that the writer shared a close enough relationship with God to feel okay with being honest and expressing his frustration.

Have you ever felt frustrated at God? I hope you answer that honestly. If you have ever prayed about anything, you know that not every prayer is answered in the way we would like. It also may not be answered according to our personal timetable.

In this Psalm, the writer is quick to also express his trust and respect for God. He also promises to praise him in front of the "great assembly." Finally in near desperation he cries out, "O Lord, you know all about this. Do not stay silent. Do not abandon me now, Lord."

These moments of personal struggle are not unlike what you may be feeling. It is really important to take note that while he is crying out in desperation, he also acknowledges that God knows all about it.

It's true. He knows all about it.

He knows what is going on in your life right now. He cares deeply about you. His view is far different than ours. You may be exhausted and think you can't go another day, but I encourage you to not give up. Cry out to God. Be honest about what you are feeling and thinking, but also be honest about who God really is and praise him even in the midst of your turmoil.

He loves you.

PRAYER

Dear God, I am at a loss for words. You know my heart. You know the thoughts that are running through my mind. Help me, Lord, please help me. When you are ready, work on my behalf. Until then I will trust you. Amen.

Let God Continue His Work

And I am certain that God, who began the good work within you, will continue his work until it is finally finished on the day when Christ Jesus returns. Philippians 1:6 NLT

Life is a journey that we all start with birth and finish with death. None of us knows when we will draw our final breath, but most of us live as though it is a long time away.

Christians or Christ-followers will approach life much differently. We have altered the pathway of our lives on this planet by giving ourselves over to following the Word of God and allowing God to guide our lives on a daily basis. This means simply that from the time of our spiritual birth, God begins a good work in us. This doesn't mean that we are perfect. It means that we are a work in progress. It means that as we follow him we learn how to really live. We learn how to put him first and to love our neighbors as ourselves. We learn the critical importance of practicing forgiveness, loving our enemies, caring for the poor, and standing for justice and peace.

Letting God work in us means that we will lean on God by praying and fasting. We will learn that money is not our security but that truly in God we should trust. By letting God continue his work we will bear spiritual fruit with our lives, and we will do to others what we would like them to do to us. We will share the good news and make disciples. With God's help we will build our lives on the solid rock of his Word.

So how are you doing? Better yet, how is God doing at continuing his good work in you? If you aren't so sure, maybe today is a good day for a reset. Make the necessary changes and allow God to start working on you and in you today. Don't allow anything or anyone to hinder God's work in you.

PRAYER

Dear God, more than anything, I need you and want you to work inside of me. Show me the way and give me the courage to follow you even when the world around me teaches me the exact opposite of your Word. Amen.

Why the Doubt?

Jesus immediately reached out and grabbed him. "You have so little faith," Jesus said. "Why did you doubt me?" Matthew 14:31 NLT

Peter saw Jesus walking on the water and asked to come to him by doing a little water walking of his own. He started out great but then started noticing things around him like strong winds and high waves. The Bible says "He was terrified and began to sink. 'Save me, Lord,' he shouted."

He actually did walk on the water. He did the unthinkable. Peter did what no one else other than Jesus has ever done. He had the faith to get out of the boat and to start toward Jesus, but something happened along the way.

In our Scripture today, I want to note three things:

- Jesus will save us even when we do dumb things.
- Sometimes we don't keep the faith we start out with.
- Jesus will always question why we don't trust him.

Walking on water is not something we should probably ask God to help us do; but Peter, being impulsive as he was, acted on a spur-of-the-moment thought. Jesus granted him permission even though the storm was raging and he knew he was likely to be overcome with fear. As our text says, "Jesus immediately reached out and grabbed him."

There are times when we may feel strong in our faith, but I need to remind you that faith should never be based on feeling. Faith should be based on fact. The fact is God is God; and if you are following him, your faith can and should be strong. When faith is based on feelings, we are liable to lose our faith when predictably fickle feelings come and go. You don't want to hear Jesus say, "You have so little faith."

When you put into context who God is, who Jesus is, and the promised abiding presence of the Holy Spirit, our faith should never waver. You are backed by the Father, Son, and Holy Spirit. You have the ability to talk to them every day. You and I can express our fears, our dreams and hopes, our anxieties, and our needs to a God that knows, sees, hears, and cares. Our goal is not to walk on water but to pass the tests of this life by keeping our faith strong no matter what may be happening around us. Open the Bible and let God's Word live in you. You may not walk on water, but you will know his abiding presence in both life and death.

PRAYER

Dear Jesus, as you rescued Peter from drowning on that day, please reach out to me today. I need you to grab my hand and pull me close to you. Help me live by faith and not by emotions or feelings. Amen.

Good Suffering

For God called you to do good, even if it means suffering, just as Christ suffered for you. 1 Peter 2:21 NLT

Nobody signs up for suffering, and yet it is a vital part of our lives. Peter is reminding us here that even while suffering we can still do good. This can be quite a challenge if one's heart and life is not surrendered to the Christ who was the great example of doing good while suffering.

While dying a horrible and dreaded death on the cross, Jesus was mindful of those killing him and asked that God would forgive them for what they were doing because of their ignorance. He also wasn't so preoccupied with his circumstances that he couldn't take time to promise the thief hanging beside him eternal life.

Perhaps the most touching scene was Jesus asking the apostle John to take care of Mary, his mother. Was he in pain? Without question he was. Was he suffering? Probably from head to foot and internally as he was gasping for breath and calling for a drink.

And yet, he did good to those around him. I don't know what you are walking through today or what I will walk through in the future, but I hope I am so locked in to Jesus that I always remember to do good. Peter is here suggesting that sometimes doing good itself will bring suffering our way. Jesus is always the example. Read about him. Study his life. Talk with him daily. The more we know him the more we can be like him.

PRAYER

Dear Jesus, give me the strength to face suffering with your grace and peace. Let me find good to do even though things are so different now. Don't let me give up or live in bitterness. Make me better. I pray in your name. Amen.

No Complaints Here

Now when the people complained, it displeased the LORD; for the LORD heard it, and His anger was aroused. Numbers 11:1 NKJV

It was not an uncommon sound in the days of Moses' leadership. God was busy rescuing the Israelites and leading them through Moses; but grumbling and complaining were far too common, and God heard it. Eventually, he reached the end of his patience.

I wonder how many times in my life I invest my emotional energy in grumbling and complaining. Even if I never share it with anyone else, how much of a toll does it take on my life and emotional health? How does my negativity affect my relationships?

There are things in life that we don't like. There may even be people we don't care for, and this may lead us to think and even speak negative thoughts. If we are not careful, we can get into a habit of complaining that is subtle. We may not have any self-awareness about it. Use today to think about your words and speech. Think about the conversations you've had recently. Are they negative or positive?

What about your conversations with God? Most people complain to God about life and eventually just stop talking to him. Even if life is not what you want it to be, don't stop talking to God. Determine that you won't be like the Israelites who forgot how much God had done for them and was doing for them. Consequently, they fell into a horrible habit of murmuring and complaining. Tell God how much you love and trust him today. In spite of what is going on around you, never quit being thankful for the life you have and for the love of a wonderful Savior.

PRAYER

Dear God, I get it. No one wants to be around a complainer, but we all like to complain. Thank you for your patience and love. I ask for your help in maintaining a positive attitude all day today. Thanks in advance. Amen.

Who Are You Searching For?

Search for the LORD and for his strength; continually seek him.
Psalm 105:4 NLT

What a wonderful reminder and admonition. Never stop seeking and searching for God in your life. Make it a lifelong journey and priority. We know that great challenges will sometimes enter our lives and cause us to doubt or feel discouragement. Too often our first reaction is to stir up our own strength to handle what has come our way. We may be successful at first; but we are only human, and eventually we will come to realize that it may be too big for us to handle.

I would encourage you not to wait till your strength is exhausted! Search for God every day in your life and you will find him. When you are connecting with him daily and things enter your life that call for great strength, your first reaction will not be to think of your own abilities, but you will seek for God's help in the beginning.

Putting God first is more than a positive suggestion. Searching and seeking for God is life-giving, life-sustaining, and faith building. God longs to hear from you and will not play hide and seek. Press in daily as close as you can to the presence of Jesus. Open his Word. Call on him in prayer. He will answer, and he will be a real friend that "sticks closer than a brother."

PRAYER

Dear Lord, please help me to never stop searching for you. Life is so full of distractions, but keep me from allowing them to interrupt my time with you. Amen.

In the Secret Place

Pray to your Father who is in the secret place; and your Father who sees in secret will reward you openly. Matthew 6:6 NKJV

Jesus was teaching the disciples about prayer when he made this statement about the Father "who is in the secret place." This devotion is not so much about prayer, but I want to think for a moment about all the things that happen in secret in our lives.

Do you have secrets? Do you have things in your life that are only known to you? Would others be surprised to learn something about you that is protected by your secret place?

What we know from the Scripture is that God is everywhere. It's always fascinating when people go to great lengths to cover their actions or to hide them from others. The fact is that God sees it all, hears it all, and knows it all. We are also reminded in Luke 12:3 that, "Whatever you have said in the dark will be heard in the light, and what you have whispered behind closed doors will be shouted from the housetops for all to hear!" Most secrets surface eventually.

The notion that God is in the secret place will either provide you with comfort or conviction. Today is a good time to think about your secret place. Do you go there to connect with God or to protect your secret actions and thoughts? Let it bring you comfort! He is there. He is waiting to hear from you. Be honest. You've got nothing to hide and couldn't even if you wanted to. Next time you are alone remember you really aren't. God is in the secret place.

PRAYER

Dear God, may I always come to you in the secret place and not try to hide from you there. Help me to remember that wherever I go you are there. Let me come to you in secret and meet with you in openness and honesty. Amen.

What Kingdom Are You Living For?

He lived in alert expectation of the Kingdom of God. Luke 23:51 MSG

This statement found in Luke 23 was written about a man named Joseph. We learn about how he lived his life because this is the man that offered his own grave for the burial of Jesus after the crucifixion.

I paused when reading this passage of Scripture because I saw these powerful words: "He lived in alert expectation of the Kingdom of God." We should all be living that way.

The world that we live in is one MAJOR distraction after another. So many things take our minds away from Christ and what he is calling us to do and be.

On this day, resolve to be alert. Alert to God's voice gently nudging you from within to do the right thing. Alert to the needs of those around you that may be going through very deep and challenging situations. Alert to what God wants to do with you today, with your words and actions.

Be intentional about your service in the kingdom of God. He is relying on you to be his hands and feet. He will use you to bless and help others if you are living in expectation of his presence every day.

Make the most of today! Do it for Jesus' sake and in his name. There is no better way to live than serving in the kingdom of God on this tragic and broken planet.

PRAYER

Dear God, I know you want men and women to work for you and to do your work. If I can do anything for you today, I hope you find me ready and willing. Amen.

Don't Let the Fire Go Out

Remember, the fire must be kept burning on the altar at all times. It must never go out. Leviticus 6:13 NLT

These two sentences are found in the Old Testament instructions given by God to Moses. Moses then passed them on to Aaron and his sons. It was important, apparently, that the fire on God's altar was never allowed to go out.

As I read these words, I felt their importance; but in my life, I don't have a real fire burning on an altar somewhere. Right?

For those of us reading this today, the fire of God should be burning on our hearts, and we should never let it go out. When our spiritual fire diminishes or goes out, we become vulnerable to the influences around us.

Do whatever you need to do to keep God's fire burning hot in your soul. Avoid anything that would suppress it in your life. Stay away from relationships that will pull you away from God's perfect plan. His fire burning in your soul will allow you to think clearly and make good choices. His fire will keep impurity from becoming a part of our life.

Fuel his fire by the Word, prayer, and worship. Practice it all day long, and stoke your spiritual fire by using the right kind of fuel. I hope this day the fire is burning in your heart and soul.

PRAYER

Dear God, please let your fire burn in my life so that there is nothing between us. Let the words of my mouth and the meditations of my heart be acceptable to you. Amen.

We All Have a Work to Finish

"My food," said Jesus, "is to do the will of him who sent me and to finish his work." John 4:34 NIV

The disciples had just returned from a trip to town to buy food, and they returned to find Jesus talking to a Samaritan woman. Not just any woman, but a woman with a very broken story and life. The disciples were taught from the time they were young Jewish kids to look down on the Samaritans. They arrived just in time to see and hear a small part of the encounter. Their first pathetic question was, "Why are you talking with her?"

These were the disciples Jesus was training to someday take over and share the good news of the gospel, but they sure needed a lot more of his grace. When finally offered food, he gave the response that is our Scripture for the day.

Jesus is now depending on us to finish the work that he started. He gave all of us the same commission. We were to be about the business of going wherever we had to go to make disciples, baptize them, teach them to obey what he said and to know that he would be with us in spirit every step of the way.

It is a struggle to put God first in our everyday lives. It takes effort and intentionality. You have to want to do his will. Like the first disciples, most of us rarely miss a meal. Our bodies and brains begin to tell us that we are hungry, and most of us find a way to take care of it. Why not try to see what God sees in the people around you today? Why not try to hear what he hears as the people around you share parts of their lives? It might be at work, the gas station, or the grocery store, but there are hurting people everywhere. Who will tell them about Jesus? Who will tell them about the everlasting water that quenches the thirst of the soul? Maybe today, God will give you a chance to eat the food that he desires most.

Dear Jesus, please allow me to follow your example and to share the good news with someone today. I know that all around me, every day, there are people in need. We often just talk about the weather or something less important. Help me to share what you have done for me. Amen.

Leading Forward

It was the transition period shortly after the death of Israel's legendary leader Moses. A young man named Joshua was to take his place. It was a formidable task. The past had some major wins but it also had some losses. Moses learned to be a great leader, but he also made plenty of mistakes; and yet Joshua was now standing on the brink of leading into the future.

Here are some thoughts from this story:

It is not wrong to acknowledge the past.

God acknowledged the past but didn't dwell there. Moses was the Lord's servant, but his time had ended and now it was time for a new leader. We should know the past history so we don't repeat the mistakes of the past. Appreciate the past and prepare to lead today!

After the death of Moses the Lord's servant, the Lord spoke to Joshua son of Nun, Moses' assistant. He said, "Moses my servant is dead. Therefore, the time has come for you to lead these people, the Israelites, across the Jordan River into the land I am giving them." Joshua 1:1-1-2 NLT

Focus on the present hour.

Now's the time! There's no time to rest on the heady days of past successes. Those days were great, but they are over. It's time to move on.

Joshua then commanded the officers of Israel, "Go through the camp and tell the people to get their provisions ready. In three days you will cross the Jordan River and take possession of the land the Lord your God is giving you." (Joshua 1:10-11 NLT)

What needs to be done today? What moves can you make to align yourself closer to God's will for your life? What would you do if you knew you wouldn't fail? Israel had been camped there for forty years and now it is time to go!

Anticipate the future.

God said, "I promise you what I promised Moses: 'Wherever you set foot, you will be on land I have given you....' No one will be able to stand against you as long as you live. For I will be with you as I was with Moses.

I will not fail you or abandon you. Be strong and courageous, for you are the one who will lead these people to possess all the land I swore to their ancestors I would give them. Be strong and very courageous. Do not be afraid or discouraged. For the Lord your God is with you wherever you go." (Joshua 1:3,4,6,7,9 NLT)

The present is only a time for transition. What we do today is always about the future and looking forward. Let God give you the courage to lead in the direction he is going.

PRAYER

Dear God, change is scary. Leading through change can be a hard road to navigate. The promise of your presence is helpful and comforting. Your promises are life changing. Thank you. Amen.

Servant Leaders

We who are strong must be considerate of those who are sensitive about things like this. We must not just please ourselves. We should help others do what is right and build them up in the Lord. For even Christ didn't live to please himself. As the Scriptures say, "The insults of those who insult you, O God, have fallen on me." Such things were written in the Scriptures long ago to teach us. And the Scriptures give us hope and encouragement as we wait patiently for God's promises to be fulfilled. May God, who gives this patience and encouragement, help you live in complete harmony with each other, as is fitting for followers of Christ Jesus. Then all of you can join together with one voice, giving praise and glory to God, the Father of our Lord Jesus Christ. Romans 15:1-6 NLT

A large part of being a Christian leader is learning to serve others. It is developing one's own gifts and strengths so that he or she may serve others and lead them to a better place. What are some characteristics of a servant leader based on this Scripture? We should practice or possess the following:

Self –Denial: *We must not just please ourselves.* People who lead others will also find that at times they have to sacrifice their wants and needs to be available to serve others.

Sharing: *We should help others do what is right and build them up in the Lord.* Sharing our knowledge with those around us will only make us more secure in our leadership role. Leaders that hang onto perceived power and position are generally not functioning at a very high level of leadership.

Strength: *For even Christ didn't live to please himself.* This strength is to be found in Christ as we remember his model of taking the insults of others directed at God. A godly leader will not have thin skin but will bear mistreatment with an eye toward forgiveness first.

Studious: *Such things were written in the Scriptures long ago to teach us.* We should always be learning and teachable. No matter how old or how long we have been around, there are always new things to learn.

Spiritual: *May God, who gives this patience and encouragement, help*

you live in complete harmony with each other, as is fitting for followers of Christ Jesus. Spiritual means simply that you follow Christ in your relationships with others. You love like Jesus. You are kind and considerate. You are filled with God's Spirit, and this allows you to lead the way in harmony and peace (most of the time).

"The way of the Christian leader is not the way of upward mobility in which our world has invested so much, but the way of downward mobility ending on the cross." —Henri J. M. Nouwen, *In the Name of Jesus: Reflections on Christian Leadership*

PRAYER

Dear Jesus, please help me lead and love like you. You put others first. You served without hesitation. May I be a reflection of you today. Amen.

Even Though

*Even though the fig trees have no blossoms, and there are no grapes
on the vines; even though the olive crop fails, and the fields lie empty and barren; even though the flocks die in the fields, and the cattle barns are empty, yet I will rejoice in the Lord! I will be joyful in
the God of my salvation!* Habakkuk 3:17-18 NLT

This classic Old Testament statement of confidence and trust in God
comes at the end of a book lamenting the suffering and bondage of
being in captivity. There is no question that the prophet Habakkuk had
some big questions for God.

It is natural to assume that because you serve God faithfully, you will
receive special favor and avoid the suffering that others go through. As
Eugene Peterson wrote, "It is not unreasonable to expect that from the
time that I become a follower, I will be exempt from dead ends, mud-
dy detours, and cruel treatment from the travelers I meet daily who are
walking the other direction. That God followers don't get preferential
treatment in life always comes as a surprise. But it's also a surprise to
find that there are a few men and women within the Bible that show up
alongside us at such moments."

Habakkuk is one of them. He knew suffering, hunger, and loss. He
cried out to God for relief and help. At one point, he even cried out,
"God, you don't even seem to make sense." Finally, in abandonment to
God's will and mercy, he cries out the words of our Scripture today. It is
a moment of great surrender and a profession of love for God no matter
what.

Maybe today you are feeling a little like Habakkuk. You have cried
and prayed. You have fasted and begged God for the answer you feel you
want and need. But it hasn't come. I encourage you to read this prayer
that the prophet wrote and mean it from your heart. It's big! Don't pray
it lightly; but if you are in a place of desperation, remind God that no
matter what happens or doesn't happen, you will trust him with your
life. Even if you die in the process, you will go into eternity trusting and
praising God. You will find joy in him when it is nowhere else.

PRAYER

Dear God. You know. You know it all, and you know my heart's cry to you today. I want the answer I want. I want things to go the way I think they should go; but today, Lord, I will love you even if there is no answer. I will find joy in you today because of the salvation I have through you. I am weak; please give me strength. Amen.

Choices Matter ... A Lot

So now I declare that I will no longer drive out the people living in your land. They will be thorns in your sides, and their gods will be a constant temptation to you. Judges 2:3 NLT

This is God speaking to Joshua and the people of Israel after they didn't completely obey his orders to destroy the altars of the false gods in the lands they were conquering.

We should find it noteworthy that our obedience matters to God. Always has and always will. When we choose to live lives of disobedience to God and his Word, we are taking on much more than most of us realize. We are opening ourselves up to less of his protection and presence.

In this case, he said the consequences of their disobedience would be the constant temptation to stray toward other gods. If they would have obeyed his commands, this would have not been the case at all. Who wants or needs more temptation?

I am left to wonder what effect the choices I make today will have on my faith moving forward. It is apparently true that my choices and actions matter way beyond the present. There are always consequences. Even though there may be forgiveness and redemption, there will still be consequences that may affect our lives moving forward.

Embrace obedience today. Love God with all your heart, mind, soul, and strength and do it in word, thought, and deed.

PRAYER

Dear God, help me to understand how much my decisions affect my life moving forward. Give me the desire and strength to always choose you in every area of my life. Help be to obey your Word always. Amen.

What Is That to You?

Jesus replied, "If I want him to remain alive until I return, what is that to you? As for you, follow me." So the rumor spread among the community of believers that this disciple wouldn't die. But that isn't what Jesus said at all. He only said, "If I want him to remain alive until I return, what is that to you? John 21:22-23 NLT

What a picture of human nature. Jealousy, gossip, and misinformation all in one biblical narrative. Jesus had just told the disciple Peter how he was going to die because he was a follower. When Peter saw John, he asked, "What about him?" Jesus quickly put Peter in his place.

It seems strange to hear Jesus ask this question. Someone might be tempted to think it was a bit snarky toward Peter, but clearly a message was sent and received.

In our walk with Jesus, the best thing we can do is to pay attention to our own spiritual journey and relationship. Jesus has a plan for all of our lives that is unique to us. Playing the comparison game is an exercise in frustration and futility.

Do you ever compare yourself to other Christians? Do you ever wonder why something happened to you but not to them? When we truly trust Jesus we won't be inclined to ask questions like this. I would not want to hear Jesus say to me, "What is that to you?" Stay in your lane. Focus on your own faith walk. Love Jesus daily with all of your heart, mind, soul, and strength. Ask God to show you how to grow in maturity with him.

PRAYER

Dear Jesus, I am probably guilty of this sometimes. It's so easy to compare myself and my life with others. Deliver me from making this a habit, and please give me the grace to walk the walk you have laid out for me. Amen.

Wholehearted Devotion

Then Solomon stood before the altar of the LORD in front of the entire community of Israel. He lifted his hands toward heaven, and he prayed, "O LORD, God of Israel, there is no God like you in all of heaven above or on the earth below. You keep your covenant and show unfailing love to all who walk before you in wholehearted devotion. 1 Kings 8:22-23 NLT

It was a very significant day when King Solomon offered this prayer. After many years and much planning, the Jewish Temple was finally built and ready for use. These were the opening lines of the dedication service.

As I read these lines, I couldn't help but think of Jesus' work on the cross as he cried, "It is finished," and the curtain in the temple was torn in two. This event opened up our ability to come to God anytime and anywhere. We can now celebrate the priesthood of believers. Jesus is our High Priest and he is praying for us every day as he is seated at the right hand of the Father.

Out of Solomon's words come these two facts about God. He keeps his covenants and he shows unfailing love. Of course, the king also says God does this for the people who walk before him in wholehearted devotion. Today I am examining myself to see about my devotion to God. There is no substitute for wholehearted devotion; it is all or nothing. God is faithful in his promises to us, and his unfailing love is legendary. Walk in them today. Walk wholeheartedly before him.

PRAYER

Dear God, I acknowledge your faithfulness. I have experienced your unfailing love. May my days on this earth be given to you with wholehearted devotion and commitment. Amen.

Power and Love

Please, Lord, prove that your power is as great as you have claimed.
Numbers 14:17 NLT

This prayer was prayed by Moses and was a plea for God to keep his word regarding forgiving the people of Israel for their sins. There are times in our lives when we may need to be this bold with God. Moses, of course, always demonstrated great respect for God and his presence, but he also was willing to plead and bargain with God when desperate.

Is there some situation in your life currently that you need for God to show his mighty power? In this request, Moses also reminds God of his unfailing love. In fact, he refers to it as "Your magnificent unfailing love."

God's love for us is indeed magnificent. We should work hard to never forget it; and when we are struggling because it seems that he is not answering our prayer, we need to remind ourselves of his love. It is unfailing.

Even when life deals us tragedy and heartbreak, we remember his unfailing love. We will have grief; we will experience sickness and even pain, but none of it changes his power or unfailing love. Draw close to the Lord today. Overcome your hesitancy. He wants to hear from you. Ask him to rise up and work on your behalf.

PRAYER

Dear Lord, please do your work today in my life. I believe that you are all powerful and can do anything. If it is in your will, show that power. If not, please give me your powerful presence and grace. Amen.

Avoiding Generational Loss

After that generation died, another generation grew up who did not acknowledge the LORD or remember the mighty things he had done for Israel. Judges 2:10 NLT

It's a thing. Generational loss in the business world is predictable. In fact, only 12% of family businesses survive into a third generation, and a mere 3% make it to the fourth, according to the Family Business Institute.

So too, denominations, churches, and even Christian families can experience generational loss. This verse describes what happened after all the amazing things God did for Israel. The context is shortly after the death of Joshua. He was a brave and effective leader, but somehow the people failed to share God's story with the younger generations.

In businesses, the loss is because by the third generation all the sacrifices and hard work have generally been accomplished. Third generations just enjoy the money and usually spend it without doing the work it takes to replenish it.

In the spiritual realm, we must never quit working to keep our hearts and relationship with God fresh and new. Children will want very little to do with their parents' God if their relationship is not dynamic and authentic. Just taking kids to church will do very little to pass on your faith to them.

Work hard to keep them in the Bible. Show them how to study it. Read it with them. Tell them and remind them often of the things God has done in your family. Encourage them to read or study the lives of Christians through whom God did amazing things. When walking through deep waters as a family, include God in the middle of it. Make him the focus. Pray with them and for them. Ask God to help you pass on the message of the gospel to your children. Don't let them forget the mighty things God has done.

PRAYER

Dear God, help me to always be willing to share your story with others. It may not be just my kids but even with the kids at the church. Let my life help them to realize what and who you are. Amen.

Obey God's Word

But don't just listen to God's word. You must do what it says. Otherwise, you are only fooling yourselves. For if you listen to the word and don't obey, it is like glancing at your face in a mirror. You see yourself, walk away, and forget what you look like. James 1:22-24 NLT

Self-awareness is an awesome gift if you have it. Most of us struggle with being aware of who we really are. Life is filled with distractions that keep our minds and souls from engaging very deeply in most things.

Sometimes as a filter for life, people will binge watch TV or movies, hoping to quiet the noise and pain that is all around them. This is a Band-Aid at best. What the writer is calling us to in these verses is much deeper and takes time to listen and learn.

Could it be that God actually expects us to do what he says? While there are theological persuasions that suggest this is impossible, I find it hard to believe that God would spend so much time in the Bible calling us to obedience if it is impossible.

The only hope we have for obedience to God's Word daily is to truly embrace what it says and pray that he will help us obey it. It means taking time to read it and think about it. Pray about it. Mediate on it. If you see that God is calling you to something, don't just read it and move on. Process it, internalize it, and make it a priority. Never forget what your soul looks like. Stay in tune and touch with your spiritual life. Be an open book before God. Wake up yearning for God and go to sleep making him the last thoughts on your mind and heart.

To obey God is always best.

PRAYER

Dear God, there is nothing I want to do more than obey you. Help me overcome my human struggles and not use my humanity as an excuse or crutch to justify sin in my life. Deliver me, O Lord, like you did for Daniel in the lion's den or the three Hebrew boys in the fiery furnace. I want to be yours completely all day, every day. Amen.

Perfect Love

God is love, and all who live in love live in God, and God lives in them. And as we live in God, our love grows more perfect. So we will not be afraid on the day of judgment, but we can face him with confidence because we live like Jesus here in this world. 1 John 4:16-17 NLT

"God is love," are three words we should never forget. These verses, however, don't stop there. We are reminded that all of us that love, do so because we live in God and he lives in us. Love is something that all of us desire and want to feel or experience. Love is more than emotion because as Christians we are instructed to love the unlovable or our enemies.

The writer really brings his thoughts to a startling conclusion when he ties our loving others on this earth with standing before God at the judgment. We will be able to stand before him without fear because we have lived like Jesus here in this world.

I find this very challenging and difficult in these days. As I write this devotion, we are experiencing lawlessness, looting, rioting, and fear-mongering at a level unseen in recent decades. I wonder what I would do if I came face to face with people whose behavior I find unacceptable or who threaten my life, and yet here we are faced with the call to love like Jesus.

John suggests that as we "live in God" our love will grow more and more perfect. God always has to be the focus or we will fail in our own strength to love with a Jesus level love.

PRAYER

Dear Jesus, oh how I want to be more like you in this area of my life. I don't want to love those that have hurt me or forsaken me, and yet I know what you want from me. Please give me grace today to allow you to love others through me. Amen.

Feeling Abandoned?

Do not abandon me, O LORD. Do not stand at a distance, my God. Come quickly to help me, O Lord my savior. Psalm 38:21-22 NLT

This prayer of desperation is not something we would pray every day of our lives. Obviously, the psalmist is struggling and needs help. Do you ever feel abandoned by God? Do you ever feel as though he is standing at a distance? I think if we are honest, all of us have felt that from time to time.

These are dangerous moments simply because it is easy to slip into a negative mindset about God and his care for us. We may be tempted to listen to the enemy of our souls when suggestions are whispered into our hearts that God really doesn't care and may not even be real.

Push ahead by faith. Declare your confidence in God no matter what may or may not be happening around you. Read the Word even more than you normally do and let it speak to your soul. Write down how you feel or journal even if it is just for this season. The psalmist declared his faith with these simple words, "Come quickly to help me, O Lord my Savior."

He is still your Lord and Savior. He is still the one who brought you this far. He is not dead. He is not asleep. He knows exactly where you are and what is happening. He will not abandon you or forsake you. The fact that you may not see him or feel him is irrelevant. He is here. He is with you now. He loves you completely.

PRAYER

Dear God, you are my Lord. You are my Savior. I will not run from you but to you all the days of my life. Today, Lord, I am leaning into you with all my being. I will trust you. Amen.

The Bottom Line

The words of the wise are like cattle prods—painful but helpful. Their collected sayings are like a nail-studded stick with which a shepherd drives the sheep. But, my child, let me give you some further advice: Be careful, for writing books is endless, and much study wears you out. That's the whole story. Here now is my final conclusion: Fear God and obey his commands, for this is everyone's duty. God will judge us for everything we do, including every secret thing, whether good or bad. Ecclesiastes 12:11-14 NLT

Most of us like hearing the bottom line, especially if we are being fed copious amounts of information and data. At some point, we will say, "Just give me the bottom line."

The writer of Ecclesiastes spends a lot of time philosophizing about life and death. He writes of seasons and times. Times for death, life, mourning, and rejoicing. He speaks of vanity and futility, and then he gets to the bottom line.

The verses above are indeed the bottom line.

There are lots of self-help opportunities, and volumes of books and writings promoting guidance and directions for our lives. They may even wear us out, but God has given us the secret to living a great life on this earth and an even better life in eternity.

The question is, are you and I willing to put God first? Here it is: "Fear God and obey his commands, for this is everyone's duty. God will judge us for everything we do, including every secret thing, whether good or bad."

This is so simple and yet it is deeply profound. It's like saying, "I love you" to someone. It's very easy to say and much harder to live out. May God enable us to fear (reverence) God and obey him daily. Even God said, "Obedience is better than sacrifice." He has always wanted a people who will follow him with their whole heart.

PRAYER

Dear God, I love you and I want to follow you with my whole heart. May it ever be so, and especially today, please give me the help I need to obey you in word, thought, and deed. Amen.

God Thinks About You

"My thoughts are nothing like your thoughts," says the Lord. "And my ways are far beyond anything you could imagine. For just as the heavens are higher than the earth, so my ways are higher than your ways and my thoughts higher than your thoughts." Isaiah 55:8-9 NLT

Do you ever wonder what God is thinking? Maybe you wonder what he is thinking about our world or even about your life. We should remind ourselves that his thoughts are different from our own.

Isaiah 55 is filled with invitations. Invitations to come and quench your spiritual thirst, come and listen with ears wide open, seek the Lord while you can find him, and call on him while he is near. These invites come from God through the prophet Isaiah. He is calling us to come close to him and spend our time and efforts on seeking to know him.

The call and invitation is to trust in God and understand that the closer you stay to him the better your life will be. This is not promising health and wealth as we often understand or desire it, but the promise of his presence. It is in him that we find our breath, faith, stamina, and the strength to persevere. It is in him that we find a rock of deliverance to stand on when the storms of life are blowing.

Stay close to his Word. Trust his thoughts about you to be in your best interest.

"How precious are your thoughts about me, O God. They cannot be numbered!" (Psalm 139:17 NLT).

PRAYER

Dear Lord, thank you for thinking of me with good thoughts. Thank you for thinking of me at all. Even when I don't understand what you may be thinking, help me to trust you and believe in you. Amen.

True Freedom

So if the Son sets you free, you are truly free. John 8:36 NLT

Freedom is a precious gift that some people never experience. It is wonderful to live in a country that enjoys freedom, but not even that compares with the freedom we find in Jesus Christ. Men and women around the world live in hostile or repressive societies but enjoy the personal freedom they find in Jesus. We can be truly free!

There is a big "if" in this Scripture. Presidents, kings, and even armies can't really and truly set us free. Only the Son can give us the freedom our soul needs.

Do you need to be set free from something or even someone today? Start with Jesus. If the Son sets you free you will truly be free! What place does Jesus hold in your life today? He is your Savior and Lord, or is he just someone you appeal to when life is falling apart. Is he your daily love and guide, or is he just someone you think about mostly on the Sabbath?

If he sets you free, he will be so much more in your life.

Allow him. Give him permission to set you free.

PRAYER

Dear Jesus, freedom is so hard to come by. Everywhere I turn I seem to be accountable to someone else. Let me live free because you make me free. Amen.

When God Gets Busy

God has rolled up his sleeves. Isaiah 52:10

When God "makes bare his arm" in the Bible it means he is about to get to work on something or he is bringing judgment. When God stops to help me, the image of him rolling up his sleeves takes me back to a different time and place.

When I was a teenager, much of my work included working for local farmers. I loved it but it was often very hard work. There is nothing quite like making hay or putting up hay on a hot mid-summer day. I remember working on a farm for a man whose father was still alive but in his later years. I can still see him in a long sleeve shirt, straw hat, and bib overalls working along with the rest of us to handle bales and endure the sun. At some point throughout the day there was a chance he might roll up his sleeves; although if it happened at all, it would be long after I would have rolled them up. This image sticks in my mind.

I love the fact that God will get down to business on our behalf. He will roll up his sleeves and get to work. Sometimes I even ask him to do this in my prayer. I don't ask lightly because I know this action is reserved for rare moments of great need.

Maybe you need to think about this image today. Allow God to work for you in your life. His strength is incomparable. His devotion and love are incomprehensible. He might just be rolling them up now for you.

PRAYER

Dear God, I love this. I love the thought of having a Father who will do whatever he needs to do to take care of me. I trust you, Lord, with my life and future. Amen.

Sin Is Never a Forever Secret

But if you fail to keep your word, then you will have sinned against the LORD, and you may be sure that your sin will find you out.
Numbers 32:23 NLT

Moses spoke these words to some Jewish men who wanted to build pens for their livestock and protection for their wives and families. The only problem with this is that they were still living out God's punishment in the wilderness. They were ordered to keep moving until God named the time and the place for them to settle down.

Now they were faced with fighting for the promised land. They could see it. Some of their friends and fellow countrymen were already engaged in fighting for it. These men decided they would be happy to just go ahead and settle down near the "promised land" instead of following God's command to go possess it.

Moses tells them in so many words that they could choose to do that but it would be disobeying what God had commanded for his people to do. It is in that context that Moses reminds them that "your sin will find you out."

Sin always finds us out. No matter how well we think it is hidden or how good we have become at masking over the reality, it will eventually become known. This word of warning to these brothers that were going to settle for less than God's best is just as timely for us today.

Don't let anything or anyone separate you from your faith. Keep your word with the Lord. If you have failed already, confess it and accept his loving forgiveness. Learn from it. Let God use it to draw you closer to him. Even failure can bring us closer to God if we don't shut him out.

PRAYER

Dear Lord, you know the power of sin and the temptations that lure me to go my own way. Sometimes it just seems the easiest thing to do; but Lord, please keep me focused on you, and don't let me fail you on my journey. Amen.

Drinking Living Water

But those who drink the water I give will never be thirsty again. It becomes a fresh, bubbling spring within them, giving them eternal life. John 4:14 NLT

Jesus said these words to a woman with a lot of sin in her life. She was broken and no doubt filled with guilt and shame as she came to a well to draw water. She was a Samaritan, and Jews had very little to do with Samaritans; so she had to be shocked to find Jesus, a Jew, even at this well and engaging her in conversation.

When I read this story and hear both conviction and compassion in the words of Jesus, I am again reminded of just who he is and who he wants to be in our lives. Of course, I have no idea what has happened in your life or what is happening as you read this. I do know there is a lot of brokenness in people's lives. Some of it is private and some is public. Regardless, the pain is still real. There may be shame, guilt, anger, and even bitterness that has built up inside of you. You may wonder what you did to deserve to be in this place, or you may know exactly why you are in this place.

As you read this today, try to hear Jesus speaking these life-giving words to you. Drink the water of salvation and forgiveness that he offers. Bow down, humble yourself, and cry out to him. What would your life be if this "fresh, bubbling spring" were within you? There is nothing he wants to give you more than eternal life.

PRAYER

Dear Jesus, you know how much I need you today. I am coming to you and asking that you free me from this burden I am carrying. Please give me a drink of your living water. In your name I pray. Amen.

Nailed to the Cross

Those who belong to Christ Jesus have nailed the passions and desires of their sinful nature to his cross and crucified them there.
Galatians 5:24 NLT

I just keep reading the words that the apostle Paul wrote, and I keep thinking of times I have struggled with the passions and desires of the sinful nature. It's not that we have to struggle, but we often do I am afraid. Why is this?

According to the Scripture, those of us that belong to Christ will nail these passions and desires to his cross and crucify them there. Have you ever thought about having a crucifixion? If you are struggling with your flesh in some way and feel like you are losing, maybe visually take your sins to his cross. Nail them there, and then stay until they are dead. I think maybe we don't stay long enough when we give things like this to God.

I love this language and the action it calls for. Nail them and crucify them. Go the whole way. Hold nothing back; and when the crucifixion is over, symbolically bury whatever is left. You can live in victory and in sweet and unbroken communion with the Lord by way of the cross.

PRAYER

Dear Jesus, there is nothing hidden from you. You know everything about my life. You know my victories and my struggles. Give me the courage to nail and crucify all that offends you. Amen.

Hate Never Wins

Hatred stirs up quarrels, but love makes up for all offenses. Proverbs 10:12 NLT

Hate is such a strong emotion, especially when it is directed toward another person. When we indulge in this emotion, it has a great negative affect on our own emotional and possibly even physical health.

Hatred certainly stirs up quarrels and divides us—sometimes from the people we should love the most. We basically have two choices in this life: we can love or we can hate. One leads to strife and war and the other to peace and safety.

How are things in your soul today? Are you filled with love, or are you wrestling with hate? I watched a few minutes of a confirmation hearing for a Supreme Court Justice today and I could have easily slipped into partisan hatred because of the unfair things being spoken and the unfounded attacks that were being directed toward the nominee.

For Christians, hate is not an option.

Cultivate love today in your heart and soul. If there is someone you are struggling to love, intentionally pray for them today. It is hard to hate people that we take to God in prayer.

PRAYER

Dear God, I realize that hate is not an option, no matter how wronged I may feel. Give the strength to forgive and move forward. Help me even love my enemies. Amen.

The Fruit of the Spirit

But the Holy Spirit produces this kind of fruit in our lives: love, joy, peace, patience, kindness, goodness, faithfulness, gentleness, and self-control. There is no law against these things. Galatians 5:22-23 NLT

Over the next three days, we will look at the fruit of the Spirit that he produces in our lives. We will take the time to focus on three fruits a day. When we are surrendered to the Spirit of God, our lives will produce spiritual fruit that cannot be duplicated outside of the Spirit. Here are three to consider:

Love is the greatest of all according to the writer of 1 Corinthian 13. Humans cannot duplicate the kind of love the Holy Spirit produces in us. To love like Jesus requires his Spirit at work in our lives.

Joy is also something beyond the scope of our abilities. We search for happiness but often find it fleeting and fickle. Deep, abiding joy can only come from God, and it remains through every circumstance of life. We find joy in him.

Peace is the most sought after agreement in the world. Nations seek it, marriages want it, neighbors long for it; and yet without, God lasting peace is impossible.

As you pray for the Holy Spirit to produce these fruits in your life, go for the long ball. Don't settle for something manufactured by yourself. Allow the Spirit to have complete access to your heart and let him bear fruit through you.

PRAYER

Dear Jesus, love, joy, and peace are three things I need to exhibit in my life today. I ask for you to help me with each one and to bear these three things today in my interactions with others. Amen.

The Fruit of the Spirit

But the Holy Spirit produces this kind of fruit in our lives: love, joy, peace, patience, kindness, goodness, faithfulness, gentleness, and self-control. There is no law against these things. Galatians 5:22-23 NLT

Today we are looking at the second fruit that is offered to those who abide in the Holy Spirit. I hope that you are taking time to really think about these fruits and if they are being produced in your life.

Patience is something that we all deal with daily probably. I think we face the need for patience at work, at home, and anywhere we deal with the public. How patient are you with people that don't do what you want them to do?

Kindness is just that, kindness. It is easy to be kind to those we love or people showing us love; but oh, how it takes a move of God's Spirit to cause us to be kind to those we disagree with.

Goodness is a virtue and fruit we probably don't think a lot about, and yet we love to encounter people with goodness. They are just that. They are filled with goodness, and they are "good people."

As you pray today, may your heart be drawn to these fruits. May they bear in your life at work, home, and in public.

PRAYER

Dear Jesus, you know that I am not always a patient person. Please let the Holy Spirit fill me with his presence so that I am a patient person filled with kindness and goodness toward everyone I encounter today. Amen.

The Fruit of the Spirit

But the Holy Spirit produces this kind of fruit in our lives: love, joy, peace, patience, kindness, goodness, faithfulness, gentleness, and self-control. There is no law against these things. Galatians 5:22-23 NLT

These fruits of the Spirit are really a good self-evaluating tool to examine your faith and the consistency of your walk. Today we are looking at the last three mentioned in this Scripture. I love Paul's last statement that clearly states with maybe a hint of sarcasm, "There is no law against these things." For law keepers, here are some you don't have to worry about keeping.

Faithfulness to God is simply living consistently and faithfully in a way that you know pleases God. It's faithfulness to commitments made, promises given, and most of all faithfulness to God and his Word.

Gentleness reminds us that our attitude should be gentle toward everyone. This is difficult I will admit, but by God's Spirit you and I can do this. Remember, we can't control others' actions, but we are responsible for our reactions.

Self-control is unique because it contains the word "self." These fruits are fruits of the Spirit, but you and I must exercise our own will to control ourselves and let God's Spirit work in our lives.

PRAYER

Dear Jesus, please bear the fruit of love, joy, peace, patience, kindness, goodness, faithfulness, gentleness, and self-control in my life. Holy Spirit, move through me, change me, and make me available to bear these fruits as needed. Amen.

Your Reasonable Service

I beseech you therefore, brethren, by the mercies of God, that ye present your bodies a living sacrifice, holy, acceptable unto God, which is your reasonable service. And be not conformed to this world: but be ye transformed by the renewing of your mind, that ye may prove what is that good, and acceptable, and perfect, will of God. Romans 12:1-2 KJV

And so, dear brothers and sisters, I plead with you to give your bodies to God because of all he has done for you. Let them be a living and holy sacrifice—the kind he will find acceptable. This is truly the way to worship him. Don't copy the behavior and customs of this world, but let God transform you into a new person by changing the way you think. Then you will learn to know God's will for you, which is good and pleasing and perfect. Romans 12:1-2 NLT

I am including two different versions of these verses for very personal reasons. It was these verses read in a King James Version of the Bible that spoke very personally and loudly to me as a teenager. They challenged me and called to me at the same time. By this time in my life, I had heard thousands of sermons and hundreds of personal testimonies as well as sat through hundreds of Sunday school classes. For whatever reason, at seventeen, these words, "it is your reasonable service," resonated with me. I had been to an altar many times as a kid after a heart-searching sermon, but this was different. This felt like the writer was just conversing with me and inviting me to follow Christ with all of my heart; and by the way, it wasn't an unreasonable ask. It was my reasonable service.

Later I came to learn that this was a classic and prolific call to follow Jesus—to worship him with my life. I was to turn from this world and all of its brokenness and follow Jesus all the way to eternity and the kingdom of God.

I wonder who may be reading this and down deep you feel a longing to know that you are following him the way he wants you to. You have forsaken this world and all of its allurement in favor of following Jesus.

In the NLT, we find the answer to our human condition: "But let God transform you into a new person by changing the way you think. Then you will learn to know God's will for you, which is good and pleasing and perfect."

I am praying for you as I write this devotion. I am praying that these words will call you to Jesus in a new and vibrant way.

PRAYER

Dear Jesus, how thankful I am for this invitation. Please transform me by the renewing of my mind. Let me always know and want your good, acceptable, and perfect will. Amen.

He Is Close

The Lord is good, a strong refuge when trouble comes. He is close to those who trust in him. Nahum 1:7 NLT

Where do you go when you are seeking a refuge? I've known people who have a physical place or prayer area set up so they can always pray in a familiar place. Some may take a drive in their vehicle and find a safe place there with no one else around.

I don't know about you, but when I need a place of refuge, or trouble has come, it's not about place for me, it's about presence. God doesn't have any actual forts or bullet and bomb proof shelters, but he is the actual fortress. It is in him that I find my protection. It is in his presence that I can feel secure.

When you trust him, you will find him to be close. As I am writing this today, I am aware of friends with great struggles going on at this moment. One is waiting on a call from the doctor regarding a cancer scan, and another is waiting to see her husband who has been in the hospital for nearly thirty days without access to family and friends. The news has the potential to be negative every day. Emotions run high and fear is often way too near.

Press in close to Jesus. Call out to him. Take time to be quiet and listen for his voice of refuge deep in your soul. Run to him. Be aware of his presence because this presence is your refuge and place of safety.

PRAYER

Dear God, who else do I have to run to for refuge but you? As good as my family and friends may be, it is you, Lord, that provides me the safety I need and long for. Please don't ever take your presence from me. Amen.

I Will Follow

Since we are living by the Spirit, let us follow the Spirit's leading in every part of our lives. Galatians 5:25 NLT

What a great goal! When is the last time you thought about the Spirit's leading in your life? I hope it was recently. When Jesus was preparing to go to the cross and then leave the earth, he spent a good deal of time teaching his disciples about the promised Holy Spirit and what he would do for them.

He is your teacher, your advocate, your helper, and the one who helps you remember the Word that is in you. He is your counselor. He is the one that will guide you into all truth.

Are you actually "living by the Spirit"? Are you following the Spirit's leading in every part of your life? If not, you can be. You can enjoy his presence in your life every day. I can't fathom living without this wonderful promised gift. The prayer today is from a song written by Edwin Hatch in 1878.

PRAYER

Breathe on me, Breath of God,
Fill me with life anew,
That I may love what thou dost love,
And do what thou wouldst do.

Breathe on me, Breath of God,
Until my heart is pure,
Until with thee I will one will,
To do and to endure.

Breathe on me, Breath of God,
Till I am wholly thine,
Until this earthly part of me
Glows with thy fire divine.

Breathe on me, Breath of God,
So shall I never die,
But live with thee the perfect life
Of thine eternity.

But Who Am I?

But who am I, and who are my people, that we could give anything to you? Everything we have has come from you, and we give you only what you first gave us! 1 Chronicles 29:14 NLT

King David uttered these words of thanksgiving to God for what had been given to Israel for the building of the temple. David himself gave all of his treasures of gold and silver to help in the construction that would be completed by his son Solomon.

He prayed this prayer of acknowledgment and praise before the whole assembly of leaders. In the middle of the prayer, he arrived at this philosophical moment and openly stated that "Everything we have has come from you."

How true that is. Your life and my life are gifts from God. The blessings and burdens come from him. Anything that we may have in our possession to give back to God came from him first. We may think that we earned it, but in reality he gave us life and health to be able to work. He gives us daily what we need mentally, physically, and even financially to live out our lives.

What joy we would experience if we realized that we are only giving back to God when we give something to him. What joy we could have if we lived with this view in mind. Live openhanded. Live with a heart that hears what God wants backs from you and eyes that sees what he sees. Care about what God cares about and be a part of it with great thankfulness. Give back to God today. Give back...

PRAYER

Dear God, many times, I look at my stuff and just think it's mine, but in reality everything comes from you. Please help me today to view my life correctly, receive, and give back to you with great gratitude for my life. Amen.

Grace and Peace

May God give you more and more grace and peace. 1 Peter 1:2c
NLT

Peter was writing to a vibrant group of Christ followers when he wished that God would give them more and more grace. One thing all of us can be certain of is that we need "more and more grace and peace."

Grace is most needed and best understood in the midst of sin, suffering, and brokenness. We live in a world of earning, deserving, and merit, and these result in judgment. That is why everyone wants and needs grace. Judgment kills. Only grace makes alive.

A shorthand for what grace is: "mercy, not merit." Grace is the opposite of karma, which is all about getting what you deserve. Grace is getting what you don't deserve, and *not* getting what you do deserve. Christianity teaches that what we deserve is death with no hope of resurrection.

Beyond that definition of grace is the grace that sustains us through the ebb and flow of life. What we know for sure is that most people have things happening around them that call for God's grace. Beyond the happy social media pictures and videos that are posted, there are things, circumstances, hurts, sicknesses, brokenness, and deep pain that is often hidden from our eyes.

My prayer for you today is that you experience this "more and more grace and peace." When God's grace is given in great measure there will be peace.

PRAYER

Dear Lord, thank you for more and more grace. Thank you for your promises of peace that you offer. Today I ask that your grace would cover those that need it so that they might know your peace. Amen.

Make the Trade

The garment of praise for the spirit of heaviness. Isaiah 61:3d NKJV

There are times in our individual lives or even in the world around us that we experience a heaviness. It may be more emotional than physical, but we feel weighted down with the cares of this life. I read words written this morning by a friend that just lost her husband to death. It was way too soon. Everything is over this morning. The calling hours have ended, the funeral was done, and yesterday there was a burial. Today is the day when reality is setting in. She wrote: "There is this dreadful, heavy weight on my chest each morning. It's not right away ... I have about two seconds before it lays down on me, pushing the air from my lungs and filling them with sadness. To breathe is hard."

It doesn't have to be a shocking and unexpected death. It can truly just be life.

The Scripture above was a prophetic description of what Jesus would come to do when he showed up as the Messiah. There are other beautiful promises in the chapter as well, but today know that he is willing to cover you with a garment of praise that will lift the heaviness. I don't know how it works but it does. When we focus on Jesus and allow ourselves to momentarily forget what is happening around us, there is a spirit of praise that even people in the most dire of circumstances have experienced. From Paul and Silas singing songs of praise at midnight in jail to the early disciples rejoicing that they were counted worthy to suffer (beaten) for Christ.

Let Jesus get to you today. Let him in on whatever is happening and stay close to him always.

PRAYER

Dear Jesus, I do feel this heaviness sometimes. Some days it is almost too much to carry. I will turn to you and I will praise you, even when I don't feel like it. Stay near me, Lord. Amen.

Urgent Prayers

First of all, then, I urge that supplications, prayers, intercessions, and thanksgivings be made for all people, for kings and all who are in high positions, that we may lead a peaceful and quiet life, godly and dignified in every way. 1 Timothy 2:1-2 ESV

When Paul wrote this to a young pastor named Timothy, the early church was living along with the Jews in a country held captive by the Roman Empire. Persecution was common, and there were many Jewish-led military insurrections against the Romans; so it was a messy and scary time. They were all being controlled by a dominating Roman rule with little sympathy for religious tolerance.

In light of our current political environment, I wanted to remind us of our responsibilities as Christians when living in a hostile society.

What it doesn't say we should do:
- Attack other people
- Argue with people on social media
- Be hateful toward enemies

What it does say we should be doing:
- Praying with supplications, prayers, intercessions, and thanksgivings
- Praying this way for ALL people
- Praying this way for kings and ALL in high positions

Goal:
- We hope to live a peaceful and quiet life, godly and dignified.

Keep connected with God when things are good so that you don't have to reintroduce yourself if and when things get bad.

Value our invitation and ability to interact with the Creator God and our Savior.

Put all your hope in Jesus Christ, no matter what that may cost you. It will be very much worth it in the end.

PRAYER

Dear Jesus, I pray for those in authority over me. I ask that you give them wisdom and guidance even if they are not seeking you. Protect us from those that would do us and our country harm. Amen.

Trusting

Don't let your hearts be troubled. Trust in God, and trust also in me. John 14:1 NLT

Often these words are shared in funerals because in the words that follow Jesus talks about going to prepare a place for us. It is mansions or rooms depending on what translations you choose to read.

Instead of looking forward, to really understand these words you have to look backwards. In John 13, Jesus washes the disciple's feet in an act of unprecedented servanthood. They are now realizing that something big is about to happen. Peter even suggests that he is ready to die for Jesus. Peter asked Jesus where he was going and if he could go with him. Jesus responds, "You can't go with me now, but you will follow me later."

Can you imagine what was going on in their heads and hearts? I am sure that fear was a major factor in their lives at that moment. Jesus came back with our devotional verse today: "Don't let your hearts be troubled. Trust in God, and trust also in me."

We have all been here at one time or the other. Can you hear him say this to you today? Can you internalize and personalize these words for you or your circumstance? He is saying this to us. In fact, this verse or quote from Jesus might be worth reading every day!

As we maneuver through our changing and sometimes unsettled world, we as Christians have a secret weapon. We don't have to carry the fear that others carry, because we trust in God and Jesus. He has gone to prepare a place. This world is not our home. Eternity is our goal and destination. Don't give up today. Bow and acknowledge your trust in God and then lift up your head as a child of the King and live out your life with confidence and trust in your Lord.

PRAYER

Dear Jesus, thank you for your words of confidence and hope. Even though life turns upside down at times, you never change, and I will trust you with my life. Amen.

It Is Possible

He replied, "What is impossible for people is possible with God."
Luke 18:27

Jesus said this. That's probably enough for those of us that practice an active faith and walk with Christ. Jesus had just laid down the details for discipleship and people were in shock. Basically he had just told a rich young man that wanted to follow him that he should sell everything that he had and give it to the poor. Of course, the young man couldn't see how to do that, so Jesus followed it up with a statement of how hard it was for a rich man to enter the kingdom of God. When the crowd said, "Who then can be saved?" Jesus responded with the quote above.

When you are walking with Christ in this daily journey, you will come up against some tough moments and great challenges.

Memorize these words. Bind them to your heart and head. Know them before the challenges hit. Nothing is impossible with God. Does that mean your impossible situation will always turn out as you want it to? Not at all. The Bible and history are loaded with stories of men and women who have walked through some deep valleys. They all have one thing in common. They didn't allow their faith to be stolen from them. Even up to the point of death, they trusted in Jesus.

When my grandfather died in the early sixties, he was hospitalized with cancer and this once-strong farmer was weak, unable to get out of bed. Knowing he was dying, he asked for my mother and father who were on either side of his bed to raise him up so he could sit up in the bed and lift his arms in praise to God. They did, he did, and then he died. He died knowing and believing that nothing is impossible with God.

Never give up your faith in the God of the impossible.

PRAYER

Dear God, I want to believe that all things are possible with you. I want to serve you knowing and trusting you with my life. Please help me today to never doubt but always believe. Amen.

Don't Worry

Then, turning to his disciples, Jesus said, "That is why I tell you not to worry about everyday life—whether you have enough food to eat or enough clothes to wear. For life is more than food, and your body more than clothing. Look at the ravens. They don't plant or harvest or store food in barns, for God feeds them. And you are far more valuable to him than any birds! Can all your worries add a single moment to your life? And if worry can't accomplish a little thing like that, what's the use of worrying over bigger things? Look at the lilies and how they grow. They don't work or make their clothing, yet Solomon in all his glory was not dressed as beautifully as they are. And if God cares so wonderfully for flowers that are here today and thrown into the fire tomorrow, he will certainly care for you. Why do you have so little faith? Luke 12:22-28 NLT

Jesus' Advice About Worry

Jesus says, Don't worry about everyday life.

Jesus says, Look at the ravens.

Jesus says, You are more valuable than ravens.

Jesus says, Look at the lilies.

Jesus says, He will certainly care for you.

Jesus says, Why do you have so little faith?

Faith means that we believe even when we don't see what we are looking for. Praying that you have strong faith today! God cares about you today. He believes in you and longs to be in the middle of your life.

PRAYER

Dear God, it is so hard for me to feel this all the time, but I want to believe that you care about me this deeply. I don't want to worry, but I want to trust you with my life. I'm looking at the lilies and ravens today. Amen.

Waiting Patiently

I waited patiently for the Lord to help me, and he turned to me and heard my cry. He lifted me out of the pit of despair, out of the mud and the mire. He set my feet on solid ground and steadied me as I walked along. He has given me a new song to sing a hymn of praise to our God. Many will see what he has done and be amazed. They will put their trust in the Lord. Psalm 40:1-3 NLT

The first three verses of Psalm 40 are classic and often used as words of encouragement. No matter what you are going for or how you might apply this today, know that these words are for you.

Here is the flow of these verses:

I waited
He turned
He lifted
He set
He gave
They will

Never give up on God. He really does know what is happening in your life at home, work, and even inside of you. He cares. While the Psalmist waited patiently, God had to turn toward him and hear his cry. Hold on. Help is coming. No one loves you like God loves you!

PRAYER

Dear God, I am waiting on you today. I come back to this Scripture again and again because it is so full of your promises. Please turn, please lift, please set my feet in a safe place. Amen.

God Is Always Watching

God looks down from heaven on the entire human race; he looks to see if anyone is truly wise, if anyone seeks God. Psalm 53:2 NLT

Invariably around Christmas, this saying will wind up on a church sign somewhere: "Wise men still seek him." It is still true, wise people will seek God daily.

Place of God:	**God is watching all of us.**
Plan of God:	**God is waiting for us.**
People of God:	**We want and worship him**

In times of storm, trouble, upheaval, and loss people often turn to God. We should be reminded today that God is looking down from heaven daily to see who is looking for him.

There is no substitute in this life for a daily, vibrant, life-altering relationship with God, not just when we need him but every day, because he needs us. He is watching and waiting for us to reach out to him, not unlike a parent longing for the attention of their child, an emotion that continues all through life.

Pause today with me and consider the ramifications of acknowledging God, worshiping him with your life, and bringing joy to him on a day-by-day basis.

PRAYER

Dear God, I am seeking you daily. I know that you are my protector and guide. I love you, Lord. Amen.

Seeking God Continually

Search for the Lord and for his strength; continually seek him. 1 Chronicles 16:11 NLT

It is clear that God wants us to search for him. Many times, we pray about something for a short time and then give up; but I am not sure that is the correct approach. I know that older Christians I have read about or known would talk about praying for someone or something for years.

I've known wives that prayed for an unsaved husband for decades, only to one day hear him express an interest in finding God in his life. No matter what it might be that you are looking for or needing strength for, you should continually seek him.

Search for the Lord and for his strength...

Are you searching for him today? Do you need him to step up on your behalf? He is available and will listen to you. He knows where you are and what is going on. Can you trust him with your life and circumstances?

PRAYER

Dear God, thank you for the encouragement found in the Bible to seek and search for you. I am doing just that. Lord, hear my prayer. Amen.

Wilderness Temptations

The Spirit then compelled Jesus to go into the wilderness, where he was tempted by Satan for forty days. He was out among the wild animals, and angels took care of him. Mark 1:12-13 NLT

I wonder if you have ever truly been in a wilderness. For me, the wilderness conjures up thoughts of deep woods with no sense of direction or human contact. I feel like it would mean just learning to survive every day trying to find the food and water needed to live.

Jesus was led or compelled by God's Spirit to go into the wilderness for a time of intense testing. It was a long and lonely time, and I assume that out among the wild animals he was taken care of by angels he could not see.

For most of us, the wildernesses we experience are circumstantial. They involve the unexpected and unwanted things that happen in our lives. They may include broken relationships or lost vocations. They may be times when our resources are low to non-existent and we wonder how we will survive.

It is in these moments that our hearts turn the most directly to God. We lay things aside that don't matter. We get a whole new set of priorities. We are careful about our life and how we are living. Sometimes in the wilderness all we can see is what is in front of us and confronting us.

If you are there and you are a servant of Jesus, know that God knows exactly where you are. He knows what is happening and the threats and weakness you face and feel. More than you know, his angels are taking care of you even though you can't see them. Don't run the other way. Sit down in the here and now and let God work. You won't always be here. There will be a better day. Life rarely stays the same. Learn all you can as you lean on your Savior. Lean into him and remember he is the Great Shepherd. Even if you are lost, he will come looking for you and bring you out of the wilderness.

PRAYER

Dear Jesus, I am desperate for you. There are questions surrounding me that I don't have answers for. I will not give up and I will not quit trusting you. Thank you for loving me. Amen.

Joy Unspeakable

Yes, joyful are those who live like this! Joyful indeed are those whose God is the LORD. Psalm 144:15 NLT

This is a new day! Each new day is a gift from God. The Bible says our days are numbered on this earth. That simply means that God knows exactly how long each of us has to live on this planet. He knows how long we have to love those around us and to be productive with our minutes, hours, days, and weeks.

We often pursue happiness in our lives. People live for the weekends. We live for the next big event or purchase; but in the end, if we are honest, rarely do things bring us lasting happiness. The psalmist gives us the simple solution to a fulfilled life. He doesn't write of happiness, but something much deeper and lasting. He writes of joy! Why is joy so different?

Joy is based on being a person who has found the secret of making God the Lord of their lives. Don't miss this. Making God LORD is a big deal. It is trusting God to the point that even if everything you know falls apart and life drastically changes that your relationship with God will not change. He is the Lord of your life; and as Lord you trust him to see you through the good, the bad, and the ugly. We don't surrender our lives to a human being, pastor, church, or anyone on this earth; but there is something incredibly safe about trusting God with our past, present, and future.

How do you do this? Know what he wants from your life and live that way. Love him with all your soul, mind, heart, and strength, and love your neighbor as yourself, Jesus said. Be honest. Avoid sin. Treat others as you want to be treated. Open the Bible and live it out. You can have joy. You can have joy even in the midst of whatever is going on around you because the Lord of all is living inside of you. Don't be afraid to make him Lord of your life.

PRAYER

Dear God, please be the Lord of my life. I realize this will affect everything I do and say with my life, but I want to find my joy in you. Amen.

Though He Slay Me

Though He slay me, yet will I trust Him. Job 13:15 NKJV

Most of us will hopefully never be as desperate as the Old Testament character Job. Everything about his life including family, fortune, and health was disappearing around him. His best friends were coming by to try to figure out what he had done wrong or how he had sinned to cause all of this loss and destruction in his life. He was near the end, covered in boils and alone, having lost everything. You can read the end of the book and see that his fortune was restored, but Job lived through an incredibly devastating season.

When we walk through tough times as a follower of Christ, we need to remember that we are human. It is okay to feel discouraged, disappointed, and even disillusioned for a time. When life hits hard, it takes time to process what we are thinking and feeling in the moment. Anger may even well up within you as you react to what seems to be unfair.

The point is that Job encountered all the human emotions we feel. Some he repented for, but most he expressed. The statement he made in Job 13:15 is one of surrender and resignation to God. It was and is the place we all must come to in our faithful walks with God. Ultimately, it is a place of peace even if the situation has not resolved like we want or prefer.

I encourage you today to do your best to live this way. Life happens every day to people, and sometimes it happens to us. Keep your eyes on God. Don't be afraid to tell God what you are feeling, but ultimately do it with respect, reverence, and trust. God loves you today no matter what is happening around you. Know this, believe it, and trust him through it all.

PRAYER

Dear God, you and you alone know the path I am walking. You know the fears and frustrations I have felt. Whatever lies ahead for me, please give me faith to endure and keep my heart from turning away from you. You are my hope. Amen.

Are You Listening?

But to you who are willing to listen, I say, love your enemies! Do good to those who hate you." Luke 6:27 NLT

Why not pause today and review your enemy list. Not forgiving others only harms you and does very little to the enemy that you won't forgive. People are flawed. We are flawed, and so it is probable that hurt will come our way; and sometimes it may even come from us. There are three things Jesus said for us to do. Here they are:

Do good ... to those who hate you.

Bless those ... who curse you.

Pray for ... those who hurt you.

I guess that's a good assignment that should keep us all busy for a while. The only way to love your enemies is to be full of Jesus in your heart and life. Corrie Ten Boom spent time in a Nazi concentration camp and watched her sister die at the hands of her captors. This is what she wrote:

"Even as the angry, vengeful thoughts boiled through me, I saw the sin of them. Jesus Christ had died for this man; was I going to ask for more? 'Lord Jesus,' I prayed, 'forgive me and help me to forgive him.... Jesus, I cannot forgive him. Give me your forgiveness....' And so I discovered that it is not on our forgiveness any more than on our goodness that the world's healing hinges, but on his. When he tells us to love our enemies, he gives along with the command, the love itself." —Corrie Ten Boom, *The Hiding Place*

PRAYER

Dear God, there is no way I can forgive those that trespass against me without your divine help. I am asking for your intervention in my life today. Don't let me walk or live with bitterness in my heart. Fill me with your love. Amen.

Be Humble

So humble yourselves before God. James 4:7 NLT

Being humble is not a subject most of us want to talk about very often. In this verse, we are being told to humble ourselves before God. What does that mean? How can you do that?

The easy answer is to humble yourself and become obedient to God's design for your life. This will touch every area of your life from loyalties, relationships, vocations, actions, and reactions, conversations, habits, entertainment, and most of all devotion. When we humble ourselves before God we make him Lord of our lives and surrender our sinfulness to his saving power.

To live humbly before God means that we come to trust and accept life as it unfolds before us. Life is filled with both blessing and burdens for all of us, but God remains that constant strength and power that we submit to and trust with both our lowest and highest moments or days.

It is the positioning of your heart to be open to God's Word. You don't just read it when you need a happy verse, but you take it in daily and let it saturate your life. It means taking the focus off yourself and figuring out what matters most to God. It means doing God's will even though it might not be popular or place you in the spotlight. It may mean serving others in a place that draws no attention to you or your actions. It means you will love others—even those who don't deserve it. It will always involve forgiveness. It might mean downward mobility, at least in spirit if not in reality.

Cry out for God's help in this. It is not easy to do in a land of wealth and riches. Even the poorest of us is wealthy from a global standpoint. Relinquish your life and loves to him. God loves a humble heart.

PRAYER

Dear God, please help me to understand what this means in my life daily. Give me the strength to love others like you would love them. Give me the courage to move forward with faith instead of fear. Amen.

Be Strong in the Lord

One day the members of the heavenly court came to present them-
selves before the Lord, and the Accuser, Satan, came with them.
"Where have you come from?" the Lord asked Satan. Satan an-
swered the Lord, "I have been patrolling the earth, watching every-
thing that's going on." Job 1:6-7 NLT

This may seem like a strange Scripture for a devotion, but in reality I think it is a timely reminder to us all that we have a common enemy. Ever since Adam and Eve fell for Satan's lies in the garden of Eden, all humans face the daily onslaught of temptations, deceptions, and lies to distract us from our faith.

I am not pretending to understand this heavenly court or why Satan was there. What I see is that he admits to patrolling the earth and watching all that is going on. As long as we are alive we will be susceptible to entities that want to turn us from our faith in God.

Paul reminded the church at Ephesus that spiritual warfare is real. He said, "A final word: Be strong in the Lord and in his mighty power. Put on all of God's armor so that you will be able to stand firm against all strategies of the devil. For we are not fighting against flesh-and-blood enemies, but against evil rulers and authorities of the unseen world, against mighty powers in this dark world, and against evil spirits in the heavenly places" (Ephesians 6:10-12 NLT).

Stay strong and stand strong. I have no idea who needs this today or even who will be reading this, but take it as a word from the Lord. He is your best friend. Always lean in his direction. Resist the devil and he will flee from you.

PRAYER

Dear God, without you I am nothing and don't stand a chance. With you I can find the power to stand for you and with you every day. Please help me resist the things that are calling for me to walk in the wrong direction today. Please help me, Lord. Amen.

Pay Attention

Pay attention to yourselves! Luke 17:3 ESV

This might seem like a strange verse to use for a devotion, but Jesus said this so we had better look at it more closely. He was teaching about the dangers of temptation and being drawn away from God. Just before saying "Pay attention to yourselves!" he had warned that if our sin causes a "little one" to sin, we would be better off for a millstone to be hung around our neck and to be tossed in the sea.

Sin is not your friend. Embracing or ignoring your sin is not God's will for you—ever. We are warned to pay attention to what we are doing. This means simply that we need to evaluate and monitor our lives closely.

I am amazed at what Christians will allow to come into minds and hearts through their ears and eyes. The so-called entertainment industry in our world, and especially in the U.S., is pretty much total filth; yet somehow we've come to a place in our sophistication or ignorance that we think it doesn't affect us. Sin happens in our lives when we allow ourselves to be led away by temptation. Temptation comes from what we allow into our hearts and minds that is not pure, wholesome, or godly.

There is no one but you that is responsible for you. That is why Jesus said, "Pay attention to yourselves." Maybe today you could ask God to make you sensitive to his Holy Spirit's presence in your life. Ask him to reveal areas of danger or behavior in your life that could lead to places of temptation or push you away from God and his will.

PRAYER

Dear God, I live in a world that calls me away from you and your Word daily. Please help me to find the strength and wisdom to be aware of what I am doing or not doing that is a danger to my spiritual walk. I need this every day. Amen.

God First

You have planted much but harvest little. You eat but are not satisfied. You drink but are still thirsty. You put on clothes but cannot keep warm. Your wages disappear as though you were putting them in pockets filled with holes! Haggai 1:6 NLT

The prophet Haggai is quoting God. This is God speaking to Israel because their priorities have become lopsided. They are celebrating and spending money on themselves and their homes while God's "house lies in ruins." God was not pleased and was holding back some very important things from them, to get their attention.

Have you ever felt this way? Have you ever felt deep dissatisfaction with your life and wondered why? I wonder how you are doing with your priorities in life. It might be wise to evaluate what is happening and what you are doing with your time, treasures, and talent. As a follower of Christ, we are to give to him first before satisfying our own needs or wants. This is a matter of faith and trust in a God who said he would supply all of our needs.

Don't be afraid to trust him with your life.

PRAYER

Dear God, I want to always honor you with my life and my possessions. I realize they are a gift from you, and I thank you for every blessing. Amen.

Shhh ... Wait on Him

Stand in silence in the presence of the sovereign LORD, *for the awesome day of the* LORD's *judgment is near.* Zephaniah 1:7 NLT

Once again, God calls his people to silence in preparation for something huge that is about to happen. Sadly, what was about to happen was not a good thing but judgment that would come with very harsh punishment for the people of Israel.

I think silence before God should be a part of our daily practice and spiritual discipline. It is in the silence that we have the best chance of hearing God's quiet voice or to feel his gentle nudge one direction or the other. It is in the silence that we receive the assurances we need to keep moving forward in the dark places.

Why not try it today? Find a quiet place, sit in the stillness, and wait on God. Turn off the distractions and embrace the silence. Let the Holy Spirit fill your heart and mind with God's thoughts.

I just did this myself. I am writing this devotion at work, so I shut my door and decided to just wait on the Lord. I failed miserably. I grabbed my phone to add some music, and I found myself actually taking a picture of a nativity in my office and realized this is a hard task. I will keep trying.

"Stand in silence in the presence of the sovereign Lord."

PRAYER

Dear Lord, please help me to learn the value and blessing of silence before you. Quiet my spirit and mind that I might hear you and sense the nearness of your presence. Amen.

The Lord Always Determines

We may throw the dice, but the Lord determines how they fall.
Proverbs 16:33 NLT

Gambling is never a good idea; but when we choose to take chances in life without involving the Lord, we are "rolling the dice" and hoping for the best. The writer of Proverbs is great with one-liners, and this one is packed full of great wisdom.

God is God and he is over all and in all. He is sovereign and in control. While we certainly have free will and can exercise our own judgment about decisions we make, the smarter response would be to always seek God's will in every matter.

He wants to be involved in our businesses and work, our relationships, our families, our churches and ministries, our hobbies, and whatever we do for him. Include him. Ask him for advice, wisdom, leadership, and guidance.

Let God determine the best way for you to navigate life. Don't gamble with your life but trust it to the grace of our merciful and all-powerful God.

PRAYER

Dear God, sometimes I make decisions without thinking about what might be best or what would be in your will. Help me to pause and wait on you as I walk through this life. Amen.

Take Courage

But Jesus spoke to them at once. "Don't be afraid," he said. "Take courage! I am here!" Then he climbed into the boat, and the wind stopped. They were totally amazed, for they still didn't understand the significance of the miracle of the loaves. Their hearts were too hard to take it in. Mark 6:50-52 NLT

The disciples were in a boat during a terrible storm. They were terrified. Ironically, they had just watched and helped Jesus feed over 5,000 people by blessing and multiplying a little boy's meager lunch. They were alone in the boat without Jesus, but no one thought about his ability to save them. When he showed up (walking on the water) and calmed the storm, they were beyond amazed.

Mark makes the point that their hearts were too hard to take in what they were seeing. They didn't even understand that if Jesus could feed over 5,000 with a few loaves and fish, he could save them from the storm even if he wasn't there. They came to understand it and learn it.

Don't be afraid today. Listen to Jesus' words, "Take courage! I am here!" He is here for you and will protect you in the storms. Call out to him in faith!

PRAYER

Dear Jesus, thank you for being in my life. Thank you for showing up in the storms. Don't let me ever forget to take courage from your presence. Amen.

Be Merciful in Jesus' Name

God blesses those who are merciful, for they will be shown mercy.
Matthew 5:7 NLT

Mercy includes our ability to show compassion to others, both friend and foe. Compassion is usually accompanied by an action. As followers of Jesus Christ we are admonished in the Bible to love our enemies, to be compassionate to "the least of these," and to love one another.

Dietrich Bonhoeffer in his classic book, *The Cost of Discipleship*, describes the first disciples, who received the Sermon on the Mount first hand, this way: "These followers of Jesus have in their life with him renounced their own dignity, for they are merciful ... they take upon themselves the distress and humiliation and sin of others. They have an irresistible love for the down-trodden, the sick, the wretched, the wronged, the outcast, and all who are tormented with anxiety.... No distress is too great, no sin too appalling for their pity. If any man falls into disgrace, the merciful will sacrifice their own honor to shield him and take his shame upon themselves."

One day those that have shown mercy will be shown the ultimate mercy from God himself as they stand before him and hear him say, "Well done, good and faithful servant."

Mathew Schmalz wrote, "But it is there in the messiness, in the conflicted and often confused ways we live our lives, that we can learn how much mercy matters to us all."

PRAYER

Dear Jesus, you modeled mercy more than anyone in history ever did. Please help me to follow your example and practice showing mercy to others in your name. Amen.

Devotions for September 1 through September 25 come from a series of devotions I did with my staff while pastoring my last church. They are a little different in format but hopefully you will find them helpful.

Invite the Misfits

He went on to tell a story to the guests around the table. Noticing how each had tried to elbow into the place of honor, he said, "When someone invites you to dinner, don't take the place of honor. Somebody more important than you might have been invited by the host. Then he'll come and call out in front of everybody, 'You're in the wrong place. The place of honor belongs to this man.' Redfaced, you'll have to make your way to the very last table, the only place left.

"When you're invited to dinner, go and sit at the last place. Then when the host comes he may very well say, 'Friend, come up to the front.' That will give the dinner guests something to talk about! What I'm saying is, If you walk around with your nose in the air, you're going to end up flat on your face. But if you're content to be simply yourself, you will become more than yourself."

Then he turned to the host. "The next time you put on a dinner, don't just invite your friends and family and rich neighbors, the kind of people who will return the favor. Invite some people who never get invited out, the misfits from the wrong side of the tracks. You'll be—and experience—a blessing. They won't be able to return the favor, but the favor will be returned—oh, how it will be returned!—at the resurrection of God's people." Luke 14:7-14 MSG

1. **The Context:** A meal with a top leader of the Pharisees.
2. **The Concern:** That those who are leaders need to have servant hearts.
3. **The Correction:** Don't exclude people. Make sure you have a balanced list of friends.
4. **The Conclusion**: Be humble, inclusive, and you will be blessed and be a blessing.

The bottom line for church leaders and staff: Don't talk to anyone longer than three minutes on Sunday morning (make an appointment) and meet someone new every service. Make sure they are not all people who look or act within your comfort zone. Serve as a servant.

Dear God, as I serve you on this earth, give me eyes to see people and reach out to them, especially in the context of church. Too often, I gravitate to my friends instead of looking for someone I need to connect to or have a conversation with.

Prayer Discovers God's Agenda

Now in the morning, having risen a long while before daylight, He went out and departed to a solitary place; and there He prayed.
Mark 1:35 NKJV

It was common knowledge among the disciples that they would find Jesus praying during the early morning hours. When they needed him, they knew to go to the place of prayer. When Judas betrayed Jesus, he led his cohorts to Jesus' place of prayer.

Every time the Lord Jesus faced an important decision, he prayed. When he was being tempted to do things by the world's methods instead of the Father's, he prayed (Matt. 4). When it was time to choose his disciples, he prayed the entire night (Luke 6:12). If the Son of God required a night of prayer in order to determine the Father's mind, how long might it take us in prayer to clearly determine our Father's will?

Because Jesus was so often surrounded by crowds, he knew he must find a quiet place so he could clearly hear his Father's voice. Jesus had many people seeking to influence the direction of his life. His disciples wanted him to go where the crowds were (Mark 1:37). The crowds wanted to crown him king (John 6:15). Satan tempted him to make compromises in order to draw a following (Matt. 4:3, 6, 9). Jesus knew that his mission was not to attract a crowd but to remain obedient to his Father. It was prayer that set the agenda for Jesus' ministry (Luke 6:12). Prayer preceded the miracles (John 11:42-43); prayer brought him encouragement at critical moments (Luke 9:28-31); prayer enabled him to go to the cross (Luke 22:41-42); and prayer kept him there despite excruciating pain (Luke 23:46).

Follow the Savior's example, and let your time alone with God in prayer set the agenda for your life. Follow his example and allow him to work through you in the area he has called you to serve in. If you are trying to grow by reading books, attending seminars, surfing the internet, networking with others in your field, or anything else, and you are not immersing yourself and your calling in prayer it will amount to nothing. While all those human efforts are great ideas and I encourage them, I believe that one man or woman with no book but the Bible and no seminars, research, or even networking can, alone with God, shake the world around them.

I offer you the secret of success. Pray, pray, pray. Learn to depend on God and embrace him because without him you and I will be like a sounding brass or a tinkling cymbal. Crowds of people and numbers do not denote success. Truly changed lives and an abundance of the Holy Spirit's power are the only standard of success that is important, and that only happens when you pray.

PRAYER

Dear Jesus, you modeled the importance of prayer for me. Help me to never go through a day without connecting with you often. Amen.

Working effectively

Let me now remind you, dear brothers and sisters, of the Good News I preached to you before. You welcomed it then, and you still stand firm in it. It is this Good News that saves you if you continue to believe the message I told you—unless, of course, you believed something that was never true in the first place.

I passed on to you what was most important and what had also been passed on to me. Christ died for our sins, just as the Scriptures said. He was buried, and he was raised from the dead on the third day, just as the Scriptures said. He was seen by Peter and then by the Twelve. After that, he was seen by more than 500 of his followers at one time, most of whom are still alive, though some have died. Then he was seen by James and later by all the apostles. Last of all, as though I had been born at the wrong time, I also saw him. For I am the least of all the apostles. In fact, I'm not even worthy to be called an apostle after the way I persecuted God's church.

But whatever I am now, it is all because God poured out his special favor on me—and not without results. For I have worked harder than any of the other apostles; yet it was not I but God who was working through me by his grace. So it makes no difference whether I preach or they preach, for we all preach the same message you have already believed.

So, my dear brothers and sisters, be strong and immovable. Always work enthusiastically for the Lord, for you know that nothing you do for the Lord is ever useless. 1 Corinthians 15:1-11, 58 NLT

None of us earned or deserved the grace of God in our lives. None of us deserves the calling he placed on us to make disciples in his name, and yet he depends on us to do the work of sharing the gospel with the world around us. Here is a good pattern for working effectively in ministry from verse 58:

- Be Strong
- Be Immovable
- Work enthusiastically

"Nothing you do for the Lord is ever useless."

PRAYER

Dear Lord, I ask that you would give me the focus I need to carry out your will for my life and ministry. Please pour out your Spirit on and in my life. Amen.

On Special Assignment for Christ

I, Paul, am an apostle on special assignment for Christ, our living hope. Under God our Savior's command, I'm writing this to you, Timothy, my son in the faith. All the best from our God and Christ be yours!

On my way to the province of Macedonia, I advised you to stay in Ephesus. Well, I haven't changed my mind. Stay right there on top of things so that the teaching stays on track. Apparently some people have been introducing fantasy stories and fanciful family trees that digress into silliness instead of pulling the people back into the center, deepening faith and obedience.

The whole point of what we're urging is simply love—love uncontaminated by self-interest and counterfeit faith, a life open to God. Those who fail to keep to this point soon wander off into cul-de-sacs of gossip. They set themselves up as experts on religious issues, but haven't the remotest idea of what they're holding forth with such imposing eloquence.

It's true that moral guidance and counsel need to be given, but the way you say it and to whom you say it are as important as what you say. It's obvious, isn't it, that the law code isn't primarily for people who live responsibly, but for the irresponsible, who defy all authority, riding roughshod over God, life, sex, truth, whatever! They are contemptuous of this great Message I've been put in charge of by this great God. 1 Timothy 1:1-11 MSG

1. **Stay on top of things:**
- To keep teaching on track.
- To pull people back into the center.
- To deepen faith and obedience.

2. **Love: The whole point:**
- No self-interest.
- No counterfeit faith.
- Keep your life open to God.

3. Moral guidance and counsel need to be given:

- The way you say it and to whom is as important as what you say.
- "Target" those who defy all authority.
- Don't allow yourself to fall into the lifestyle of this culture: "riding roughshod over God, life, sex, truth, whatever!"
- Avoid being contemptuous of the gospel message.

Con-temp´tu-ous a. manifesting or expressing contempt or disdain; scornful; haughty; insolent; disdainful. A proud, contemptuous behavior. —Hammond.

PRAYER

Dear Jesus, please give me the courage to stand for the Word of God. Help me to love people enough to not comprise the truth but to always share what the Bible teaches even if it goes against the culture. Amen.

He Went Out on a Limb...

I'm so grateful to Christ Jesus for making me adequate to do this work. He went out on a limb, you know, in trusting me with this ministry. The only credentials I brought to it were invective and witch hunts and arrogance. But I was treated mercifully because I didn't know what I was doing—didn't know Who I was doing it against! Grace mixed with faith and love poured over me and into me. And all because of Jesus.

Here's a word you can take to heart and depend on: Jesus Christ came into the world to save sinners. I'm proof—Public Sinner Number One—of someone who could never have made it apart from sheer mercy. And now he shows me off—evidence of his endless patience—to those who are right on the edge of trusting him forever. Deep honor and bright glory to the King of All Time—One God, Immortal, Invisible, ever and always. Oh, yes!

I'm passing this work on to you, my son Timothy. The prophetic word that was directed to you prepared us for this. All those prayers are coming together now so you will do this well, fearless in your struggle, keeping a firm grip on your faith and on yourself. After all, this is a fight we're in. There are some, you know, who by relaxing their grip and thinking anything goes have made a thorough mess of their faith. Hymenaeus and Alexander are two of them. I let them wander off to Satan to be taught a lesson or two about not blaspheming. 1 Timothy 1:12-20 MSG

The Reality:

"He went out on a limb."

The Requirements:

What are your credentials?

The Remedy:

"But I was treated mercifully because I didn't know what I was doing—didn't know Who I was doing it against! Grace mixed with faith and love poured over me and into me. And all because of Jesus."

The Reminder:

"Here's a word you can take to heart and depend on: Jesus Christ came into the world to save sinners."

Our Response:

"All those prayers are coming together now so you will do this well, fearless in your struggle, keeping a firm grip on your faith and on yourself. After all, this is a fight we're in."

No Relaxing:

"There are some, you know, who by relaxing their grip and thinking anything goes have made a thorough mess of their faith."

PRAYER

Dear Lord, I know that you went out on a limb to save and call me to your work. Let me always serve you at home, work, and at play. Wherever I am, may I always stay in your service. Amen.

Pray Every Way You Know How...

The first thing I want you to do is pray. Pray every way you know how, for everyone you know. Pray especially for rulers and their governments to rule well so we can be quietly about our business of living simply, in humble contemplation. This is the way our Savior God wants us to live.

He wants not only us but everyone saved, you know, everyone to get to know the truth we've learned: that there's one God and only one, and one Priest-Mediator between God and us—Jesus, who offered himself in exchange for everyone held captive by sin, to set them all free. Eventually the news is going to get out. This and this only has been my appointed work: getting this news to those who have never heard of God, and explaining how it works by simple faith and plain truth. 1 Timothy 2:1-7 MSG

We are called to ministry; and because of this, we are foolish to think that we can minister to anyone successfully without prayer. E. M. Bounds wrote about ministry and said that ministry "cannot rise in its life-giving forces above the man. Dead men give out dead sermons, and dead sermons kill. Everything depends on the spiritual character of the preacher." Ministry—period—will never truly be effective if not accompanied by and saturated in prayer.

Bounds went on to write, "Talking to men for God is a great thing, but talking to God for men is greater still. He will never talk well with real success to men for God who has not learned well how to talk to God for men."

1. **Praying for who?**
   a. Everyone you know
   b. For those in authority

2. **Praying for what?**
   a. A non-distracted, simple life
   b. Contemplation

3. **Praying why?**
   a. The salvation of others
   b. The sharing of truth
   c. To be able to explain in relevant terms simple faith and plain truth

Prayer is the key to everything we do with our lives and for others. It is not education, as good as that may be. It is not having the right tools and settings but prayer that makes even the inferior special when God is in it. God has done some amazing things through some very unimpressive men and women that knew the power of prayer.

PRAYER

Dear Jesus, it is an honor to pray to you. I ask to be drawn to prayer over and over again in my life. May prayer be like breathing for me. Jesus, I come to you. Amen

Salvation Only Comes to Those Who Continue...

Since prayer is at the bottom of all this, what I want mostly is for men to pray—not shaking angry fists at enemies but raising holy hands to God. And I want women to get in there with the men in humility before God, not primping before a mirror or chasing the latest fashions but doing something beautiful for God and becoming beautiful doing it.

I don't let women take over and tell the men what to do. They should study to be quiet and obedient along with everyone else. Adam was made first, then Eve; woman was deceived first—our pioneer in sin!—with Adam right on her heels. On the other hand, her childbearing brought about salvation, reversing Eve. But this salvation only comes to those who continue in faith, love, and holiness, gathering it all into maturity. You can depend on this. 1 Timothy 2:8-15 MSG

This is a very interesting and often ignored part of 1 Timothy. Most people don't want to deal with the "restrictions" that appear to be placed on women. In reality, I see Paul giving females in that culture instruction on how to participate in the faith and in the church. There are some who are very uncomfortable with the teaching, but let's look at it a little closer.

1. The invitation: Humility is for everyone.
2. The instruction: Hunger for God trends, not world trends.
3. The interpretation: Honor the system.
4. The inheritance: Holiness comes to those who pursue it.

Regardless if you are reading this as a man or a woman, the message is the same. Keep pursuing God. Pray like you mean it. Never give up. God uses men and women to do great things for him. You qualify if you pray.

PRAYER

Dear Jesus, I lift up holy hands to you. Please use me however you want. I am available for you now and always. Amen.

Leadership, There Are Preconditions...

If anyone wants to provide leadership in the church, good! But there are preconditions: A leader must be well-thought-of, committed to his wife, cool and collected, accessible, and hospitable. He must know what he's talking about, not be over fond of wine, not pushy but gentle, not thin-skinned, not money-hungry. He must handle his own affairs well, attentive to his own children and having their respect. For if someone is unable to handle his own affairs, how can he take care of God's church? He must not be a new believer, lest the position go to his head and the Devil trip him up. Outsiders must think well of him, or else the Devil will figure out a way to lure him into his trap.

The same goes for those who want to be servants in the church: serious, not deceitful, not too free with the bottle, not in it for what they can get out of it. They must be reverent before the mystery of the faith, not using their position to try to run things. Let them prove themselves first. If they show they can do it, take them on. No exceptions are to be made for women—same qualifications: serious, dependable, not sharp-tongued, not over fond of wine. Servants in the church are to be committed to their spouses, attentive to their own children, and diligent in looking after their own affairs. Those who do this servant work will come to be highly respected, a real credit to this Jesus-faith." 1 Timothy 3:1-13 MSG

There are always going to be conditions and rules no matter how much we dislike them. Currently there is a generation entering leadership that loves to challenge and break the rules. To some extent, most generations challenge the status quo of those that have gone before them. There is an overwhelming spirit of rebellion toward anything structured or anything that has a pattern or form. The funny thing about this is that structure and standards of behavior are not just a church thing. Successful businesses function smoothly because of the performance standards that they have in place. Even Starbucks, the Gen. X shrine, has rules and guidelines that they demand from their employees.

Paul is simply writing to inform young Timothy that these are the job requirements for leading in the church. If you can't keep these you forfeit your right to lead. In fact, you do much more damage when you try to lead through these kinds of inconsistencies instead of dealing with them before you lead.

These should be the preconditions that we look for in people we put in leadership within the church.

The preconditions:
1. Must be well thought of.
2. Committed to their wife or husband.
3. Cool and collected.
4. Accessible and hospitable.
5. He must know what he's talking about.
6. Must not be over fond of wine.
7. Not pushy but gentle.
8. Not thin-skinned.
9. Not money-hungry.
10. He or she must handle his own affairs well, attentive to his own children and having their respect.
11. He must not be a new believer.
12. Outsiders must think well of him.
13. Serious, not deceitful.
14. Not in it for what they can get out of it.
15. They must be reverent before the mystery of the faith, not using their position to try to run things.
16. Let them prove themselves first. If they show they can do it, take them on.
17. No exceptions are to be made for women—same qualifications: serious, dependable, not sharp-tongued, not over fond of wine.
18. Servants in the church are to be committed to their spouses, attentive to their own children, and diligent in looking after their own affairs.

There is a lot here. Be sure you read it over and really take it in.

PRAYER

Dear Jesus, do I qualify for ministry? I hope so, because I want to serve you every day and share the message of good news with others. Let me live out these standards of behavior in my life. Amen.

A Great Mystery, Far Exceeding Our Understanding...

I hope to visit you soon, but just in case I'm delayed, I'm writing this letter so you'll know how things ought to go in God's household, this God-alive church, bastion of truth. This Christian life is a great mystery, far exceeding our understanding, but some things are clear enough: He appeared in a human body, was proved right by the invisible Spirit, was seen by angels. He was proclaimed among all kinds of peoples, believed in all over the world, taken up into heavenly glory. 1 Timothy 3:14-16 MSG

In the final words of chapter 3, Paul has just given Timothy a list of characteristics that leaders must have to be qualified to lead in the church. He states that he has done this because he may not be able to visit as soon as he would like. As he closes, he makes a most astonishing statement from one as knowledgeable as Paul. He declares that the Christian life is a great mystery, far exceeding his understanding. He then declares the things that we do know, things that are clear.

1. **Know how God wants the church to work.**
2. **Know how God wants us to seek his wisdom.**
3. **Know God and his ways.**

For anyone reading this, these are the things that are important to know.

PRAYER

Dear Lord, I have such a hunger to know and understand your Word. Help me to understand what you want me to do at church and in the world around me. Amen.

We're Banking on the Living God. . .

The Spirit makes it clear that as time goes on, some are going to give up on the faith and chase after demonic illusions put forth by professional liars. These liars have lied so well and for so long that they've lost their capacity for truth. They will tell you not to get married. They'll tell you not to eat this or that food—perfectly good food God created to be eaten heartily and with thanksgiving by Christians! Everything God created is good, and to be received with thanks. Nothing is to be sneered at and thrown out. God's Word and our prayers make every item in creation holy.

You've been raised on the Message of the faith and have followed sound teaching. Now pass on this counsel to the Christians there, and you'll be a good servant of Jesus. Stay clear of silly stories that get dressed up as religion. Exercise daily in God—no spiritual flabbiness, please! Workouts in the gymnasium are useful, but a disciplined life in God is far more so, making you fit both today and forever. You can count on this. Take it to heart. This is why we've thrown ourselves into this venture so totally. We're banking on the living God, Savior of all men and women, especially believers. 1 Timothy 4:1-10 MSG

When you open a bank account the general idea is to make deposits that will grow the account or at the very least keep enough in the account to cover your debts. To be a Christ follower means that we believe that he is who he says he is and that the Bible is the Word. The Word of God given to us as a guide; and to use an investment term, in some ways the Bible is a prospectus.* We look at it and the God it represents and embrace it as truth. We make the investment.

1. Be earnest about pursuing God's way and Word (verse 5).
2. Be exercising daily; embracing a disciplined life (verses 7-8).
3. Be empowered for today and tomorrow (verse 8).

To be a soldier in the army of the Lord requires much from us. It is not a sloppy, undisciplined, careless way of living. It is intentional, focused, and requires an amazing amount of commitment. You can do it! Let go and let God lead you in a closer path.

*Prospectus: A formal written document relating to a new securities offering that delineates the proposed business plan or the data relevant to an existing business plan / Information needed by investors to make educated decisions whether to purchase the security.

PRAYER

Dear Lord, you are the living God and I am indeed "banking on you." I want to throw myself all in to your kingdom and work. Lead me and I will follow. Amen.

Knowing, Being, and Doing

Get the word out. Teach all these things. And don't let anyone put you down because you're young. Teach believers with your life: by word, by demeanor, by love, by faith, by integrity. Stay at your post reading Scripture, giving counsel, teaching. And that special gift of ministry you were given when the leaders of the church laid hands on you and prayed—keep that dusted off and in use.

Cultivate these things. Immerse yourself in them. The people will all see you mature right before their eyes! Keep a firm grasp on both your character and your teaching. Don't be diverted. Just keep at it. Both you and those who hear you will experience salvation. 1 Timothy 4:11-16

Do these verses really need any comments? There is no doubt what qualifies you as a spiritual leader according to what Paul wrote in this letter to Timothy.

You can break this down into knowing, being, and doing.

1. **What we need to know:** You have the special gift of ministry. You are working to bring salvation to others and yourself. Know that your age doesn't have to matter. Know that faithfulness to God brings maturity.

2. **What we need to be:** Faithful. "Teach believers with your life: by word, by demeanor, by love, by faith, by integrity."

3. **What we need to do:**
   a. Get the word out.
   b. Teach all things.
   c. Stay at your post: reading Scripture, giving counsel, teaching (work ethic).
   d. Cultivate and immerse yourself in God and his ways.
   e. Keep a firm grasp on character and your teaching.
   f. Don't be diverted.
   g. Keep at it!

Again, as I have said before in these devotional thoughts, if you want to be a leader, here is the pattern. Paul has been very clear. Ministry is tough and demands our total devotion, our affection, and our faithfulness. There is the standard and it is a tough one. May those of us who lead realize our weakness is made perfect in his strength.

PRAYER

Dear Jesus, I want to thank you for your Word. Without it, I am useless. Help me, Lord, to know that only with your wisdom and being obedient to your Word am I able to lead others to salvation and a life with hope. Amen.

Doing Ministry Well

The elders who direct the affairs of the church well are worthy of double honor, especially those whose work is preaching and teaching. For the Scripture says, "Do not muzzle the ox while it is treading out the grain," and "The worker deserves his wages." Do not entertain an accusation against an elder unless it is brought by two or three witnesses. Those who sin are to be rebuked publicly, so that the others may take warning.

I charge you, in the sight of God and Christ Jesus and the elect angels, to keep these instructions without partiality, and to do nothing out of favoritism. Do not be hasty in the laying on of hands, and do not share in the sins of others. Keep yourself pure. Stop drinking only water, and use a little wine because of your stomach and your frequent illnesses. 1 Timothy 5:17-23 MSG

1. **Administration matters!** "...who direct the affairs of the church well"
2. **Accusations matter.** "Those who sin are to be rebuked publicly."
3. **All people matter.** "...do nothing out of favoritism."
4. **Abiding matters.** "...do not share in the sins of others. Keep yourself pure."
5. **Affliction matters**. "...because of your stomach and your frequent illness."

In the fifth chapter of 1 Timothy, Paul spends a great deal of time dealing with how to care for widows and the elderly. At the end of the chapter he begins to wrap up some loose ends. We are looking at those loose ends in this devotional. For those who would be leaders in the church, these are important truths to add to those Paul has already written.

The bottom line is no matter what a generation may teach or think about the church, you have to go back to the Word of God as the standard. Usually generations are sidetracked due to hypocrisy or apathy on the part of those who are older.

While this is understandable, it is a dangerous and devastating pursuit to deny the foundational truth of Christianity because of others' actions or inaction. I won't write or talk about it now, but Gnosticism is alive and well, and unfortunately it seems to have attracted a whole generation of young people who could make such a difference if they would focus on living close to God instead of seeing how much like the culture they can live. Christians are different. It has always been a fine line that is hard to maintain, but let's be honest: the early Christians didn't lose their lives because they were cool, hip, or no different than the culture. They lost their lives because they stood for righteousness in a pluralistic society.

What is it that is worth dying for? I wouldn't give two cents for the weak, messy, grace-abusing trivial faith that is commonly thought to be the new wave of Christianity. By the way, I wouldn't give two cents for the anemic, weak, selfish faith of the nominal church today either. Churches that are going through the motions without touching and changing the culture around them are revolting, and I understand the longing for change; but change must come in a way that calls us to the holiness and standard that God lays out in the Word and not the call to embrace sinful ways of this world. If we are just poor, miserable, sinning people, what do we have to offer the poor, miserable, sinning people we live and work with? Holiness to the Lord, now and forever!

PRAYER

Only you, Lord. Only you, Lord. Help me in my weakness to follow only you, Lord. When I stray, pull me back to where I belong with only you, Lord. Thank you for your lovely grace and mercy; may I offer more to others. Amen.

Sin Will Never Be Secret Forever

The sins of some people are blatant and march them right into court. The sins of others don't show up until much later. The same with good deeds. Some you see right off, but none are hidden forever. 1 Timothy 5:24-25 MSG

Sin is something we have to deal with from time to time in the church. The church does really well at celebrating the forgiveness of a sinner on the front end of their salvation; but if you happen to fall into a devastating sin after you have been a Christian for a good length of time, they are ill-equipped to know what to do.

Paul deals with this in prior verses and says we are to "call them on the carpet" if someone falls into sin, especially a leader. He also in other places calls for restoration. His admonition in these two verses should be remembered. Sin will always show up at some point—if not here, in the final judgment. Also our good deeds may not be recognized, especially in leadership roles, but they will not be hidden forever. Trust God with your walk and work. If you fall into sin, repent and seek the Lord. If you do a good deed, let God be glorified and let all honor go to him. You will get your recognition soon enough.

PRAYER

Lord Jesus, please forgive me for my downfalls, for when I fall I sin against you. Lord Almighty, full of grace and mercy, thank you for your restoration. Amen.

Living and Loving for Real

Whoever is a slave must make the best of it, giving respect to his master so that outsiders don't blame God and our teaching for his behavior. Slaves with Christian masters all the more so—their masters are really their beloved brothers! These are the things I want you to teach and preach. If you have leaders there who teach otherwise, who refuse the solid words of our Master Jesus and this godly instruction, tag them for what they are: ignorant windbags who infect the air with germs of envy, controversy, bad-mouthing, suspicious rumors. Eventually there's an epidemic of backstabbing, and truth is but a distant memory. They think religion is a way to make a fast buck. A devout life does bring wealth, but it's the rich simplicity of being yourself before God. Since we entered the world penniless and will leave it penniless, if we have bread on the table and shoes on our feet, that's enough. But if it's only money these leaders are after, they'll self-destruct in no time. Lust for money brings trouble and nothing but trouble. Going down that path, some lose their footing in the faith completely and live to regret it bitterly ever after. 1 Timothy 6:1-10 MSG

1. **Behavior matters:** Our actions reflect on God and our teaching.
2. **Beliefs matter:** There is not a lot of room for personal interpretation.
3. **Being yourself:** Wealth is more than money. It is found in simplicity.
4. **Be vigilant:** There are wrong roads out there.

If you are called by God to be a leader in ministry, the standard remains high. In the prior chapter Paul reinforces the need to pay those who are leading, but here he challenges some who are abusing the system. Being called to serve God and the church is not just another vocation. You don't go to job fares to see if maybe you want to be in full-time ministry. While I believe strongly in the priesthood of believers, there is something unique about the call of God and the responsibility that comes with it. It is simple: serve God every day all day with all your heart, mind and soul. (I really believe all Christians should live by this same standard.)

O Holy Spirit, be with me and give me a spirit of discernment to know where only Christ is being taught and lived out. Every place that I am, let me see you that I might reflect you in the way I believe and how I behave. Thank you for your guidance. Amen.

Pursue the God-Life

But you, Timothy, man of God: Run for your life from all this. Pursue a righteous life—a life of wonder, faith, love, steadiness, courtesy. Run hard and fast in the faith. Seize the eternal life, the life you were called to, the life you so fervently embraced in the presence of so many witnesses. I'm charging you before the life-giving God and before Christ, who took his stand before Pontius Pilate and didn't give an inch: Keep this command to the letter, and don't slack off. Our Master, Jesus Christ, is on his way. He'll show up right on time, his arrival guaranteed by the Blessed and Undisputed Ruler, High King, High God. He's the only one death can't touch, his light so bright no one can get close. He's never been seen by human eyes—human eyes can't take him in! Honor to him, and eternal rule! Oh, yes.

Tell those rich in this world's wealth to quit being so full of themselves and so obsessed with money, which is here today and gone tomorrow. Tell them to go after God, who piles on all the riches we could ever manage—to do good, to be rich in helping others, to be extravagantly generous. If they do that, they'll build a treasury that will last, gaining life that is truly life. And oh, my dear Timothy, guard the treasure you were given! Guard it with your life. Avoid the talk-show religion and the practiced confusion of the so-called experts. People caught up in a lot of talk can miss the whole point of faith. Overwhelming grace keep you. 1 Timothy 6:11-21 MSG

1. **Pursue life:**
   a. Our life in God is full of wonder, faith, love, steadiness, and courtesy.
   b. It is eternal.
2. **Seize eternal life:**
   a. You have been called.
   b. Embrace it.
3. **Trust God with your life:**
   a. He is life-giving.
   b. He shows up at the right time.
   c. He is a bright light.

4. **Teach others to go after the God life:**
   a. Let God live and love through you.
   b. Put your "money" in God's bank!
5. **Guard God's gift with your life:**
   a. Avoid slick religion.
   b. You don't need to be an expert.
   c. You don't need to talk about it; just live it for real.

Run away from sin as fast as you can go. Run away from a lust for money. Run in God's direction daily. Pursue a godly and holy life.

Dear Lord, I turn to you. As I daily turn my mind away from all the things that distract me from your love, may I run toward you. Thank you for your grace. Amen.

All the Best

I, Paul, am on special assignment for Christ, carrying out God's plan laid out in the Message of Life by Jesus. I write this to you, Timothy, the son I love so much. All the best from our God and Christ be yours! Every time I say your name in prayer—which is practically all the time—I thank God for you, the God I worship with my whole life in the tradition of my ancestors. I miss you a lot, especially when I remember that last tearful good-bye, and I look forward to a joy-packed reunion. That precious memory triggers another: your honest faith—and what a rich faith it is, handed down from your grandmother Lois to your mother Eunice, and now to you! And the special gift of ministry you received when I laid hands on you and prayed—keep that ablaze! God doesn't want us to be shy with his gifts, but bold and loving and sensible. So don't be embarrassed to speak up for our Master or for me, his prisoner. Take your share of suffering for the Message along with the rest of us. We can only keep on going, after all, by the power of God, who first saved us and then called us to this holy work. We had nothing to do with it. It was all his idea, a gift prepared for us in Jesus long before we knew anything about it. But we know it now. Since the appearance of our Savior, nothing could be plainer: death defeated, life vindicated in a steady blaze of light, all through the work of Jesus. 2 Timothy 1:1-10 MSG

Paul is once again writing to his "son" in the faith. Timothy is engaged in ministry and Paul is his mentor and spiritual father. In this section of the letter Paul is admonishing and encouraging Timothy. He is reminiscing and in the process remembers some things worth remembering.

1. **We need supportive people around us.** People who care. Verse 4
2. **We need to honor our calling.** Nurture God's gifts. Verse 6
3. **We need to "just do it."** (ministry) Verse 7
4. **We need God's power.** Verse 8

Again, Paul is writing some practical leadership advice. These writings from the Word are very relevant to anyone in ministry today. A call to God's service is not a title nor is it an entitlement. It is a gift to be embraced, strengthened, protected, worked, lived out, loved, and fulfilled as God opens the doors of opportunity. This call to ministry is to all of us.

PRAYER

Dear Lord, I know that you have every right to call me and ask me to do anything for you. Please give me the courage to believe in your calling and the strength to see it through. Amen.

I Couldn't Be More Sure...

This is the Message I've been set apart to proclaim as preacher, emissary, and teacher. It's also the cause of all this trouble I'm in. But I have no regrets. I couldn't be more sure of my ground—the One I've trusted in can take care of what he's trusted me to do right to the end. So keep at your work, this faith and love rooted in Christ, exactly as I set it out for you. It's as sound as the day you first heard it from me. Guard this precious thing placed in your custody by the Holy Spirit who works in us. I'm sure you know by now that everyone in the province of Asia deserted me, even Phygelus and Hermogenes. But God bless Onesiphorus and his family! Many's the time I've been refreshed in that house. And he wasn't embarrassed a bit that I was in jail. The first thing he did when he got to Rome was look me up. May God on the Last Day treat him as well as he treated me. And then there was all the help he provided in Ephesus—but you know that better than I. 2 Timothy 1: 11-18 MSG

1. **We have been set apart for ministry.** Verse 11
2. **Ministry rarely means trouble free or easy.** Verse 12
3. **Focus is critical:**
   a. Keep at your work.
   b. Let faith and love be rooted in you through Christ.
   c. Guard what has been given you by the help of the Holy Spirit.
4. **Sometimes you will feel deserted.** Not everyone will get it or be willing to take the journey with you. Let those who do get it and who want to be a part love you and provide the care you need.

God has called all of us to this unique place of service. We have been called to this time in the history of the church to be as faithful as possible to the great commission. Our "job" is to lead others to do ministry and share the message that has been entrusted to us.

Paul assures Timothy that he "couldn't be more sure of his ground," even though he has been in prison. Are you sure today of your ground? Are you sure of your calling? Seek every day to know the mind of Christ and let his Spirit live and work through you.

PRAYER

Dear Jesus, please allow me to see and hear your calling in my life. Even when there are challenges, let me stay the course and follow you with complete trust. Amen.

Throw Yourself into This Work...

So, my son, throw yourself into this work for Christ. Pass on what you heard from me—the whole congregation saying Amen!—to reliable leaders who are competent to teach others. When the going gets rough, take it on the chin with the rest of us, the way Jesus did. A soldier on duty doesn't get caught up in making deals at the marketplace. He concentrates on carrying out orders. An athlete who refuses to play by the rules will never get anywhere. It's the diligent farmer who gets the produce. Think it over. God will make it all plain. 2 Timothy 2:1-7 MSG

1. **Multiplying:**
Our church endeavors to be a place where Christ-followers reproduce/multiply Christ-followers, leaders reproduce/multiply leaders, and churches reproduce/multiply other churches.

Verse 2 is clearly teaching that reproduction/multiplication is a biblical principle.

2. **Reality checks:**
   a. Sometimes the way will get rough. Verse 3
   b. Stay focused. Verse 4
   c. Systems matter. Verse 5
   d. Stick to it. Verse 6
   e. Spend time meditating on these things. Verse 7

We have been called to this church to be leaders. Leaders should not be on a pedestal or think of themselves as being better than others. It is our job to see that others respond to the call of God in their lives. We are to mentor, empower, and bless others by supporting them in their ministries.

PRAYER

Dear Jesus, when you are at work things will multiply. I offer my ministry to you so that you can expand whatever it is you want me to do. Show me the way. Keep me focused. Amen.

Fix This Picture Firmly in Your Mind...

Fix this picture firmly in your mind: Jesus, descended from the line of David, raised from the dead. It's what you've heard from me all along. It's what I'm sitting in jail for right now—but God's Word isn't in jail! That's why I stick it out here—so that everyone God calls will get in on the salvation of Christ in all its glory. This is a sure thing: If we die with him, we'll live with him; If we stick it out with him, we'll rule with him; If we turn our backs on him, he'll turn his back on us; If we give up on him, he does not give up—for there's no way he can be false to himself. Repeat these basic essentials over and over to God's people. Warn them before God against pious nitpicking, which chips away at the faith. It just wears everyone out. Concentrate on doing your best for God, work you won't be ashamed of, laying out the truth plain and simple. Stay clear of pious talk that is only talk. Words are not mere words, you know. If they're not backed by a godly life, they accumulate as poison in the soul. Hymenaeus and Philetus are examples, throwing believers off stride and missing the truth by a mile by saying the resurrection is over and done with. Meanwhile, God's firm foundation is as firm as ever, these sentences engraved on the stones: GOD KNOWS WHO BELONGS TO HIM. SPURN EVIL ALL YOU WHO NAME GOD AS GOD. 2 Timothy 2:8-19 MSG

1. **Know Christ, know him really well.**

He is the focus of our faith. He is to be the focus of our life and the direction our life takes, not just day by day but minute by minute. When our focus is on Christ and who he is, the issues of daily life don't seem so intimidating.

2. **Know these principles:**

"If we die with him, we'll live with him; If we stick it out with him, we'll rule with him; If we turn our backs on him, he'll turn his back on us; If we give up on him, he does not give up—for there's no way he can be false to himself.

3. **Know the godly life.**

Concentrate...

PRAYER

Dear Lord, you and you alone are my focus. Whatever is done through me will always be because of you. Help me to know the godly life so that I may always be in your will. Amen.

What Kind of Container Are You?

In a well-furnished kitchen there are not only crystal goblets and silver platters, but waste cans and compost buckets—some containers used to serve fine meals, others to take out the garbage. Become the kind of container God can use to present any and every kind of gift to his guests for their blessing. 2 Timothy 2:20-21 MSG

In a wealthy home some utensils are made of gold and silver, and some are made of wood and clay. The expensive utensils are used for special occasions, and the cheap ones are for everyday use. If you keep yourself pure, you will be a special utensil for honorable use. Your life will be clean, and you will be ready for the Master to use you for every good work. 2 Timothy 2:20-21 NLT

Those who cleanse themselves from the latter will be instruments for special purposes, made holy, useful to the Master and prepared to do any good work. 2 Timothy 2:21 NIV

Run away from infantile indulgence. Run after mature righteousness—faith, love, peace—joining those who are in honest and serious prayer before God. Refuse to get involved in inane discussions; they always end up in fights. God's servant must not be argumentative, but a gentle listener and a teacher who keeps cool, working firmly but patiently with those who refuse to obey. You never know how or when God might sober them up with a change of heart and a turning to the truth, enabling them to escape the Devil's trap, where they are caught and held captive, forced to run his errands. 2 Timothy 2:22-26 MSG

1. God's call is always to be holy

Holiness is not an elective or option for only the super spiritual. It is God's standard for his followers. Down through history, God always uses people who will practice the presence of God every day all day long. Being holy should be the daily desire and goal for all of us. We are commanded to teach others this standard of biblical truth.

2. **God's call always involves relationships**
   a. Run away from personal indulgences that take you away from godliness.
   b. Run toward maturity: righteousness, faith, love, and peace. PRAY.
   c. Refuse to be drawn into petty conversations. Be patient.
   d. Realize that God's goal is always redemption.

PRAYER

Dear Jesus, fill me with your holiness so that I can serve you with no reservations. I don't want to hold anything back from you, ever. Amen.

They'll Make a Show of Religion...

Don't be naive. There are difficult times ahead. As the end ap-proaches, people are going to be self-absorbed, money-hungry, self-promoting, stuck-up, profane, contemptuous of parents, crude, coarse, dog-eat-dog, unbending, slanderers, impulsively wild, sav-age, cynical, treacherous, ruthless, bloated windbags, addicted to lust, and allergic to God. They'll make a show of religion, but be-hind the scenes they're animals. Stay clear of these people. These are the kind of people who smooth-talk themselves into the homes of unstable and needy women and take advantage of them; women who, depressed by their sinfulness, take up with every new religious fad that calls itself "truth." They get exploited every time and never really learn. These men are like those old Egyptian frauds Jannes and Jambres, who challenged Moses. They were rejects from the faith, twisted in their thinking, defying truth itself. But nothing will come of these latest impostors. Everyone will see through them, just as people saw through that Egyptian hoax. 2 Timothy 3:1-9 MSG

1. **Don't be naïve**

The bottom line is there are always going to be difficult times. When everything is going smoothly, we are probably not challenging anybody very deeply. "As the end approaches" is the beginning of an accurate por-trayal of society and culture. We need to find ways to touch the culture without buying into the culture.

2. **Stay clear of certain people**

We need to ask ourselves why we should stay away from certain peo-ple. What are the negative results that could come from contact?

3. **Trends, fads, and truth**

In the church world, we seem to be especially vulnerable to running after "Christian celebrities." Sometimes we are much too quick to equate crowds with blessing or God's approval. We should always seek to know and embrace truth. We should ask God for the vision he wants for our church specifically and not ask what is the church across town doing.

PRAYER

Dear Jesus, these are strange days we live in and I ask that you will give me the ability to know your will and way. Let me serve you with my whole heart. Amen.

There's Nothing Like the Written Word of God...

You've been a good apprentice to me, a part of my teaching, my manner of life, direction, faith, steadiness, love, patience, troubles, sufferings—suffering along with me in all the grief I had to put up with in Antioch, Iconium, and Lystra. And you also well know that God rescued me! Anyone who wants to live all out for Christ is in for a lot of trouble; there's no getting around it. Unscrupulous con men will continue to exploit the faith. They're as deceived as the people they lead astray. As long as they are out there, things can only get worse. But don't let it faze you. Stick with what you learned and believed, sure of the integrity of your teachers—why, you took in the sacred Scriptures with your mother's milk! There's nothing like the written Word of God for showing you the way to salvation through faith in Christ Jesus. Every part of Scripture is God-breathed and useful one way or another—showing us truth, exposing our rebellion, correcting our mistakes, training us to live God's way. Through the Word we are put together and shaped up for the tasks God has for us. 2 Timothy 3:10-17

1. **Ministry would be great if it weren't for people!** Verses 10-13

Paul and Timothy had been through a lot together, but Paul always seems to come back to the suffering. It was a common part of his faith. God always rescued him, but God never kept him from experiencing suffering. Verse 12 is quite startling in its directness. It reminds us once again that those who really follow Christ will without doubt be tested and tried. The Christian life is certainly not about health and wealth.

2. **Make the Word of God your manual for living.** Verses 14-17

These verses really are some of the most understandable and practical in all the New Testament. Anyone reading them should be able to "get it." The problem often comes for those in ministry when we start operating on our own knowledge and experience. There is no one in ministry that doesn't need to be living in the Word of God. It is the Word, held up against our lives, that shapes and guides us in our pursuit of God.

Find something every day from the Word of God that you can hang onto all day long. Love it, learn it, and live it.

Dear Jesus, Please let me live on and in your Word. I ask that nothing or no one in this world will cause me to be distracted as I pursue your calling in my life. Amen.

God Is Looking Over Your Shoulder

I can't impress this on you too strongly. God is looking over your shoulder. Christ himself is the Judge, with the final say on everyone, living and dead. He is about to break into the open with his rule, so proclaim the Message with intensity; keep on your watch. Challenge, warn, and urge your people. Don't ever quit. Just keep it simple. 2 Timothy 4:1-2 MSG

Paul is winding up this letter with a sense of urgency. He really believes that what he is about to write needs to leave a lasting impression on Timothy. Without much warning he announces, "God is looking over your shoulder."

What a great thought to temper our daily actions and reactions. It doesn't feel negative unless you are doing something you know you shouldn't be doing. It is more like having a mentor and friend who is behind you in your endeavors. Christ will someday have the final say regarding how we have lived our lives and particularly how we have done our ministry. With that in mind we should:

1. **Proclaim the message with intensity. Passion**
2. **Keep your watch. Patience**
3. **Challenge, warn, and urge people. Priority**
4. **Don't quit. Ever. Persistence**
5. **Keep it simple. Purpose**

PRAYER

Dear Jesus, the notion of you looking over my shoulder is both comforting and challenging. I welcome you, Lord, into every area of my life, including when no one else is looking. I am all in for you. Amen.

Keep the Message Alive...

You're going to find that there will be times when people will have no stomach for solid teaching, but will fill up on spiritual junk food—catchy opinions that tickle their fancy. They'll turn their backs on truth and chase mirages. But you—keep your eye on what you're doing; accept the hard times along with the good; keep the Message alive; do a thorough job as God's servant. 2 Timothy 4:3-5 NLT

Paul is writing about seasons of spiritual decline that individuals, churches, and even denominations go through. We must be very vigilant and full of wisdom to be able to discern genuine moves of God verses man made movements. Right now it is a strange and defining time in the church world, especially in America. Take these words to heart and note the action steps laid out by Paul:

1. **Keep your eye on what you are doing.**   **Evaluation**
2. **Accept the hard times along with the good.**   **Endurance**
3. **Keep the message alive.**   **Evangelism**
4. **Do a thorough job as God's servant.**   **Excellence**

Keep the message alive. Our work should always be about the life-changing gospel message. Always.

PRAYER

Dear God, I am and always want to be your servant. Help me keep my eye on what's important. Make me more like you. Amen.

Depend on it . . .

You take over. I'm about to die, my life an offering on God's altar. This is the only race worth running. I've run hard right to the finish, believed all the way. All that's left now is the shouting—God's applause! Depend on it, he's an honest judge. He'll do right not only by me, but by everyone eager for his coming. 2 Timothy 4:6-8 MSG

Paul is nearing the end of his life and the race that he has run for God. He has mentored Timothy to be a young leaders and pastor. He has urged him to be the shepherd God called him to be. And now these are his final words. We can find great instruction for our own lives if we live them with Paul's words in view. Here is what he left Timothy and us to ponder:

Our life is a gift to God: For Paul, his life was an offering on God's altar. I love this analogy. My prayer for us is that our lives will stay on His altar till the day we die.

Our race has a fantastic goal: Paul reminds us that the godly life is the only race worth running. He has run hard all the way to the finish. All that is left is the shouting.

Our prize at the end will be His grace: Paul says, *"God's applause!"* I can't imagine receiving that prize someday. By His grace, we will be judged and He will do it right according to His word and promises.

Be eager for His coming and return. Always know that heaven is far better than anything on this earth. Keep eternity in view.

PRAYER

Dear Lord, I can't imagine what I will feel at the end of my life, but I know I want to leave this world trusting you with my eternity. Let me live in your house forever. Amen.

God Is Always Searching

The Lord looks down from heaven on the entire human race; he looks to see if anyone is truly wise, if anyone seeks God. Psalm 14:2 NLT

We are living through strange times. These days are unlike anything most of us have experienced in our lifetime.

As you pause today to consider God's Word, I want to encourage you to take advantage of this time. Use this time to do some things you didn't think you had time to do in the past. Spend more time in the Bible, pray more, help others, focus on your family, either in person or by electronic means.

Today we are looking at a verse of Scripture from Psalm 14. We are looking at verse 2 and this is what it says:

1. God is always searching (looking)
2. We should always be seeking him (leaning)

God is always searching.

He searches for men and women who are serving him and trusting in him. God blesses these people! These are the people that God loves to support.

So know that God has his eyes on you! This is a great thing!

He is looking for people who will depend on him.

He is looking for people who will trust him when they can't see the future.

He is looking for people who will not give up their faith when life turns upside down.

He is looking for people who will look to him in their weakness and failure.

He is looking for men and women who feel insecure and anxious.

The bottom line is that he is looking for you and me.

If God is always looking at us, then we should always be seeking him.

Sometimes when life becomes a struggle, we will turn every other direction seeking help and forget that God is watching and waiting for us to turn to him. Nothing should keep you from seeking God. No matter where you are living in your life or what may be going on around you, never give up seeking God.

We know that the Bible teaches us that if we draw near to God, he will draw near to us.

Dear God, please keep looking for me. Make my heart hungry to know more about you and to know you more. I am seeking you. Amen.

Vanishing Love

"O Israel and Judah, what should I do with you?" asks the Lord.
*"For your love vanishes like the morning mist and disappears like
dew in the sunlight."* Hosea 6:4 NLT

The words of God to Israel and Judah are haunting in some ways.
How easy it is to forget our relationship with God if we are not careful. Israel enjoyed the special calling of God and yet they were never
happy. They were constantly seeking help from false gods, false religious
leaders, and generally ignoring God and his desire for relationship.

When I read this verse, I paused and spent some time reflecting on
God's words. "For your love vanishes like the morning mist and disappears like dew in sunlight." I never want for him to feel that way about
my relationship with him. He longs for us to be true to him, faithful to
him, and in love with him. Our relationship should be so rooted in love
and trust that nothing or no one possesses the ability to turn our heads
or call us away from his path.

And yet, sometimes great people have fallen. The Bible is full of stories of men and women that blew it. Like with Israel and Judah, God was
there to provide restoration and redemption; but more than anything,
God wants our whole hearts.

Spend some time today examining your love for God. Don't be afraid
to be honest with God about it since he knows anyway. View him as a
friend looking to hear from you each day. View him as the love of your
life who longs to know and experience your love.

PRAYER

*Dear God, please allow me to grow stronger in my love for you. I
don't want the things of this world. I want to be free from their pull
and to be fully devoted to you. Amen.*

Christ's Ambassadors – 1

And all of this is a gift from God, who brought us back to himself through Christ. And God has given us this task of reconciling people to him. For God was in Christ, reconciling the world to himself, no longer counting people's sins against them. And he gave us this wonderful message of reconciliation. So we are Christ's ambassadors; God is making his appeal through us. 2 Corinthians 5:18-20 NLT

Never forget what your role is if you are a Christian. We represent Christ and his message in a very lost world. You are his ambassador. He is "making his appeal through us."

Most of the time when there is a change in presidents there are new ambassadors appointed around the world. They have very clear instructions given on what they are to do, and they become students of the culture where they are to serve.

When I graduated from Franklin University's Graduate school, I was contacted and sent a notebook. I officially became a Graduate Outreach Agent. It is amazing the lengths they went to in order to insure that the university and its mission would be represented well.

Topics in this notebook included:

10 Tips for Successful Public Speaking.

Tips for Public Speaking.

Professional Attire for Men and Women.

12 Tips for effective Networking.

Networking No-No's.

6 Tips for a Good Handshake.

Negotiating Tips.

Introductions.

Manners Mom Never Taught You.

The bottom line is that if we are truly Christ followers we are enlisted as ambassadors of the gospel. The question becomes: What kind of an ambassador are you? Who are you representing? What does it take to be an ambassador?

In the next devotion I will try to answer those questions. What do you think it means to be an ambassador for Christ?

Dear God, this is really a big deal. Enable me to come to an understanding of what it means for me to represent you as an ambassador. I want to represent you well every day. Amen.

Christ's Ambassadors – 2

This means that anyone who belongs to Christ has become a new person. The old life is gone; a new life has begun! And all of this is a gift from God, who brought us back to himself through Christ. And God has given us this task of reconciling people to him. For God was in Christ, reconciling the world to himself, no longer counting people's sins against them. And he gave us this wonderful message of reconciliation. So we are Christ's ambassadors; God is making his appeal through us. 2 Corinthians 5:17-20 NLT

I want to revisit this passage of Scripture and think a little deeper about what it means to be an ambassador for Christ. There is no question that this calling is for all Christians. It is not optional for just a handful. So what does it mean for you and I? Please notice that I added verse 17 to today's Scripture.

The Marks of an Ambassador
a. **All things are new.** "This means that anyone who belongs to Christ has become a new person. The old life is gone; a new life has begun."
b. **All things are of God.** "And all of this is a gift from God."

The Message of an Ambassador
a. **We are reconciled:** "who brought us back to himself through Christ."
b. **We are reconcilers.** "And God has given us this task of reconciling people to him."

The Ministry of an Ambassador
a. **We are to represent God.** "So we are Christ's ambassadors."
b. **We are to work with God.** "God is making his appeal through us."

PRAYER

Dear Jesus, I am so glad you allow me to represent this wonderful message of reconciliation and forgiveness. I want to be your ambassador until I draw my last breath. Use me as you will. Amen.

Practicing Restraint

*So this is what the Lord says to his people: "You love to wander far
from me and do not restrain yourselves."* Jeremiah 14:10 NLT

Wandering away from God is something that all of us must be aware
of in our spiritual life. It is very easy to be distracted by the things
of this world or even the cares of our lives. People can be distracting.
Work can be distracting. Family can be distracting.

We must value our time with God daily and not forsake or sacrifice
it for any reason. We must restrain ourselves and ask ourselves often,
"What does God think about what I am doing?"

His Word enables us to find the path or the narrow road or gate that
Jesus referred to in the Sermon on the Mount. He said only a few ever
find it, and that says to me that you and I must be diligent about our
faith. We must give ourselves to God daily in a way that puts him first in
every decision.

In 1758, Robert Robinson wrote these words that became the song
"Come Thou Fount of Every Blessing." Make this your prayer today:

PRAYER

Come, thou Fount of every blessing,
Tune my heart to sing thy grace;
Streams of mercy, never ceasing,
Call for songs of loudest praise.
Teach me some melodious sonnet,
Sung by flaming tongues above.
Praise the mount, I'm fixed upon it,
Mount of thy redeeming love.
O to grace how great a debtor.
Daily I'm constrained to be!
Let Thy goodness, like a fetter,
Bind my wandering heart to thee.
Prone to wander, Lord, I feel it,
Prone to leave the God I love;
Here's my heart, O take and seal it,
Seal it for thy courts above.

Instead, Be Kind

Instead, be kind to each other, tenderhearted, forgiving one another, just as God through Christ has forgiven you. Ephesians 4:32 NLT

This! This is the way to live as a human being. Of course, to really live this way you need Christ living in you. We are at our best when we are following Jesus in word, thought, and deed.

Being kind to others is such an appealing way to live. To live out kindness you must have a tender heart, meaning you must be sensitive to the feelings, needs, and presence of those around you. How would you rate your tenderheartedness today?

When I think of this question, I try to measure myself against the actions of Jesus when he was on this earth. He was tenderhearted toward a woman with a twelve-year hemorrhage. He was tenderhearted toward the parents of a little girl that died by raising her back to life. He was full of compassion for blind Bartimaeus and for a father with a demon possessed son. He was moved by a sinful woman at a well one day, and he is moved with compassion and tenderheartedness for you. Even from the cross, Jesus prayed for those who were killing him.

Because he forgave us, we are to forgive others, practice tenderhearted kindness, and spread the love of Jesus to all we meet daily.

Let his love shine through you today!

PRAYER

Dear Jesus, please give me a tender heart and a kind, loving spirit. Teach me to know the power of forgiveness on others and me. Let my love as you love. Amen.

Pray, Pray, and Pray Some More

Never stop praying. 1 Thessalonians 5:17 NLT

Prayer is a gift to all that will use it. It is best to pray every day and not just when the crisis hits. God wants to hear from you always. He delights in your presence through prayer.

I wonder if you have ever tried staying in touch with God all day long. In other words, wherever you are, you find yourself mentally accenting and acknowledging God's constant presence in your life. It doesn't have to be a distraction for you or those around you. I have found that I can quietly acknowledge God throughout my day and whisper a prayer including him in whatever is going on around me.

Why not try that today if you don't already practice it? Let God be the constant partner that is with you every hour of every day. Who knows how an intentional awareness of his presence might change a lot of things about your day!

PRAYER

Dear Jesus, help me learn to practice your presence in the mundane things of life. Give me an awareness and a hunger to include you in all that I do daily. Amen.

I've Got the Joy, Joy, Joy, Joy...

This is the day the Lord has made. We will rejoice and be glad in it. Psalm 118:24 NLT

Every day is a day created by God! Let that thought sink in for a moment or two. It is a gift. It is his creation. It will be filled with opportunities and moments of grace. Sometimes you will receive grace, and sometimes you may be the one extending it.

The psalmist is calling us to acknowledge and celebrate the day! We are to find joy and gladness in our day. I must be quick to tell you that some days the only joy you might find is in your relationship with Christ.

I have had unexpected moments of joy because of someone's kindness, a grandchild encounter (that can go both ways), or the licks and wagging tail of a puppy.

I love the declaration in this verse. "We will rejoice and be glad in it." When I officiate funerals I generally will pray this verse at the beginning in acknowledgment of God's creation of even days filled with sorrow and grief. Be so trusting of God that no matter what happens you can find a way to rejoice with gladness at the day you are now living in.

No matter what happens, God made the day! Find your joy in him!

PRAYER

Dear God, thank you for this day! You made it. You know everything that will happen and that has happened. I rejoice in you and lift up my voice of thanksgiving to you today. Amen

I Can

For I can do everything through Christ, who gives me strength.
Philippians 4:13 NLT

When you pair your weakness with Christ's strength, nothing is impossible for you to do if God is calling you to do it.

This is one of the most powerful verses in the entire Bible. No matter who reads it, or where they are from around the world, this verse is for them. As followers of Christ, we are promised that his power will empower us to do whatever he wants us to do. It also means that he will supply the grace to enable us to endure the things we encounter in our lives.

There is such disparity in the world with the majority of the population living in some form of neglect or poverty, and yet those that seek Jesus learn about his abiding power and presence. I wonder what God wants you to do today. I encourage you to not be too quick to respond with a negative answer, or an answer based on your insecurities and weaknesses.

We are reminded in 2 Corinthians 12:9 that God said, "My grace is sufficient for you, for my strength is made perfect in weakness." Rethink whatever is going on around you today. Open yourself to his call and promises. Look for Jesus to show up when you need him most. That doesn't mean every prayer gets answered the way we want or wish, but it means he will be in the middle of whatever is happening in our lives.

Connect with Jesus Christ and let him work in you and through you!

PRAYER

Dear Jesus, thank you for this amazing promise. Help me to really believe and embrace these words every day of my life. Amen.

He Is the Beginning and the End

"I am the Alpha and the Omega—the beginning and the end," says the Lord God. "I am the one who is, who always was, and who is still to come—the Almighty One." Revelation 1:8 NLT

This verse written by John was a direct quote from God. It should bring us great comfort and hope to realize that our Lord is the beginning and the end of all things.

He is the only one that brings true and lasting hope into our lives. It is in Jesus that we find hope. It is not in politics, politicians, money, human power, education, relationships, networking, or anything else that we tend to put our trust in.

He reminds us, "I am the one who is, who always was, and who is still to come."

As I look around me and observe what is happening, personally and in our world, I might be tempted to be discouraged at times. Then I remember that as a Christ-follower, I am connected to the first and the last, the beginning and the end of all things. If that is not enough, I remind myself that he is "still to come."

For the true followers, the second coming of our Lord is to be hoped for and longed for and to provide us with confidence and comfort. Lift up your heads. Keep your eyes open and your heart waiting for the one who is to come. When Jesus left this earth, the angels reminded the disciples who were staring up into the sky when Jesus had just gone (a dramatic and even traumatic moment) by saying, "Why are you standing here staring into heaven? Jesus has been taken from you into heaven, but someday he will return from heaven in the same way you saw him go!"

He is coming back someday! For some that may produce fear, but for most of us it should produce a sense of destiny and eternity, calmness and confidence and faith and hope.

PRAYER

Dear Lord, I am reminded today that you are the great I Am. You are everything to me, and I am longing for your return with much anticipation and expectation. Amen.

Are You Listening?

Have you never heard? Have you never understood? The LORD is the everlasting God, the Creator of all the earth. He never grows weak or weary. No one can measure the depths of his understanding. He gives power to the weak and strength to the powerless. Isaiah 40:28-29 NLT

I have to wonder what Isaiah was feeling and thinking when he wrote these words and questions. They feel emotional and almost desperate to get someone to listen. He wants us to know who God is. He wants us to know what he does and that he never grows weary. God has more understanding than we can comprehend. He gives power to the powerless!

Well, there you have it. Whatever is on your mind today, this week, this month, or even this year should be filtered through these powerful verses. His ways are indeed higher than our ways, so we trust him with our lives. We trust him with our circumstances. We allow him to walk with us through the deep waters that sometimes threaten us.

Why not today, really think about the role God plays in your life. Do you have a personal, daily relationship with the Creator of all the earth, or do you just call on him when life turns upside down? I would not want to walk through this life without God as my counselor and heavenly Father. I grow weak but he does not. I sometimes don't understand, but he always does. I get weary with life, but he gives strength when I need it most.

Have you not heard? Have you never understood?

PRAYER

Dear God, sometimes I forget. I have heard and I know who you are, and I want you to be in my life. Please guide me through the seasons of my life. Please fill me with your strength and power so that I will follow you with all my heart every day. Amen.

The Love of God

Keep yourselves in the love of God, waiting for the mercy of our Lord Jesus Christ that leads to eternal life. Jude 1:21 ESV

As you know, this world is full of distractions. We are often consumed with all the things that are happening around us. Life happens, and most of it is beyond our control. Phone calls come and we are summoned into someone's needs, problems, or drama. Even on our strongest and best days, it can be exhausting.

Here we have an answer. "Keep yourselves in the love of God."

How can I keep myself in the love of God? I am pondering that. I think today that I will remind myself repeatedly of how much he loves me. I will think about his love and allow him to love me. What happens when I "keep myself in his love" is that I begin to think about how much I love him. When I think about it, I become grateful for what he has done and does in my life every day. Circumstances on this earth will always be a challenge, but his love never wavers. His love gives us the hope of life after the struggles of this earth have ended. We are to "wait for the mercy of our Lord Jesus that leads to eternal life."

The lyrics of the first verse to the song "Hold to God's Unchanging Hand" provide a good reflection.

> *Time is filled with swift transition,*
> *Naught of earth unmoved can stand,*
> *Build your hopes on things eternal,*
> *Hold to God's unchanging hand.*

PRAYER

Dear Jesus, thanks for this reminder to keep myself in your love. Your love is all I really need. My hope is in what happens after this life. Amen.

404

Devote Yourself

Devote yourselves to prayer with an alert mind and a thankful heart. Colossians 4:2 NLT

There is a notion strongly suggested in this verse that we bear some responsibility to make prayer work. It's a simple but profound directive: "Devote yourselves." I think this means that you and I have to be devoted to prayer. Devotion means we possess love, loyalty, or enthusiasm for a person, activity, or cause. In this case, it would be for a person, Jesus, and the activity of talking with him in an intimate way.

When we love someone, we stay in contact with him or her. We think nothing of calling, texting, emailing, or seeing them as much as possible. How much more should we be in love with Jesus? How much more should we communicate with him daily than sometimes we do?

Today would be a good day to talk with him often. Practice awareness of his presence all day long. Pray is the key to heaven. Stay devoted and alert. Pray often. Jesus is coming back and he will be looking for the faithful.

PRAYER

Dear Jesus, with your help I will devote myself to prayer today. I will have an "alert mind and a thankful heart." Thank you for your invitation daily to talk with you. Amen.

His Love Endures Forever!

Give thanks to the LORD, *for he is good. His faithful love endures forever.* Psalm 106:1 NLT

With all the things to be thankful for, the last five words of this verse sum it all up. "His faithful love endures forever." God's love is faithful; and while he may allow us to experience the consequences of our sins, or the struggles that sometimes come to us because we live in a very broken world, his love never fails. His love endures forever.

You may be thinking about things you have done that you wish you wouldn't have done. Words spoken, actions or reactions, or maybe even broken commandments.

Thankfulness should be practiced every day. Spend some time during this devotional time thinking of all the things you are grateful for every day.

Find things to be thankful for this week. Know how good God is and ponder that his faithful love endures forever. His love is over the top. He is crazy about you!

PRAYER

Dear Jesus, may I never forget to be thankful for your enduring and everlasting love. I rejoice in it today and want you to know my gratefulness. Amen.

The Ultimate Rescue

He reached down from heaven and rescued me; he drew me out of deep waters. 2 Samuel 22:17 NLT

All of us have the potential to get in over our heads. When life is threatening, don't panic. God is able to reach you and rescue you. The thought of the literal hand of God reaching down from heaven would certainly be sensational. Of course, we know that he doesn't need human hands to move, reach down, or draw us out of our circumstances.

God does rescue us in due time, but it rarely fits our timetables. When we pray, we want an answer now. Oftentimes we may be in our circumstances for a while to allow us to learn lessons we would never learn without adversity. It is in crisis that we often draw the closest to God.

You may feel like you are drowning today in anxiety or even panic. Don't listen to the lies that Satan would have you believe. You are safe in God's hands. He will see you through whatever is happening. Draw close to him, even cling to him until he comes to your rescue. He knows exactly where you are!

PRAYER

Dear Jesus, oh how I wish I could see your hands. I wish I could see them protecting me today and guiding me through this life. Thank you, Lord, for always being there even if I can't see it or know it at the time. Amen.

God's Sanctuary

Let me live forever in your sanctuary, safe beneath the shelter of your wings! Psalm 61:4 NLT

In a world that sometimes appears to be spinning out of control, most of us want something or someone that will provide us safety and security. Surely, the psalmist must have been feeling this need when he wrote these words. What a prayer! Could you pray this prayer today?

"Let me live forever in your sanctuary, safe beneath the shelter of your wings!"

I can't think of a better place to live or exist than in the shelter of his wings and the sanctuary of the Lord. Of course, for now, it is not a literal place; but thinking of God in these terms can be so helpful to those wrestling with the issues of life. Run to him today. Find this place of safety. If the idea of his sanctuary is not enough, draw even closer to the shelter of his wings. He knows exactly where you are and what is going on. He will protect you and hold you in these times.

God's sanctuary is not limited to a building; however, there is great strength to be found in being in community with God's people. Make sure you are a part of the body of Christ. Don't walk through this life without him.

PRAYER

Dear God, how many times I have longed to feel you near. Today I need you to be near me and to protect me. Protect my heart and mind from the attacks by the enemy of our soul. Amen.

Waiting Quietly

Let all that I am wait quietly before God, for my hope is in him. He alone is my rock and my salvation, my fortress where I will not be shaken. My victory and honor come from God alone. He is my refuge, a rock where no enemy can reach me. Psalm 62:5-7 NLT

"Let all that I am wait quietly before God." Waiting quietly before God is not always easy. The writer bases his quietness on the facts that he believes about God. God is his hope. God is his rock, his salvation, and his fortress. He is his refuge and most of all a place where no enemy can touch him.

Sometimes these kinds of verses are hard to read, especially if you are dealing with something that has touched your life deeply and in a negative way. You may want to ask, "What about the line that says no enemy can reach me, yet here I am." Disease, divorce, or even death has come to your life and you are living with the consequences.

For me, when I read theses verses, I feel as though it is my soul that no enemy can touch or reach. Paul wrote this to the Christians at Corinth: "Therefore we do not lose heart. Even though our outward man is perishing, yet the inward man is being renewed day by day" (1 Corinthians 4:16 NKJV). Your outward life might be experiencing severe trauma of some kind; but your soul, if surrendered to God, is offered protection of the best kind: God's protection. You have been given that today, and that allows you to quiet yourself and wait before him.

Whatever you are facing in your life, or whatever we may face in the future, God and God alone is the safest place of refuge. Dark days come, seasons change, life and death happen, but God never changes. Let him be your fortress and rock.

PRAYER

Dear God, you alone have my back 24/7. You know me and what is going on in my life and the lives of people I love. I will wait quietly before you today as you protect me and work on my behalf. Amen.

Be Tenderhearted

Finally, all of you should be of one mind. Sympathize with each other. Love each other as brothers and sisters. Be tenderhearted, and keep a humble attitude. 1 Peter 3:8 NLT

The call to love others is a consistent call throughout the Bible. Peter here reminds us that we should show sympathy for each other. We should love each other as brothers and sisters. There are times in our lives when certain people, even family, can be a challenge to love. No matter what may be happening to cause our love to fall short, we should work hard to let Christ's love be in us and show through us.

Maybe the answer is to be tenderhearted and humble as Peter suggests. Think of someone today that you can practice on by loving them and showing them tenderness. Maybe it will be a complete stranger that crosses your path today, or maybe it will be someone you have lost contact with recently. Show kindness and tenderheartedness. Surprise them in a creative way. Ask God to show you the person. Make it a habit by being of one mind with Christ.

As followers of Jesus Christ, we should work hard to emulate him in our love for others. Maybe today you will find opportunities to be kind, tenderhearted, and serve others. Let the mind of Christ be in you...

PRAYER

Dear God, please give me the mind of Christ and make me willing to love everyone, including those that may not love me back. Give me a tender heart and humble attitude that I might be a blessing for you on this earth. Amen.

Staying True

Therefore, my dear brothers and sisters, stay true to the Lord. Philippians 4:1a NLT

Words from the apostle Paul to the new first century church in Philippi. Paul had started it and given them their primary lessons in what it meant to be a follower of Jesus Christ or a Christian.

After leaving and going on to other places to spread the gospel of Christ and start other churches, he would write letters to be written and shared with the whole church.

When you see the word "therefore" in Scripture I have always been told that you should look at the verse before the word and see what it is referring to. I chose this verse for a devotion because of Paul's admonition to "stay true to the Lord." That in and of itself is a life principle to adopt.

Whatever you do today, stay true to the Lord. Whatever you say today, stay true to the Lord. In all your decisions, actions, reactions, and pursuits, stay true to the Lord.

About those verses before and the word therefore, here is what he wrote: "But we are citizens of heaven, where the Lord Jesus Christ lives. And we are eagerly waiting for him to return as our Savior. He will take our weak mortal bodies and change them into glorious bodies like his own, using the same power with which he will bring everything under his control" (Philippians 3:20-21 NLT).

Therefore, my dear brothers and sisters, stay true to the Lord.

Stay strong today. Love God and give him everything in your life. Believe that he loves you and will never leave or forsake you. Stay true to him always, as true as an arrow to the center of a target.

PRAYER

Oh God, may this be the desire of my heart every day. Let me know what you want from me. Help me to do everything I possibly can to carry out your plan for my life. I will stay true. I won't look to the left or the right but keep my eyes, heart, and mind on you. Amen.

Tested, Tried, and True

Fire tests the purity of silver and gold, but a person is tested by being praised. Proverbs 27:21 NLT

All of us crave affirmation and even praise to one degree or another. Some people suffer from low self-esteem and are looking for some kind of positivity they can hang onto regarding themselves.

When fire tests silver and gold, it is refining and removes all the impurities, leaving only the pure gold or silver. When refined it is at its highest value.

According to the writer of this proverb, we are tested by praise. I think what we can take away from this is the fact that often praise may bring out the worst in a human being. At least, we are tested when popularity, success, financial or material growth, or even notoriety come our way. It is then that we must decide who gets the credit for who we are or what we have achieved. The godly will always defer to God with credit and praise. The self-centered will take it personally and over time begin to believe that they are truly better than other people.

St. Gregory wrote these words around 560 A.D., "Praise of one's self tortures the just, but elates the wicked. But while it tortures, it purifies the just; and while it pleases the wicked, it proves them to be reprobate. For these revel in their own praise, because they seek not the glory of their Maker."

When praise comes your way the next time, if you are a Christian, defer to the grace of God and his work within that has allowed you to achieve some measure of success. The apostle Paul wrote about this when he was asking God to take something away from him that seemed to be holding him back:

"So to keep me from becoming proud, I was given a thorn in my flesh, a messenger from Satan to torment me and keep me from becoming proud. Three different times I begged the Lord to take it away. Each time he said, "My grace is all you need. My power works best in weakness." So now I am glad to boast about my weaknesses, so that the power of Christ can work through me. That's why I take pleasure in my weaknesses, and in the insults, hardships, persecutions, and troubles that I suffer for Christ. For when I am weak, then I am strong" (2 Corinthians 12:7-10 NLT).

It is God that is working in you and making you whatever you are or are becoming. "For God is working in you, giving you the desire and the power to do what pleases him" (Philippians 2:13 NLT).

PRAYER

Dear God, I ask that you would allow me to be free from the love of praise and affirmation. Please don't let the words of those around me, spoken or unspoken, control who I am in you. I am always thankful when others find something I've done helpful or worthy of some reaction; but I know, Lord, that it is you at work in me. Amen.

Remember My Chains

Remember my chains. Colossians 4:18b NLT

What a strange verse for a devotion you may be thinking. It is a part of the historical record of the early church and of the apostle Paul. He spent a considerable amount of time in prison because of his willingness to follow Jesus Christ. While incarcerated because of his faith he wrote letters to individual Christians and churches he felt connected to or had started. His letters were instructive, motivating, corrective, and encouraging the early believers to keep themselves in Christ daily.

I think I am using this verse as a reminder that serving Christ or following him as a Christian is no guarantee that life won't be full of challenges. Some of the things that happen to us in a lifetime may be unfair, unexpected, and even unnerving; but if we are followers of Christ, he will not leave us or forsake us.

The apostle Paul wrote this letter to the church at Colosse and spent the most of his words encouraging the saints and spurring them on to greater faith and focus as they pursued godly lives. He reminded them and us with these classic words:

"Since God chose you to be the holy people he loves, you must clothe yourselves with tenderhearted mercy, kindness, humility, gentleness, and patience. Make allowance for each other's faults, and forgive anyone who offends you. Remember, the Lord forgave you, so you must forgive others. Above all, clothe yourselves with love, which binds us all together in perfect harmony. And let the peace that comes from Christ rule in your hearts. For as members of one body you are called to live in peace. And always be thankful" (Colossians 3:12-15 NLT).

"And let the peace that comes from Christ rule in your hearts."

Whatever may be happening in your life, know that you are not alone. Some of God's finest people throughout the centuries have faced insurmountable challenges. Around the world, God's people are facing persecution, torture, famine, extreme poverty, and even death. Maybe like Paul you could say, "Remember my chains." It's not the first thing you say or talk about, but you could use some prayer. I doubt that it is chains, but something you are facing is out of your control. Know that as I wrote this devotion I remembered you. I prayed for you.

Dear Jesus, what a great honor it is to follow you. I know you invited us to share in your suffering, and yet none of us really want to do that. When it comes my way, Lord, give me the grace I need to keep caring for others and following you every day of my life. Amen.

Living a Godly Life

By his divine power, God has given us everything we need for living a godly life. We have received all of this by coming to know him, the one who called us to himself by means of his marvelous glory and excellence. 2 Peter 1:3 NLT

The greatest gift for all of humanity is the gift of God given to us through Jesus Christ. It is by his presence in our lives that we excel in living the Christian life. Let his power be in you daily as you walk and navigate life in this world.

To live a godly life, we must rely on his divine power. He has given us everything we need to live for him, but we have to want to live his way. When you know Christ as your Savior and have answered his call to follow, you are a recipient of his marvelous grace and excellence.

Ponder the relationship you have with Christ. Does it grow you daily to be more like him? Do you feel like he has given you what you need to live a godly life? The more you know him, the more you will know how to emulate him and share the good news of his gospel.

He calls you every day to live a godly life. He is calling today, and he will empower you to do the right things at the right time. Keep close to Jesus and let him guide you with his divine power.

PRAYER

Dear Jesus, you offer so much to make my life better and godly. Give me the strength to never quit pursing you with all of my heart, mind, soul, and strength. Amen.

What's a Day in God's House Worth?

A single day in your courts is better than a thousand anywhere else! I would rather be a gatekeeper in the house of my God than live the good life in the homes of the wicked. Psalm 84:10 NLT

Ultimately, this world will fail you. If you have all your confidence and hope in the world we live in, you will be disappointed in a grand way. For those that follow Jesus, there is nothing more appealing than being in his presence.

This may mean that you enjoy attending a church with like-minded people. You have found community and you love being there. It may mean that you have found the joy of prayer and spending time in God's presence throughout your day.

In reality, it means that we flourish in God's presence. Our souls were made to worship him; and when we get the chance to experience him, those moments are better than moments of entertainment, sports, or even relaxing. One day in his presence is better than any number of days without his presence. His presence sustains us. His presence guides us and encourages us. His presence is offered to you today. Don't hold back. Lean into him and acknowledge him, even if you feel like a gatekeeper. Even the gatekeeper gets glimpses of and encounters with the master.

I love that illustration. Although I've preached thousands of times in hundreds of churches and even around the world, I would rather be a gatekeeper in God's house than be up front. Just to be in his presence is more than enough.

PRAYER

Dear Lord, someday I will see your courts for real. For now, let me live in the awareness of your presence every day of my life. There is no place I would rather be. Amen.

The Father's Compassion

You must be compassionate, just as your Father is compassionate.
Luke 7:36 NLT

When God is our Father we are not given a choice, we will be compassionate to others. If you read in the verses before this one, you will find we are to love our enemies. Many communities these days seem to be polarized around one cause or the other. This often leads to misunderstanding or the inability to see from the perspective of others.

When separation happens, it becomes easy to pull back or excuse yourself from being loving and compassionate. Of course as Christians, we don't have the option of not practicing compassion. We should be the most ardent supporters of the marginalized. Jesus spoke often about caring for the poor, the widows, the orphans, and the imprisoned.

Compassion costs more than money. It may cost us our time and even personal space. It may mean that we lose our comfort zone. Remember, Jesus is saying the standard is to be compassionate as your Father in heaven is compassionate.

Figure out some compassionate things to do today. Work compassion into your life. Become aware of things that are happening around the world as well as your neighborhood. Lead the way and help others be compassionate.

Working hard on this in my own life. Encouraging you to practice compassion today toward those that might not deserve it.

PRAYER

Dear Jesus, fill me with compassion so that I will serve others with the compassion of our Father in heaven. Amen.

What Makes You Cry?

"Dear woman, why are you crying?" the angels asked her. "Because they have taken away my Lord," she replied, "and I don't know where they have put him." John 20:13 NLT

Mary Magdalene went to the tomb of Jesus early on that first Easter. At first, she was part of a group; but after seeing the tomb empty, all the others went back home. She did not. She loved Jesus because of what he had done for her. She was delivered from seven devils that possessed her. After Jesus, she was free of their torment. She loved him and followed him with great devotion. Now she utters this astonishing statement in answer to why she is crying: "Because they have taken away my Lord."

For her, she had seen Jesus in the flesh and didn't know what it was like to have to have faith in a Jesus you couldn't see, talk to while looking at his face, or even touch him when necessary. The others that gathered at the tomb processed the opened tomb and John wrote: "Then the disciple who had reached the tomb first also went in, and he saw and believed—for until then they still hadn't understood the Scriptures that said Jesus must rise from the dead. Then they went home."

For most of us, this is the way we live every day. We know the tomb is empty, but for them it was a moment of belief. All of a sudden they understood all that Jesus had been telling them.

Nobody can take away your Lord as Mary said. No politician, no atheist, no evil dictator or even an ungodly person in your family or at work. We see him by faith. We trust him by faith. We talk to him whenever we want by faith. We walk by faith and work by faith. We hold his hand by faith and follow him through the seasons of our lives, both good and not so good.

Whatever you may be experiencing today, just know that Jesus is with you. He has not forsaken you or walked away. Yes, it would be nice to see him, and that day will come soon enough. For today, enjoy his presence. Talk to him and tell him what is on your heart and mind. He cares deeply about you!

Dear Jesus, there are times when I wish like Mary that you were right in front of me. I wish that I could hear your voice and feel your touch. Today I will listen for your voice in my heart and I will love you, Lord. I believe and look forward to that day when my faith will be sight. Amen.

Are You on the Run?

That is why I ran away to Tarshish! I knew that you are a merciful and compassionate God, slow to get angry and filled with unfailing love. You are eager to turn back from destroying people. Jonah 4:2b NLT

The story of Jonah was always fascinating to me as a child. Jonah running from God, the terrifying storm at sea, thrown overboard to calm the sea, the storm calming, the great fish that swallowed Jonah, and then him surviving all of that to be coughed up back onto land to finish what God told him to do. It was captivating.

As an adult, you process the story differently and wonder why Jonah was so upset that God wanted him to preach repentance to a sinful city of about 120,000 people and his chief complaint was that God would not destroy them for their wickedness but turn back to them and accept their repentance. Maybe he was just a weary and tired prophet; but even after the storm and the great fish, when God changed his mind and was merciful to the city of Nineveh, Jonah was still mad about it. But look at those words!

No matter what you have done, God wants you to come back to him more than anything in this world. Jonah describes him as a God that is a "merciful and compassionate God." He says He is "slow to get angry and filled with unfailing love." He says he is "eager to turn back from destroying people."

His love and compassion have never changed. God's mission has always been to save this world and the people in it. We know that the majority of people will not listen or serve God or turn from their sins, but it doesn't mean you and I can't. You can let him take away your past and make everything new starting today. What a great comfort to live in his will and his way. Celebrate God's unfailing love and mercy today. Remember his compassion and willingness to change his mind for a city that was willing to repent.

PRAYER

Dear God, your love, mercy, and compassion are beyond what I can understand, but I am so thankful for them. I am thankful for you and the life you offer us to live by following your will and way. Help me to live this way every day. Amen.

Finding Life

Come to me with your ears wide open. Listen and you will find life.
Isaiah 55:3 NLT

When God sends an invitation, you probably should respond. In Isaiah 55, God is calling out to Israel and inviting them to come to Him. He is offering them their best life now even when they chose to not see it most of the time.

I wonder how many times we miss what God has for us because we are too busy to come to him, or when we do come to him our mouths are open instead of our ears. Listen, God says! Listen and you will find life.

You may say or even want to scream back, "I've listened and I don't ever hear anything." Keep listening. Keep your ears open. God will speak into your life when he is ready and when you absolutely need it most. Listen for his voice. You won't hear him speak, but you will hear him in a sermon, a verse, a song, or maybe even through the voice of a friend.

Come to me, open your ears, listen... "you will find life."

I would not want to live in this world without an authentic relationship with God. He is my source of life. This world will fail you. People will let you down and disappoint you, but God will never fail. Remember even the angel said that to Mary the mother of Jesus, "The word of the Lord will never fail." Stand on it. Count on it. Listen to it and for him to speak life into you.

PRAYER

Dear God, my ears are open and I am listening. Amen.

Forgiveness Is not Optional

If you forgive those who sin against you, your heavenly Father will forgive you. But if you refuse to forgive others, your Father will not forgive your sins. Matthew 6:14-15 NLT

Forgiveness is a big deal for a follower of Jesus Christ. Forgiveness is a big deal in the life of every human to be honest. When we have been wronged but don't find a way to forgive the person that has wronged us, the damage is far worse to our soul and life than it is to theirs.

Harboring unforgiveness is destructive to us emotionally, mentally, and spiritually. When we hang on to things that others have done, somehow it slowly destroys us from the inside. More often than not we descend into bitterness, and that effects every other relationship we try to have.

Jesus knew this, and so he included this teaching throughout his Word. He even modeled it from the cross by praying for those that were executing him and asking God to forgive them because they were ignorant about what they were doing.

I wonder today if there is anyone in your life that you have not forgiven. There is something very freeing and wonderful about that moment of time when forgiveness is extended to someone else. For the Christian, it is not optional. If you want your sins forgiven you must forgive others. That's what Jesus said and taught. It could be a major step forward in your spiritual journey and relationship with God and others.

Pray about it. Think about it. Act on it. Pick up the phone. Write an email or talk to them in person. You can do this and for your sake and theirs, you ought to do it.

PRAYER

Dear Jesus, you know of course every detail of my life, past, present, and future. You know things that have happened; and if there is unforgiveness in me, please soften my heart and make me willing to extend forgiveness to others as you have forgiven me. Amen.

No Pretenders Allowed

Don't just pretend to love others. Really love them. Romans 12:9
NLT

In this section of Romans 12, the writer gives us some character traits that mark us as true followers of Jesus Christ. Authentic Christ followers love all people. That is a really big statement, but if you follow Christ's teaching you will learn that we are called to even love our enemies.

To love others—really love them—means that we will often put others first. It can also mean a surrender of our own rights and may even sometimes feel unfair. It might mean that we love and don't receive it back in return. The only way we can love like this is to have the love of Christ active in our own lives.

The apostle Paul asked some great questions in Philippians 2: "Is there any encouragement from belonging to Christ? Any comfort from his love? Any fellowship together in the Spirit? Are your hearts tender and compassionate?"

Maybe today is a good day to reflect on your level of love for the people in your life. Too often we excuse our lack of love on their behavior, personality differences, or some other challenge that takes genuine love to overcome. Let the love of Christ grow in you. Pray for it. Ask God to give you love that is beyond your own human capacity.

PRAYER

Dear Jesus, I do find your love comforting. Please give me the ability to love others as you have loved me. Please make my heart tender and compassionate. Amen.

I Will Pick Up My Cross

Then he said to the crowd, "If any of you wants to be my follower, you must give up your own way, take up your cross daily, and follow me. If you try to hang on to your life, you will lose it. But if you give up your life for my sake, you will save it. And what do you benefit if you gain the whole world but are yourself lost or destroyed? Luke 9:23-25 NLT

Jesus spoke these words to his first disciples, but they are for anyone that wants to follow him. In fact, that is what he implies that sets up the rest of this invitation; you must have a desire to follow him. We don't always feel or hear this call from Jesus, so it is important that when God is stirring around in your life, heart, or mind that you respond.

If you have a desire to follow him, then the next step is to deny and give up your way of thinking. We lay our way down and pick up his way, which is the way of the cross or surrender. We deny ourselves but follow him with determination, even determination to whatever cross following him may cause us to bear.

The end result? We save our lives through Jesus Christ. We become devoted followers of Christ. You may gain all of this world and much of what it has to offer; but when it comes your time to die, you will take nothing with you from this world. What we take with us into eternity is how we respond to this call from Jesus.

Are you walking your way or his way? Is your life surrendered to him or are you doing it however you want to do it on a daily basis? When this life wraps up, and more specifically your life, you will wish with all your heart you had done it his way.

Start with desire. Deny yourself, and with determination pick up your cross and let him lead you to a life of devotion.

PRAYER

Dear Jesus, may my desire always be to follow you. Give me the courage to deny myself and follow you wherever it may lead me. I am determined to live my life for you. Amen.

Help Wanted

Never be lazy, but work hard and serve the Lord enthusiastically.
Romans 12:11 NLT

It's not a verse that most people memorize from the Bible but I'm not sure why not. Maybe it's because instead of being a promise to bless us, it is a call for us to do something on our own. It's easier to remember promises over verses that prod us.

The writer here is calling us to serve the Lord with passion and enthusiasm. How are you doing with that? I realize that some people who read this may not know what it is to be in a relationship with God on a daily basis. For those of us that do, this may speak more directly to us.

Serving God and being in a genuine and personal relationship with him is unique in many ways. Not the least of which is our inability to see him, hear him, or even know for sure that he is in the room. Even in the best earthly relationship, there are times when we have to work on our enthusiasm level. Sometimes we may grow weary of the work it takes or focus on someone's weaknesses, and in those moments enthusiasm may run low.

With God, we are to serve him enthusiastically. Don't be lazy, but work hard at it, the writer says. Our enthusiasm for the Lord will be strong the more we live in his Word, the more we trust him with our lives, and the more we learn about him by focusing on him every day. When we find a way to serve God—and keep in mind that we are serving him by serving others—our enthusiasm has a better chance of survival and life!

Serve him today. Here is what the writer said in the next few verses. Try applying your energy and enthusiasm to these admonitions:

"Bless those who persecute you. Don't curse them; pray that God will bless them. Be happy with those who are happy, and weep with those who weep. Live in harmony with each other. Don't be too proud to enjoy the company of ordinary people. And don't think you know it all!" (Romans 12:14-16 NLT).

Dear God, this is a lot! Give me the courage and strength to serve you enthusiastically today. Help me to live out your Word and not just be someone that hears it and forgets or doesn't apply it to my life. Let me love others in your name today, even my enemies. Amen.

Peace

And Jesus said to the woman, "Your faith has saved you; go in peace." Luke 7:50 NLT

She was an immoral woman. That's what Luke wrote about her in his Gospel account. Even the Pharisees said she was a sinner and professed total shock that Jesus would allow her to wash his feet with her hair and the expensive perfume she poured lavishly on them.

The fact is, for whatever reason she came searching for Jesus and she was on a mission. We don't know for sure why she came to him or why she showed such extravagant love. She wasn't welcome in the home where Jesus was a guest, but she came anyway. She was an outcast in society, but she came anyway. She had a bad reputation, but she came anyway. She no doubt heard the comments and felt the shock and reaction of those watching her actions, but she did them anyway. The fact is, she came to Jesus.

No matter what you have done or not done. No matter your background, current situation, or past, Jesus welcomes you to come. Bring him your brokenness, your anxieties, your shame, your sins, your past and present. Jesus wants you to come to him and to follow him. He knows more about you than you know about yourself, so nothing you are or can say will scare him away.

Confess in your heart that you need him. Let him forgive you. Allow him to lead you in a better direction. Give him your life and let him make you a new person. The best thing that could ever happen to you today is to hear Jesus say these words, "Your faith has saved you; go in peace."

PRAYER

Dear Jesus, you know everything about my life, including my closest secrets. You know the things I struggle with, and I want you to come into my life today. Bring me the peace that only you can give. Amen.

All the Good Things

And I am praying that you will put into action the generosity that comes from your faith as you understand and experience all the good things we have in Christ. Philemon 1:6 NLT

These words were written in a personal letter from the apostle Paul to a man named Philemon. This sentence contains a call and challenge that should be a great reminder for you and I today. He was praying that Philemon would "put into action the generosity" that comes from the faith Christians experience. We also experience "good things we have in Christ."

A focused follower of Christ will not allow the things of this world to blind them to the good things that are happening in their souls and in their lives. Society may be falling apart all around us. Life may be dealing out challenges that effect you mentally, emotionally, physically, and other ways; but there will still be good things happening because you are in Christ. Your life is directed, ordered, and guided by him.

Because of this, practice generosity! I remember once going through a personal trauma and experience that my wife and I didn't ask for or want. Months later, we realized that because of our pain we were working it into every conversation we had with others. We made an effort to be self-aware and to stop sharing it constantly. One thing that helps is to be generous with those around you. Listen to them instead of talking. Help them when you can. Pass along kind and affirming words. Be sensitive to the pain of others. Look for hurting people to bless. Be creative. Do it often. You might just be amazed at how much you forget about what is happening in your own life.

PRAYER

Dear Jesus, life is really hard sometimes, but you have given me so much of yourself. Your grace has been extended to me. Give me the ability to share generously with others even when I don't feel like it. Amen.

Have Mercy

Please remember what you told your servant Moses: "If you are unfaithful to me, I will scatter you among the nations. But if you return to me and obey my commands and live by them, then even if you are exiled to the ends of the earth, I will bring you back to the place I have chosen for my name to be honored." Nehemiah 1:8-9 NLT

Nehemiah hears about the destruction of Jerusalem and its walls and gates that have been torn down and destroyed. Something in him stirs him to appeal to God. In the first part of his prayer (verses 6-7) he confesses the sins and waywardness of the people of Israel, and he even confesses the sins of his own family. He is reminding God of his promises of mercy and restoration.

I wonder what you need mercy for today. I wonder if there is anything you would like God to restore. There is a way, and Nehemiah knew it.

He humbled himself before God.

He confessed his sin and was honest with God.

He promised to honor God with his life.

He specifically asked God to hear his prayer and answer.

God wants to hear from us. God longs for us to repent when necessary and to turn or return to him. Think about it as a course correction. Our common enemy that wants to destroy our faith and soul would push us to think that things are hopeless or even that we are hopeless.

With God, all things are possible. Seriously push yourself to practice humbling yourself, being honest, and honoring him. He will turn and hear your prayer. Return to him and you will find his open arms.

PRAYER

Dear God, too often I don't want to be honest with You. I am ashamed when I fail or when my life is a mess or in ruins. I will turn to you today. I am even now kneeling in my heart and soul before you. Lord, hear my prayer. Amen.

Overcoming Fear

There was also Benaiah son of Jehoiada, a valiant warrior from Kabzeel. He did many heroic deeds, which included killing two champions of Moab. Another time, on a snowy day, he chased a lion down into a pit and killed it. 1 Chronicles 11:22 NLT

Mark Batterson wrote a great book about Benaiah entitled, *In a Pit With a Lion on a Snowy Day.* The heart of the book celebrates the heroics of Benaiah and his willingness to chase a lion into a pit and to kill it. The point is obvious. He was a brave man who was not afraid of something that would scare you and I. If we were to chase a lion and it fell down into a pit we would most likely be content with that as an ending to our heroics. Apparently, it wasn't enough for Benaiah. He upped the risk by fighting a lion on a bed of slippery and wet snow!

Fear is a paralyzing part of our lives. There are things and even people that may cause us deep angst and fear. More often than not it seems far easier to run the other way or even hide from what causes us fear.

It just might be that whatever has you in hiding and fear needs to be faced head on. I'm not talking about physical fighting of course. I am talking about facing your fears and allowing God to give you the strength and grace to confront and conquer the things that have held you back from being spiritually, mentally, and emotionally whole.

On this snowy day as I write this devotion, I am thinking of the lions in my life that I should consider chasing. I will pick them carefully and prayerfully. I will probably only chase one lion at a time. May God give us the grace and courage to face whatever has been chasing us and causing unnecessary fear.

PRAYER

Dear God, you know what I am afraid of the most. You alone know what I feel inside of me when I think about facing my fears. Please give me the strength I need to do what needs to be done. Amen.

In Word, Thought, and Deed

I pray that from his glorious, unlimited resources he will empower you with inner strength through his Spirit. Then Christ will make his home in your hearts as you trust in him. Your roots will grow down into God's love and keep you strong. Ephesians 3:16-17 NLT

The apostle Paul wrote these words from jail to the church at Ephesus. He was praying for them and asking God to empower them through his Spirit. The result that he was looking for in the end was two-fold:

1. For Christ to make his home in their hearts.

2. For their spiritual roots to grow deep into God's love.

God makes his home in our hearts when we trust him, and allowing ourselves to be deep in his love will keep us strong. Is Christ living in your heart? Has he made your heart his home? Are you trusting him with everything and everyone around you?

Are you practicing your faith in a way that allows your spiritual roots to go deep into God's love? Do you know him better day by day? Are you willing to let go of things that distract you away from spiritual growth?

To be a Christ follower simply means that we will follow him daily in word, thought, and deed. We will love and serve him in word, thought, and deed. Check your heart and make sure it is his home and not filled with things that only are attractive to you. Do something this week that will send your spiritual roots deep into his love. You might be surprised how God will respond to your intentional actions.

PRAYER

Dear God, please live in me! Give me the courage to make room for you in my heart and life. Don't let me hold anything back from you, and may my roots be grounded in your eternal love. Empower me by your Spirit. Amen.

Attitudes of Gratitude:
Dancing!

Not all of us have happy feet, nor do we consider ourselves to be dancers. Here is the story of a man so filled with gratitude to God that he expressed it by allowing himself to dance before God—not just dance, but dance with total abandon. This is unusual for most, and we have all seen people who may just like to be the center of attention; but in this story it was about being thankful to God. It was in the street and it was a king that did the dancing. He danced before God and his people.

After the men who were carrying the Ark of the Lord had gone six steps, David sacrificed a bull and a fattened calf. And David danced before the Lord with all his might, wearing a priestly garment. So David and all the people of Israel brought up the Ark of the Lord with shouts of joy and the blowing of rams' horns. (2 Samuel 6:13-15 NLT)

It was a high moment of gratefulness and celebration and David couldn't contain himself. He danced with all his might in total abandon to God. Of course, not everyone was happy about it. The daughter of the former king saw him dancing and called him out for doing things unbecoming for a king. Here is his response: "I was dancing before the Lord, who chose me above your father and all his family! He appointed me as the leader of Israel, the people of the Lord, so I celebrate before the Lord. Yes, and I am willing to look even more foolish than this, even to be humiliated in my own eyes!" (2 Samuel 6:21-22 NLT).

I don't know that dancing is required to express thankfulness; but if you feel it in your feet, don't be afraid to let yourself go in honor of God's goodness.

- "You have turned my mourning into joyful dancing. You have taken away my clothes of mourning and clothed me with joy" (Psalm 30:11 NLT).
- "Praise his name with dancing, accompanied by the tambourine and harp" (Psalm 140:3 NLT).
- "Praise him with the tambourine and dancing; praise him with strings and flutes!" (Psalm 150:4 NLT).

Think of things today that might just make you stand on your feet and reach out to God. Express your devotion and love for him and don't be afraid.

PRAYER

Surrounded by your glory. What will my heart feel? Will I dance for you, Jesus, or in awe of you be still? Will I stand in your presence, or to my knees will I fall?
Will I sing hallelujah? Will I be able to speak at all? I can only imagine, I can only imagine. Amen. (– Lyrics from "I Can Only Imagine," Bart Millard)

Attitudes of Gratitude: Love!

Six days before the Passover celebration began, Jesus arrived in Bethany, the home of Lazarus—the man he had raised from the dead. A dinner was prepared in Jesus' honor. Martha served, and Lazarus was among those who ate with him. Then Mary took a twelve-ounce jar of expensive perfume made from essence of nard, and she anointed Jesus' feet with it, wiping his feet with her hair. The house was filled with the fragrance. But Judas Iscariot, the disciple who would soon betray him, said, "That perfume was worth a year's wages. It should have been sold and the money given to the poor." Not that he cared for the poor—he was a thief, and since he was in charge of the disciples' money, he often stole some for himself. John 12:1-6 NLT

In this rare and rather intimate moment in the home of Jesus' friends, Mary, the sister of Lazarus and Martha, performs the extravagant act of anointing Jesus with perfume and wiping his feet with her hair! It was an act of love. Pure, simple love for this one that graced their home and shared a friendship with them. Mary acted recklessly in the eyes of Judas. It's hard to even process a love that would give the equivalent of a year's wages. But she did it and Jesus accepted it.

How do you love Jesus? How do you express your love to him? Probably the best way is to tell him often. Even better is to love him by living the way he intended us to live. Love him with all of your heart, soul, mind, and strength. Don't allow anything or anyone to take priority over your relationship with Jesus.

PRAYER

Dear Jesus, I give you everything. If I am holding anything back, please show me and give me the courage to give it all to you. Amen.

Attitudes of Gratitude: Rejoicing!

In the very familiar story of Paul and Silas, we find them imprisoned for sharing their faith and the message of Jesus. Here's the scriptural reference:

A mob quickly formed against Paul and Silas, and the city officials ordered them stripped and beaten with wooden rods. They were severely beaten, and then they were thrown into prison. The jailer was ordered to make sure they didn't escape. So the jailer put them into the inner dungeon and clamped their feet in the stocks. Around midnight Paul and Silas were praying and singing hymns to God, and the other prisoners were listening. (Acts 16:22-25 NLT)

They were praying and singing and it was not a sad song. They were rejoicing to be suffering for Jesus. They were following in the Lord's steps. They were "picking up their crosses" and following him and they were joyful about it. This attitude of rejoicing in the first century Christians was consistent. In Acts 5 we read:

"They called in the apostles and had them flogged. Then they ordered them never again to speak in the name of Jesus, and they let them go. The apostles left the high council rejoicing that God had counted them worthy to suffer disgrace for the name of Jesus" (Acts 5:40-41 NLT).

Paul and Silas and these other apostles were so thankful to be sharing in the shame of Jesus' name and message that they were filled with rejoicing. As we go through our days, it is unlikely that we will be physically beaten or tortured for our faith. If it happens, though, we shouldn't be surprised because every day men and women around the world are tortured for their faith. For most of us, we will get up and go through our routines. We will be relatively safe. We will drive our cars and leave and come back to our comfortable homes. Today, think about things that make you joyful in Christ.

"Always be full of joy in the Lord. I say it again—rejoice" (Philippians 4:4 NLT).

PRAYER

Dear Jesus, just as you gave Paul and Silas the strength to sing in their cell, may my mouth be full of singing and thanksgiving to you. Amen.

Attitudes of Gratitude:
Singing!

Israel was fleeing years of slavery at the hand of the Egyptians. Led by Moses, this million plus group of people crossed the Red Sea miraculously because God opened up a path and they marched through on dry land. When the pursing Egyptian army was in the middle of the sea, God allowed the walls of water to come crashing down. The Egyptians were destroyed and God was given credit for this miracle.

But the people of Israel had walked through the middle of the sea on dry ground, as the water stood up like a wall on both sides. That is how the Lord rescued Israel from the hand of the Egyptians that day. And the Israelites saw the bodies of the Egyptians washed up on the seashore. When the people of Israel saw the mighty power that the Lord had unleashed against the Egyptians, they were filled with awe before him. (Exodus 14:29-31 NLT)

In their overwhelming moment of thankfulness and gratitude, we read that they burst out in song.

"Then Moses and the people of Israel sang this song to the Lord: 'I will sing to the Lord, for he has triumphed gloriously; he has hurled both horse and rider into the sea. The Lord is my strength and my song; he has given me victory'" (Exodus15:1-2 NLT).

This song goes on and on and is followed by Moses' sister also singing her own song! They sang their gratefulness to God. Singing one's praise to God is found throughout the Bible.

In the New Testament we read the words of the apostle Paul admonishing: "Don't be drunk with wine, because that will ruin your life. Instead, be filled with the Holy Spirit, singing psalms and hymns and spiritual songs among yourselves, and making music to the Lord in your hearts. And give thanks for everything to God the Father in the name of our Lord Jesus Christ" (Ephesians 5:18-20 NLT).

PRAYER

Dear Jesus, today I want to sing my thanksgiving and praise to you. Fill my heart with a song of praise and I will lift my voice in worship to you. Amen.

Attitudes of Gratitude:
Surrendering

This may seem a bit odd at first; but in reality when we are deeply thankful to God for something he has done, it reduces us to total trust and surrender. We realize that only God could have answered our prayer, and we are humbled by his response. There is a dynamic example of this in the Old Testament. In 1 Samuel we find the story of Hannah. She was childless. She was bullied by others because of her barrenness. She was reduced to grief at a level unknown to most. One day while pouring her heart out to God in the temple, the priest noticed her and assumed she was intoxicated because of her brokenness. She was crying out to God and asking for a child. God gave her a boy. She named him Samuel, and she was so grateful for this answer to prayer that she literally surrendered him back to God. She took him to the temple and handed him over to be raised and groomed to be a prophet of the living God.

Hannah was in deep anguish, crying bitterly as she prayed to the Lord. And she made this vow: "O Lord of Heaven's Armies, if you will look upon my sorrow and answer my prayer and give me a son, then I will give him back to you. He will be yours for his entire lifetime." (1 Samuel 1:10-11 NLT)

She made good on that promise. As soon as Samuel was old enough, she and her husband returned to the temple; and this was her response to the priest: "'I am the very woman who stood here several years ago praying to the Lord. I asked the Lord to give me this boy, and he has granted my request. Now I am giving him to the Lord, and he will belong to the Lord his whole life.' And they worshiped the Lord there" (1 Samuel 1:26-28 NLT).

With a heart full of thanksgiving she surrendered her most precious gift from God. Today think of the blessings in your life and hold them lightly because all of them come from God. The air we breathe is a gift from God. It's best to just live in an attitude of surrender to our God. Let him know today that all you have is given as an offering of thanksgiving to him.

PRAYER

Gracious God, you alone are the source of my living a surrendered life. Because of my trust in you, I am able to live the surrendered life with gratitude and trust. Amen.

Attitudes of Gratitude:
Thankfulness

Thankfulness is an attitude. It is a choice that we make every day. Is it only to be used when receiving something, or can it be expressed at other times? Possessing a thankful heart is a principle of godly living that we shouldn't ignore.

One day ten men with leprosy approached Jesus and loudly pled with him for healing. In a moment of time, he restored all of them to perfect health. Here is what happened next: *One of them, when he saw that he was healed, came back to Jesus, shouting, "Praise God!" He fell to the ground at Jesus' feet, thanking him for what he had done. This man was a Samaritan. Jesus asked, "Didn't I heal ten men? Where are the other nine? Has no one returned to give glory to God except this foreigner?" And Jesus said to the man, "Stand up and go. Your faith has healed you."* (Luke 17:16-19 NLT)

Jesus was bothered by their ingratitude. Thanklessness and ingratitude are sadly a common part of our society. Children are not taught to be appreciative or express it. Many people feel entitled and therefore feel no need to be thankful.

In Romans 1:21, people who rebel against God and practice ingratitude are indicted with these words: "Yes, they knew God, but they wouldn't worship him as God or even give him thanks" (Romans 1:21 NLT).

It is easy to forget this attitude and to let it slip out of our life. Work at it. Own it and believe how much it means to God when you turn back and thank him.

- Give thanks today!
- Make a list of blessings and pray through this list.
- Do it every day.
- Today, only pray words of thankfulness. Don't ask for anything from God.
- Take moments today to acknowledge God's blessing to you.
- Whisper thankfulness to him all day long.
- Be thankful to God and others.

"And let the peace that comes from Christ rule in your hearts. For as members of one body you are called to live in peace. And always be thankful" (Colossians 3:15 NLT).

Dear Lord, may the words of my mouth be full of thankfulness every day of my life. May I truly always be thankful. Amen.

Attitudes of Gratitude: Worship!

She was a young unmarried girl and God chose her to be the earthly mother of the Son of God. God's angel came to Mary and gave her the news. She was in shock; but while visiting her cousin Elizabeth, who was pregnant with a boy that would become John the Baptist and prepare the way for Jesus, she came to accept this role and responsibility. She broke out in spontaneous worship.

Oh, how my soul praises the Lord. How my spirit rejoices in God my Savior! For he took notice of his lowly servant girl, and from now on all generations will call me blessed. For the Mighty One is holy, and he has done great things for me. (Luke 1:46-49 NLT)

Worship is too often only equated with singing or a time of music during a church service. Nothing could be further from the truth. We worship God with our lives. It happens wherever we are and when we do things that honor him. Mary worshiped God in that moment. She was in her cousin's home, but it became a sanctuary of thankfulness for God's blessing.

In a very different setting, we read about King David in the Old Testament. He was known for being a man after God's own heart. He killed the giant Goliath and was a victorious warrior. He also wrote many of the Psalms that are in the Bible. He also was known for a moment of great failure in his personal life: adultery, murder, and deceit made up his story of failure. When the baby born as a result of his affair with Bathsheba became sick, David fasted and prayed for seven days. The child died. Here is how it happened: "Then on the seventh day the child died. David's advisers were afraid to tell him. 'He wouldn't listen to reason while the child was ill,' they said. 'What drastic thing will he do when we tell him the child is dead?' When David saw them whispering, he realized what had happened. 'Is the child dead?' he asked. 'Yes,' they replied, 'he is dead.' Then David got up from the ground, washed himself, put on lotions, and changed his clothes. He went to the Tabernacle and worshiped the Lord" (2 Samuel 12:18-20 NLT).

In the worst of times, David found the strength to go and worship the Lord. What depth of worship do you think he felt? What emotions must have been flowing? After seven days of prayer and fasting, maybe he didn't have anything left to feel; but he went and worshiped. Even when life is not joyful, may God grant us the grace to always worship him with thanksgiving. It's the attitude of Job who in the middle of his loss of family, wealth, and health stated his faith with this famous sentence: "Though He slay me, yet will I trust Him" (Job 13:15 NKJV).

Worship God with thanksgiving and trust. He loves you and knows what you are experiencing, whether blessing or burden.

PRAYER

Dear Lord, I will worship you with my whole heart and life. You are worthy of all the praise I can possibly give to you. Receive my praise today. Amen.

Serve Him Wholeheartedly

But as for me and my family, we will serve the Lord. Joshua 24:15
NLT

Joshua was about to die and he was instructing the people of Israel and giving them a chance to declare their loyalty to God. In the process, he declares his own loyalty for himself and his family.

We all have options every day. We are faced with many choices that will either bring us closer to God or push us away. How important it is that we make the right choice! Choosing unwisely can have negative effects on our families for generations.

Make sure today that you do everything you can to guide those around you in the right direction. Seek God's help in understanding his Word so that it becomes a trusted and true guide for your daily walk.

PRAYER

Lord, today will you give me wisdom as I make choices for myself and even my family. Let us serve you with our whole hearts today and for the rest of our lives. Amen.

Taking the Examination

Examine your motives, test your heart, come to this meal in holy awe. 1 Corinthians 11:28 MSG

Let a person examine himself, then, and so eat of the bread and drink of the cup. 1 Corinthians 11:28 ESV

Examine means to test and prove your sincerity. To test by implication. Is the evidence there that you are truly following Christ? It is a serious blessing to have self-awareness. When we lose touch with self-awareness we assume that others view us far differently than they do. More importantly, God views us far differently than we view ourselves.

Below are some questions used by John Wesley and his followers over 200 years ago. These questions were what kept them focused and allowed them to examine themselves on a regular basis.

1. Am I consciously or unconsciously creating the impression that I am better than I really am? In other words, am I a hypocrite?
2. Am I honest in all my acts and words, or do I exaggerate?
3. Do I confidentially pass on to another what was told to me in confidence?
4. Can I be trusted?
5. Am I a slave to dress, friends, work, or habits?
6. Am I self-conscious, self-pitying, or self-justifying?
7. Did the Bible live in me today?
8. Do I give it time to speak to me every day?
9. Am I enjoying prayer?
10. When did I last speak to someone else about my faith?
11. Do I pray about the money I spend?
12. Do I get to bed on time and get up on time?
13. Do I disobey God in anything?
14. Do I insist upon doing something about which my conscience is uneasy?
15. Am I defeated in any part of my life?
16. Am I jealous, impure, critical, irritable, touchy, or distrustful?
17. How do I spend my spare time?

18. Am I proud?
19. Do I thank God that I am not as other people, especially as the Pharisees who despised the publican?
20. Is there anyone whom I fear, dislike, disown, criticize, hold a resentment toward, or disregard? If so, what am I doing about it?
21. Do I grumble or complain constantly?
22. Is Christ real to me?

When examining yourself, be honest before God. Allow the Holy Spirit to search every area of your life.

PRAYER

Search me, O God, and know my heart: try me, and know my thoughts: And see if there be any wicked way in me, and lead me in the way everlasting. Amen. Psalm 139:23-24 NLT

Do You Care Enough to Care?

Then Jonathan said, "Tomorrow we celebrate the new moon festival. You will be missed when your place at the table is empty." 1 Samuel 20:18 NLT

Are you living in a way that will make those around you miss you when you are gone? Jonathan and a young man named David were best friends. Jonathan's father was the first king of Israel and his name was Saul. For many reasons he was jealous of David and probably knew that David would replace him someday as king.

Jonathan and David were close friends and acted more like brothers. David was on the run and hiding from Jonathan's father who was trying to kill him. This greatly affected their friendship and time together. Jonathan was grieving the absence of his friend and the ability to celebrate in the same place.

I officiate quite a few funerals, and it is always fascinating to see the void that is or isn't left by the deceased. When I ask people to tell me about the deceased, they never talk about money, titles, or positions. They talk about how the person showed them that they cared. They talk about how they expressed their love and compassion for others. They talk about chocolate chip cookies baked and shared or "the day they took me out of school to go fishing."

Prioritize your time around the people that will be crying at your funeral. Occasionally I officiate at the funeral of someone that cared more about themselves than the people around them. It's always a short and awkward conversation with the family.

It wasn't David's death that prompted Jonathan's lament but the lack of his presence. Love deeply today. Take time even when you don't think you have time. Care for someone intentionally today.

PRAYER

Dear God, may I live my life today and every day in a way that others will feel your love through me. Help me to think less about myself and more about others. Amen.

Hearing from Heaven

At times I might shut up the heavens so that no rain falls, or command grasshoppers to devour your crops, or send plagues among you. Then if my people who are called by my name will humble themselves and pray and seek my face and turn from their wicked ways, I will hear from heaven and will forgive their sins and restore their land. My eyes will be open and my ears attentive to every prayer made in this place. 2 Chronicles 7:12-15 NLT

Prayer is often a challenge; however, embedded in these words from God is a helpful pattern for successful praying. These words were spoken from God upon the completion of Solomon's building of the temple. God had a long history with Israel and knew their propensity to wander away from God's ways. They were often short on obedience, and he would allow things to happen to them to cause them to turn back to him.

As leaders of a Christian ministry, we are called to lead others to connect with Christ through what he has done in our own lives. Our interactions with those we lead, when done with Christ's love and guidance, will be redemptive and helpful in their personal growth as well.

Successful praying based on these verses will include:

A Right Attitude: *"Then if my people who are called by my name will humble themselves and pray..."*

It's a big deal to stay humble, but the Bible clearly calls us to this. Everything we are is because of God's grace, mercy, and goodness. When we forget, it is important to remember and humble ourselves.

A Reverent Aim: *"and seek my face"*

This simply means putting God first. Again, it is a challenge to keep him first in our lives, especially in the marketplace; but that is where we need him to work through us the most. Sitting in church calls for no special grace or strength. It is in our everyday walk that he wants to show up and work through us.

A Restoring Adjustment: *"and turn from their wicked ways"*
In Revelation, God talks about losing our first love. He talks about laxity and lukewarmness in our spiritual lives. The answer to this is to "turn back" to him. Set your heart and affections on him.

The Results: God says
I will hear...
I will forgive...
I will heal...

"My eyes will be open and my ears attentive to every prayer made in this place" (2 Chronicles 7:15 NLT).

PRAYER

Dear God, give me the courage to be open and honest before you. I turn today from any wicked way that might be in me. I am seeking your face. Humble me, Lord, before you. Amen.

Are You Willing?

Jesus had just informed his disciples that he was going to Bethany in Judea to deal with his friends Lazarus's sickness and death. The disciples quickly reminded him that only a few days earlier in the same area people had tried to stone and kill him. After refusing all their reasoning, Jesus simply says, "Come, let's go see him." Then the disciple Thomas speaks up: *That's when Thomas, the one called the Twin, said to his companions, "Come along. We might as well die with him."* John 11:16 MSG

Thomas is also a disciple that has been referred to as "Doubting Thomas." It's an unofficial name and refers mostly to his hesitancy to believe that Jesus was raised from the dead unless he could see and touch the fresh wounds that would have marked his body.

I've read and re-read his statement above to try to discover the nuances and context of his declaration. Was he sarcastic? Was he fatalistic? Was he sincere in believing that death was a part of following Jesus? I'm leaning toward the first two. Jesus had said: "If any of you wants to be my follower, you must give up your own way, take up your cross daily, and follow me" (Luke 9:23 NLT).

What are we willing to "die" for? Sometimes in ministries the outlook may seem bleak. There may seem to not be answers no matter how hard we try to find them. At some point, men and women down through the centuries learned the power of surrender and total trust.

It doesn't mean you won't actually die, but it means you work and think in a way that honors Jesus Christ because your ministry bears his name.

- Don't hold back because of fear of the unknown or of others.
- Don't hesitate because of a lack of trust.
- You will always be safe as long as you are following Jesus.
- Sometimes surrender doesn't come until you are in the middle of the biggest storm.
- Don't be afraid to carry a cross ... it's part of the deal.

When Jonah tried to run from God the boat he was in was enveloped in a horrific storm. He confessed his story and suggested that he be thrown overboard. No one wanted to do that, so we read: "Nevertheless, the men rowed hard to get back to dry land, but they could not, for the sea was raging against them more and more" (Jonah 1:13 NLT).

You can row hard or you can trust God. You can run from your cross or pick it up and follow. Following Jesus is always the right answer. Always.

Love Your Enemies

But I say unto you, Love your enemies, bless those that curse you, do good to those that hate you, and pray for those who speak evil about you, and persecute you. Matthew 5:44 JB

Jesus shared a lot of teaching and truth in what is referred to as the Sermon on the Mount. There is nothing more poignant than his teaching about loving one's enemies. Most people try to live without making enemies, but it is inevitable that at some point in your life you may find yourself with people that may not like you or want anything to do with you. Sometimes this reaction may not be your fault, and sometimes it is the result of some decision, action, or reaction you have demonstrated in your life. Regardless of reason, Jesus comes along and says, "Love your enemies." These are startling words when taken to the extreme. Is that what Jesus meant? Are we really supposed to love a person or people that hate us? The short answer is, "Yes."

The ramifications cover international, national, state, and local relationships. Enemies come in all shapes and sizes, but for the most part we all can identify if we have them. From Muslim terrorist to the man or woman next door, we have to find the capacity to love.

Jesus offers us this simple outline:

- Love your enemies
- Bless those that curse you
- Do good to those that hate you
- Pray for those who speak evil about you and persecute you

The outline is simple in its words and complex in its call to action or reaction. Someone once said that we are not responsible for others' actions but we are responsible for our reaction to them. And so Jesus says, love, bless, do good to, and pray for those that hate you, speak evil about you, and persecute you. If you can't start with love, then start by praying for them and work backwards through the list.

It is possible in our lifetime that we may face persecution for our faith. Around the world this often leads to tragic deaths. The most powerful testimonies come from those who find the ability to love their torturers and executioners.

PRAYER

God help me to love like you love. Give me the desire and ability to love those that hate me, persecute me, or speak evil of me. Amen.

"I can no longer condemn or hate a brother for whom I pray, no matter how much trouble he causes me." —Dietrich Bonhoeffer

Whatever it Takes

On one of the days while Jesus was teaching, some proud religious law-keepers and teachers of the Law were sitting by him. They had come from every town in the countries of Galilee and Judea and from Jerusalem. The power of the Lord was there to heal them. Some men took a man who was not able to move his body to Jesus. He was carried on a bed. They looked for a way to take the man into the house where Jesus was. But they could not find a way to take him in because of so many people. They made a hole in the roof over where Jesus stood. Then they let the bed with the sick man on it down before Jesus. When Jesus saw their faith, he said to the man, "Friend, your sins are forgiven."

The teachers of the Law and the proud religious law-keepers thought to themselves, "Who is this man who speaks as if he is God? Who can forgive sins but God only?" Jesus knew what they were thinking. He said to them, "Why do you think this way in your hearts? Which is easier to say, 'Your sins are forgiven,' or, 'Get up and walk'?

"So that you may know the Son of Man has the right and the power on earth to forgive sins," he said to the man who could not move his body, "I say to you, get up. Take your bed and go to your home." At once the sick man got up in front of them. He took his bed and went to his home thanking God. All those who were there were surprised and gave thanks to God, saying, "We have seen very special things today." Luke 5:17-39 NLT

It's a compelling story that speaks deeply to any that will listen. A friend yesterday lamented the fact that they never had a conversation about salvation with a suddenly deceased acquaintance. I know that feeling and have experienced it myself. These men were determined to save their friend. As you read this story and the outline of the Scripture, allow God to burden your heart today with someone that you may need to bring to Jesus.

1. **They shared in his sickness: They had a desire to help**
Some men took a man who was not able to move his body to Jesus.

2. **They shared in his solution: They were determined in their mission**
He was carried on a bed. They looked for a way to take the man into the house where Jesus was. But they could not find a way to take him in because of so many people. They made a hole in the roof over where Jesus stood. Then they let the bed with the sick man on it down before Jesus.

3. **They shared in his salvation: He was delivered from his sins**
When Jesus saw their faith, He said to the man, "Friend, your sins are forgiven."

4. **They shared in God's story: God deserved the praise he received.**
At once the sick man got up in front of them. He took his bed and went to his home thanking God. All those who were there were surprised and gave thanks to God, saying, "We have seen very special things today."

PRAYER

Dear Jesus, allow me to bring others to you. There are people in my life that are sin-sick and need you so desperately. Please give me the words to speak that will compel them to come to You. Amen.

What Are You Wrestling?

This left Jacob all alone in the camp, and a man came and wrestled with him until the dawn began to break. When the man saw that he would not win the match, he touched Jacob's hip and wrenched it out of its socket. Then the man said, "Let me go, for the dawn is breaking!"

But Jacob said, "I will not let you go unless you bless me."

"What is your name?" the man asked. He replied, "Jacob."

"Your name will no longer be Jacob," the man told him. "From now on you will be called Israel, because you have fought with God and with men and have won."

"Please tell me your name," Jacob said.

"Why do you want to know my name?" the man replied. Then he blessed Jacob there.

Jacob named the place Peniel (which means "face of God"), for he said, "I have seen God face to face, yet my life has been spared." The sun was rising as Jacob left Peniel, and he was limping because of the injury to his hip. Genesis 32:24-31 NLT

One of the most dramatic moments in all of Scripture. Jacob wrestling with God all night was indeed a battle for his soul. We have to ask ourselves periodically, "What am I wrestling for?" This world clamors for our attention and allegiance.

Are we overcome with the search for positions, possessions, and pleasure? Maybe it is the seven deadly sins of pride, envy, gluttony, lust, anger, greed, or slothfulness. Regardless, we must battle for our soul.

We have two invitations from God while we are on this earth. One is to join the "kingdom of heaven" and the other is to "participate in the divine nature." Both of these ready our soul for the movement of God in us and through us. But we wrestle for our soul. There is no resting. Fight the good fight. We don't necessarily wrestle with God, but the Bible says,

"Finally, my brethren, be strong in the Lord and in the power of His might. Put on the whole armor of God, that you may be able to stand against the wiles of the devil. For we do not wrestle against flesh and blood, but against principalities, against powers, against the rulers of the darkness of this age, against spiritual hosts of wickedness in the heavenly places. Therefore take up the whole armor of God, that you may be able to withstand in the evil day, and having done all, to stand. Stand therefore" (Ephesians 6:10-14a NKJV).

Like Jacob, never let go of God. Hold on to your faith. Wrestle and fight for it to the end.

PRAYER

Dear God, I don't want to wrestle with you. Please help me to identify and surrender to you the things that challenge me the most. Amen.

Love and Loyalty

Don't lose your grip on Love and Loyalty, tie them around your neck; carve their initials on your heart. Earn a reputation for living well in God's eyes and the eyes of the people. Proverbs 3:3-4 MSG

Losing your grip is something none of us want to experience. You don't want that to happen in a tennis, racquetball, or pickleball game, and you don't want it to happen in rock climbing. You also don't want to lose your grip in doing life.

Life and relationships can sometimes be a challenge. When we interact with others at work or even at home it can be a test of our endurance and grace.

The writer of Proverbs offers us the suggestion that love and loyalty are so important that we should tie them around our necks, and to take it a step further carve their initials on our hearts!

In researching this Scripture and the phrase "love and loyalty" I read 27 other translations of the Bible. Here are a few of the words I found in different combinations which give even more definition to what we are supposed to grip relentlessly:

Love and faithfulness NIV

Loyalty and kindness NLT

Steadfast love and faithfulness ESV

Kindness and truth NASB

Mercy and truth KJV

A vast majority of the translations used the phrase "mercy and truth." Does that change its meaning? Not necessarily.

For us it means that we embrace these expressions of love. We bind them to us and imprint them on our hearts. We make sure that we remember to practice these with the people we are around the most. When we forget to love with mercy and to be loyal and faithful to those we know the best, it is a sign that we need some internal work.

God promises us that loving like this is possible. Through the power and presence of the Spirit of God in our lives, we will be loving and loyal.

"But the Holy Spirit produces this kind of fruit in our lives: love, joy, peace, patience, kindness, goodness, faithfulness, gentleness, and self-control. There is no law against these things!" (Galatians 5:22-23 NLT).

Dallas Willard writes about a "well-kept heart." We have to work at it, but the payoff is well worth the effort. When we practice this love and loyalty we "Earn a reputation for living well in God's eyes and the eyes of the people."

It is this "living well" and loving well that draws others to the grace of God that is at work in us.

Action Steps: Grip, Tie, Carve, and Earn...

PRAYER

Dear God, bind love and loyalty to my soul. Let me always walk the path you point me to. May my heart be ever yours in every area of my life. Amen.

Plan for God to Work with You

Good planning and hard work lead to prosperity, but hasty short-cuts lead to poverty. Proverbs 21:5 NLT

Planning strategically is a foundational principle of leadership. "Good planning," as stated by the writer, leads to prosperity. Prosperity in this verse really is better defined as success. The Message Bible translates it this way, "*Careful planning puts you ahead in the long run.*"

"*Good planning and hard work,*" are linked together as equally important and in the ESV it reads this way: "*The plans of the diligent lead surely to abundance.*"

Follow up visionary plans with the hard work that makes it happen. Linking these two together allow us to enjoy the fruit of our labors. Successful people plan well and perform well. They strategize and they sweat to bring things to life. They make a plan and follow it with passion.

When we follow this spiritual advice from the Proverb writer, we are going to benefit in many ways:

We will build strong character.

We will find profit instead of poverty (brought on by "*hasty short-cuts.*")

We will create a path for others to follow.

We will provide for ourselves and those around us.

We will be disciplined leaders.

We will be successful leaders.

We will find that success doesn't just find us we have to go after it.

Serving God opens up practical opportunities in our lives to follow His guidelines for living and leading.

PRAYER

Dear God, Please help me to be willing to work diligently at whatever my hand finds to do. May my work ethic always be strong even when my body isn't what it used to be. Amen

Thankful for the Benefits

O my soul, bless God. From head to toe, I'll bless his holy name. O my soul, bless God, don't forget a single blessing! He forgives your sins—every one. He heals your diseases—every one. He redeems you from hell—saves your life! He crowns you with love and mercy—a paradise crown. He wraps you in goodness—beauty eternal. He renews your youth—you're always young in his presence. Psalm 103:1-5 MSG

Practicing thankfulness to God should be a daily habit. Hopefully this is something you do every day and every time you pray. All of us have a lot to be thankful for in our lives even if not everything is perfect or maybe the way we think it should be.

"He forgives your sins—every one."

Having one's sins forgiven is the most important element of human life. Our lives lived out on this side of eternity are but a fraction of time in comparison with that endless and coming forever. This is our testing ground. Our life here is like a boot camp to prepare us for eternal life with God or without him. Jesus Christ came to this earth to die in our place as a sacrifice for our sins. He offered us eternal life if we would but turn from our wicked ways and embrace his ways. I hope that you know the assurance of sins forgiven. I hope that you have experienced the peace that comes from God and the joy that fills a redeemed soul.

Pause today and remember where and what Jesus saved you from.

Pause today and reflect on how different your life would have been without him.

Pause today and renew a spirit of thanksgiving for your salvation. Your sins have been forgiven!

If you don't know that your sins are forgiven, pause today and repent or turn from them by asking Jesus to forgive you. He longs for us to do this. He wants to give you salvation. He will forgive your sins—every one!

PRAYER

Dear God, having my sins forgiven brings me to my knees in gratefulness to you. My life, my future and my family are in your hands. Please hear my thankfulness today as I express it to you. Amen.

Thankful for the Benefits

O my soul, bless God. From head to toe, I'll bless his holy name. O my soul, bless God, don't forget a single blessing! He forgives your sins—every one. He heals your diseases—every one. He redeems you from hell—saves your life! He crowns you with love and mercy—a paradise crown. He wraps you in goodness—beauty eternal. He renews your youth—you're always young in his presence. Psalm 103:1-5 MSG

"He heals your diseases – every one."

Could this be true? Does God heal all our diseases? The spirit of this Psalm is one of continuation from the previous sentence. Not only does God forgive us our sins but he begins the healing process from the inside out.

All of us bear the scars of sinfulness. Our lives and our stories are often marred by decisions we made, relationships that were broken, the haunting memories of dysfunction, and many other scars. When we allow Jesus to become our Savior he doesn't stop with the gift of eternal life. He begins the process of inner healing. As we surrender our past, many times over years, he brings his healing touch to the effects of our former lives.

It's a deep thought I suppose, but maybe today is a good time to remember what he saved you from. Remember who you used to be before his grace invaded your life. Maybe this is a day where not only do you thank him for his promised healing, but you allow him to have complete access to your past, present, and future.

Let him heal your memories, your hurts, your bitterness, your unforgiveness, or anything else that may be weighing you down. Trust him with your life. Trust him with your emotions. Trust him and thank him today because he loves you as you are, not as you should be. He will heal you!

PRAYER

Dear Lord, I firmly believe that you have the power to heal the bodies you have given us. I also know that healing doesn't always happen the way I would like or when I would like it to. I trust you with all my diseases. Amen.

Thankful for the Benefits

O my soul, bless God. From head to toe, I'll bless his holy name. O my soul, bless God, don't forget a single blessing! He forgives your sins—every one. He heals your diseases—every one. He redeems you from hell—saves your life! He crowns you with love and mercy—a paradise crown. He wraps you in goodness—beauty eternal. He renews your youth—you're always young in his presence. Psalm 103:1-5 MSG

"He redeems you from hell - saves your life!"

At first glance, you might think this is a summation of the first two blessings, but that is not the case. In more traditional translations, it is rendered this way, "Who redeems your life from destruction."

Remember this is a Psalm of David. A short recap of his personal story will remind you that he needed his life to be redeemed from destruction. He messed up. He really, really messed up. When faced with the truth about his actions he fell on God for forgiveness and mercy.

I don't know how David would fare today among the people called Christians, but I can assure you that God forgave him and redeemed a tragic and horrible life event. It came with consequences for sure, but God's grace was in the midst of the tragedy.

Like David, if you have ever allowed your focus to be distracted away from God and stumbled your way into failure, it doesn't have to be final. He will redeem your life from destruction. He will redeem you from hell. He will save your life.

For this, offer gratitude today.

PRAYER

Most merciful God, today I thank you for your grace and willingness to forgive the broken and bruised. Thank you for your grace toward the fallen and failing. Thank you for loving me and for redeeming my life. Amen.

Thankful for the Benefits

O my soul, bless God. From head to toe, I'll bless his holy name. O my soul, bless God, don't forget a single blessing! He forgives your sins—every one. He heals your diseases—every one. He redeems you from hell—saves your life! He crowns you with love and mercy—a paradise crown. He wraps you in goodness—beauty eternal. He renews your youth—you're always young in his presence. Psalm 103:1-5 MSG

"He crowns you with love and mercy—a paradise crown." "He wraps you in goodness – beauty eternal."

Simply put, when you belong to God, he covers you from head to foot. We are covered with love and mercy on our heads. The above verses are from The Message so they are a little different than more traditional renderings of these verses. You might be familiar with interpretations like, "He fills my life with good things" or "He satisfies your desires with good things."

Regardless of the translation of these verses, the spirit is the same. When we look to God for satisfaction, we will be satisfied. When we believe that his mercy and love are enough, we will be the adopted children of a King. We will be crowned with his compassion and wrapped in his goodness. This makes our lives beautiful even when they may not appear to be from those looking on from the outside. We may at times get distracted by the circumstances or people that threaten to steal our joy.

As you praise and thank him today, also ask him to give you the eyes needed to see with a godly perspective. You are blessed if you are crowned with his mercy and love and wrapped in his goodness. You have beauty eternal!

PRAYER

Dear God, help me to really embrace this thought today. I am so thankful for your love, mercy, and goodness. You crown me and you wrap me in your beauty. Thank you for this. Amen.

Count your Blessings!

Let us come to him with thanksgiving. Let us sing psalms of praise to him. Psalm 95:2 NLT

Thanksgiving should be more than a once a year holiday. Life can be distracting. Many times our focus will fixate on what we don't have instead of being thankful for what we do have. I am going to suggest that starting today you pause, either in the morning before you get up or sometime throughout the day, and just be thankful. Do it for a week, or better yet a month, and see if it develops into a habit.

It's really not that hard once you get started. We live in a world with many people that live way below the standard of living we have come to expect. They struggle for food, housing, clean water, money, and even in some cases clothing.

For me it is easy to come up with things to be thankful for, and here are a few of them:

God

My salvation through Jesus

Health

The ability to walk up stairs or across a parking lot

Eyes that see and my ears that hear

My job, my family, my ability to pay for gas, food, clothes, and to provide a home for my family

My church

My car that is working today, and my furnace and hot water heater that function day after day

Food

Water

Friends

To be loved

Music

Laughter

Books

Smiles given and received

Freedom

Safe landings
Sleep
Peace
Emotions
Forgiveness
Joy
Time
Whisper your thankfulness to God all day long.

Dear God, thank you!

Everything?

"In everything give thanks" 1 Thessalonians 5:18 NKJV

Everything is a big word! The only way to be able to be thankful for everything is to be fully surrendered to God and to trust him with all of our days. Pause and be thankful today. You are loved.

It is easy to be thankful for the good things, but push yourself today to be thankful for all things. If we learn to be thankful when minor setbacks occur and practice self-awareness by pushing ourselves to be thankful, we will not find it as hard when major events come along that take our breath away.

Most of us aren't very good at this, especially if we live in the United States or some other country known for consumerism and expectations to be met on demand. Too often I am afraid we emotionally respond with shock, anger, agitation, frustration, and even grief. There are times where these emotions are probably acceptable, but ultimately our resting position should be one of thankfulness to God for his presence in our lives through it all.

See what God will do with you today if you can practice thankfulness all day long.

PRAYER

Dear Jesus, you know that I am not always good at saying thanks, especially for the negative things in my life. Give me the grace I need to be thankful in all things. Amen.

What Is the Cross to You?

The message of the cross is foolish to those who are headed for destruction! But we who are being saved know it is the very power of God. 1 Corinthians 1:18 NLT

Most people are not ashamed of a cross as long as it is on a necklace or some form of jewelry. It might even be in a picture or some kind of decoration; and of course, we are okay with that as well.

But the message of the cross is more than just a fashion statement. It is the very power of God!

If you have knelt before the cross, figuratively speaking, and given your life to Jesus Christ, you know that power and the change that takes place in your life. The way you live your life on this planet is drastically and forever different. You will no longer desire the ways of this world or be charmed by the culture. You will hunger and thirst for more of God in your life and do whatever is necessary to draw closer to him. Your eyes will be open to the needs of those around you, and you will see the pathetic and destructive path that many choose to take. A path that leads to destruction.

What is the cross to you? Is the cross a symbol of the salvation that you enjoy, or is it just part of a story that seems barbaric and bloody? Do you love being associated with the cross and the Savior that died on it to provide you forgiveness of sins, or does it just seem like a story you would rather not identify with?

Embrace the cross and the Christ that hung there in scorn and shame. Make sure that you have offered your life and prayed a prayer of repentance so that you are walking in a relationship with the Savior of the world.

PRAYER

Dear Jesus, I don't ever want to be ashamed of the cross or think that it is foolish. I am sorry for my sins and ask you to forgive me through the blood you shed on the cross. Live in me, Jesus, and let me be a part of your story in the world. Amen.

Standing Watch

I will stand my watch and set myself on the rampart, and watch to see what He will say to me, and what I will answer when I am corrected. Habakkuk 2:1 NKJV

I will place myself in the right position

The writer is clearly looking for a message from God, so he is standing watch. He is where he is supposed to be. We should always live in a right position before God. Be faithful to his Word. Be aware of what he wants from you daily. He does want something from you. He wants you to be available to be his hands and feet. He wants you to speak with him both words of praise and petition. Be in the right place at the right time because you desire to hear from God. Standing watch over your soul is recommended all throughout the Bible. Are you in the right position?

I will learn to listen to what God says

When you are in the right position to hear from God, meaning that you have forsaken the sins that are devastating to your spiritual life, you can learn to listen for his voice. Of course, he doesn't speak out loud; but he will speak. He speaks to us through his Word, sermons, songs, books, and even in nature. He may speak through someone you know and in rare cases even a stranger. You and I have to want to hear what he is saying. When we desire to hear from him he will find a way to communicate to our minds and hearts. Are you learning to listen?

I will care about his corrections

When parents love their children, they will love them enough to correct them and lead them in the way that they should go. So, too, your heavenly Father will bring correction into your life. The writer here is concerned about how he will respond to God's correction. It's a good thing to think about, because correction will make us better or bitter. We will take it and grow from it or we will reject it and continue on in the same destructive paths we have been walking. God's corrections are always in our best spiritual interest. They may even save us from dangerous outcomes if we care and don't persist in our own ways. Are you caring about his corrections?

Being a Christian is primarily about being in a relationship with God. It is about caring about what he cares about, loving what he loves, and doing what he wants you to do. What an amazing opportunity you have today to be in a relationship with the Creator God. Think about that today. Reach out to him and see what he wants to say to you.

PRAYER

Dear God, it is an amazing and awesome gift to be able to live in your presence. I will stand watch over my life, and I will learn to listen for your voice. Give me the ability to respond in the way I should every day. Amen.

Mourning and Fasting

When I heard this, I sat down and wept. In fact, for days I mourned, fasted, and prayed to the God of heaven. Nehemiah 1:4 NLT

Nehemiah had just visited with some people from his hometown of Jerusalem, and he received bad news. It was reported to him that the people were in trouble, living in disgrace, and that the wall of Jerusalem had been torn down and the gates destroyed by fire. His response was to sit down and weep. For days he mourned, fasted, and prayed. If you know the rest of the story, you know that he also did something about it by getting permission to leave his job as the king's cup-bearer. He was living in luxury, but he was compelled to leave the comfort and go home to repair the walls.

I can't remember the last time I heard a message calling me to fast and pray before God. I fear it is something that many of us never practice. We certainly all have our share of concerns, needs, and burdens; but I think it is easier to just dash off a prayer than it is to intentionally fast by denying ourselves food for a meal or two in the interest of focused prayer.

Why not try it next time you are overcome by a need? Nehemiah sat down and wept. He was shaken by the news. He was unashamed to cry, and he was deeply touched and moved to prayer. He was in mourning, and he fasted for days. Why not one day this week skip a meal and use that time to pray for something in particular? When I was in Bible College, Thursdays were a day for prayer and fasting. Many of us would meet in the chapel and pray and it focused my mind on the needs I was praying about. It also made dinner that much sweeter when it finally rolled around.

I am challenging you today to make fasting a real part of your faith journey with God. We can also give up other things that waste our time like TV, our phones, computers, and social media. Refocus your time when you give something up so that you are connecting with God. It really does make a difference.

PRAYER

Dear God, I am going to fast before you. Whatever it takes to bring focus and purpose back to my life. Align me, Lord, with your purposes, and give me a heart that follows your heart in this world. Amen.

Troubled Hearts

Don't let your hearts be troubled. Trust in God, and trust also in me. John 14:1 NLT

Last evening I was called to visit and pray with a lady that was dying. She was sitting on the couch in her daughter's home. She had decided the treatments were too much; and now, a week or so later, hospice was called in and I found myself sitting in front of her having a deep but brief conversation about life. She was a pastor's wife for years. She was a God-loving lady that had modeled her faith for her family for decades. Her three daughters were around her as I prayed for her and with her.

When I asked her if everything was okay with her heart/soul, she replied with confidence that it sure was, and she didn't understand how anybody could live without Jesus. I read this verse to her and reminded her of the fact that Jesus had just told his disciples that he was going away and that they couldn't follow him. And then he said this:

"Don't let your hearts be troubled. Trust in God, and trust also in me. There is more than enough room in my Father's home. If this were not so, would I have told you that I am going to prepare a place for you? When everything is ready, I will come and get you, so that you will always be with me where I am."

At 11:30 last evening she slipped away from this world and went to be with Jesus. Just three hours before her death she looked me right in the eyes with great confidence and assured me of her love for her Lord. Now she is with him. Everything was ready, and he came to get her.

I was moved by it all. I am resolved to not let the distractions of this disgusting and Godless world turn me away from my trust in Jesus. Whatever it is today that is going on around you, trust in God and trust in Jesus. They care deeply for you, and someday you will be with them if you trust in them now.

PRAYER

Dear Jesus, I want to trust you with my life now and always. Give me a confidence and hope that nothing can diminish in my life. Let me love you more today than I ever have. Amen.

Follow the Good

Dear friend, don't let this bad example influence you. Follow only what is good. Remember that those who do good prove that they are God's children, and those who do evil prove that they do not know God. 3 John 11

In the early churches there were men and women who began to take advantage of their leadership positions. Before long they departed from orthodox truth as preached by the apostle Paul, John, Peter, and others.

The test between good and evil has always been discovered in the actions of the person being tested. If you are demonstrating evil behaviors in your life that are contrary to the Word of God, you can be assured that you are practicing evil. If your life matches with the principles and commands of the Bible, you can know that you are practicing good.

The Bible commands us to love one another. We are told to take care of orphans and widows and to be generous toward the poor. We are told to let the Spirit of God bear fruit through us, like love, joy, peace, patience, kindness, goodness, faithfulness, gentleness, and self-control. We are told to make disciples and love our neighbors as ourselves. Most of all, we are told to love God with all of our heart, mind, soul, and strength.

"Follow only what is good." I hope that is what you are doing. If not, start today. Turn around. It's never too late to head in the right direction.

PRAYER

Dear Jesus, for sure I want to be on the good side and not the evil side of life. Always show me my heart and actions in light of your Word. Amen.

Guarding the Truth

Hold on to the pattern of wholesome teaching you learned from me—a pattern shaped by the faith and love that you have in Christ Jesus. Through the power of the Holy Spirit who lives within us, carefully guard the precious truth that has been entrusted to you.
2 Timothy 1:13-14 NLT

Writing to a young ministry protégé, the apostle Paul urges him to never let go of the pattern for Christian living that he was given. All of us have experienced some form of Christian teaching handed to us from others. We've heard a sermon, had a conversation, listened to a teaching, or at some point been given a pattern of Christian behavior to follow.

We should never compare ourselves to other Christians, because they are not the standard we are called to follow. We are called to follow the Word of God as our guide. We learn this Word from personal study but also from others called to share God's message in spoken or written word.

Here is a breakdown of this Scripture for you to ponder today:

Grace: There is a pattern of wholesome teaching ... shaped by faith and love in Jesus Christ.

We live wholesome lives because we love Jesus Christ and have faith in him daily. Our lives should be a reflection of his love in our relationships and interactions with friends, family, and foe.

Gift it: There is the power of the Holy Spirit that lives in us.

The Holy Spirit is referred to as a gift in the Bible. We received him as a guide to lead us and empower us to serve the Lord on this earth. We are called share this gift with others.

Guard it: This is precious truth entrusted to us.

Don't allow the enemy of our souls, who goes around seeking whom he may devour, to attain any foothold in your life. Guard your mind, your heart, and your soul. Stay connected to Jesus daily. Cultivate your love for him and talk with him every day even if it is casual conversation. Love him most. Put God first. Keep him first.

"There is no joy in the soul that has forgotten what God prizes."
—Oswald Chambers

"All change comes from deepening your understanding of the salvation of Christ and living out the changes that understanding creates in your heart." — Tim Keller

PRAYER

Dear Jesus, don't let me ever let go of the truth of your Word. Help me always guard my heart and what you have allowed me to learn about life and living for you. Amen.

Gentle for the Win

A gentle answer deflects anger, but harsh words make tempers flare. The tongue of the wise makes knowledge appealing, but the mouth of a fool belches out foolishness. Proverbs 15:1-2 NLT

We've all been around people who have anger issues. Many times this person will lose self-control and open their mouth no matter where they are or who they are around. It's that awkward moment at the grocery store when two adults allow their fight to escalate to the point that you can't avoid hearing and seeing what is going on. It's the dad or mom at a sporting event that loses control and in the process embarrasses their child and family but may not even be self-aware enough to notice.

The Proverb writer is suggesting that our words are powerful and can make us look foolish or wise. They can escalate or deescalate a situation. I wonder what you are thinking as you read this. Are you thinking about someone you know or about yourself? If it is you that you are thinking about, why not ask God to help you with the issue. Ask him to take away the anger that seems uncontrollable. Ask him to soften your heart and to give you a more quiet response. Rest your soul in him. Trust him to change you from the inside out.

PRAYER

Dear Jesus, you are the best model I know of restraint and soft words. You endured so much and didn't retaliate or demand your own way. Teach me to be more like you in my responses to others. Guard my heart and my mouth. Amen.

Let Me Be in the Moment

So encourage each other and build each other up, just as you are already doing. 1 Thessalonians 5:11 NLT

What a great reminder for all of us as we encounter the hustle and bustle of one of the busiest months of the year. Be aware of the people around you today, and be sensitive to what may or may not be going on in their lives.

This includes family, friends, co-workers, neighbors, the people who serve you in the service industry, and even strangers you might encounter. How can you emulate the unconditional love that you experience in Jesus to the people in your life? What are some things you could do today to make a difference for them? Here are a few suggestions:

Pray for them.

Listen to them.

Care about them.

Ask God to love them through you.

Share with them.

Be engaged with the people you meet or talk to today. Slow down and be in the moment. Hear their words with your heart and not just your head. Be the eyes and ears of Jesus today. Someone may need you more than you know. God is looking for people that will care for others, so get ready if you take the challenge. Be the channel for God's love today.

PRAYER

Dear Jesus, in this month when we celebrate your birth, please give me the ability to be aware of your presence moment by moment. Thank you for coming to this earth! Amen.

When God Chooses You

Jews were aware that a Messiah was promised, but I am not sure that Mary thought it would happen through a human birth. I'm not sure she could have imagined that someone would be chosen to carry and bear the Son of God in a very human birth. God picked her. God chose her for a reason.

Like Mary, God has something unique for all of us to do. In Mary's case the announcement came from an angel who said to her that she was highly favored and blessed among women. She was understandably afraid, and the angel went on to tell her again that she had found favor with God and would conceive and bear a Son.

"You will conceive and give birth to a son, and you will name him Jesus. He will be very great and will be called the Son of the Most High. The Lord God will give him the throne of his ancestor David. And he will reign over Israel forever; his Kingdom will never end!" Mary asked the angel, "But how can this happen? I am a virgin."

The angel replied, "The Holy Spirit will come upon you, and the power of the Most High will overshadow you. So the baby to be born will be holy, and he will be called the Son of God.... For the word of God will never fail."

Mary responded, "I am the Lord's servant. May everything you have said about me come true." And then the angel left her. Luke 1:31-35,37-38 NLT

That was it. Short and straight to the point. God wants you to do something. Any questions? She asked the obvious one and heard the how and why. "God's word never fails," said the angel. And she responded and submitted to being God's servant.

It's a daily call for all of us. We don't have to birth the Son of God but every day there is something that God has on our agenda to accomplish for him. Finding it is to find the sweet spot of your calling. We are called to love the unlovable. We are called to care for people less fortunate than ourselves. We are called to share the Good News of Jesus Christ to all people.

Mary was his mother and raised him for thirty years. We know very little about those years. All we know is that she was faithful to the call. She responded with the right answer. Here's a big secret. The answer to God is always ... YES!

PRAYER

Dear God, I want to always be available for you and willing to do whatever you call on me to do. May my faith be strong, and may I always believe that your Word never fails. Amen.

What's Your Soul Worth?

And what do you benefit if you gain the whole world but lose your own soul? Mark 8:36 NLT

This time of year, our minds turn toward the giving and accumulation of things. Family members begin asking for lists of gifts you might like to receive. You may begin thinking about what gifts you are going to give to others.

Sometimes people are fueled by their passion for collecting things. There is a thrill in finding some elusive collectible, and there is the excitement of the hunt. We enjoy sharing the stories of our stuff with others who will take the time to see what we have, and we really love it when they ask questions. Depending on your budget, there is something for almost everyone to collect or own.

The writer of this Scripture simply reminds us to not allow anything or anyone to distract our heart, mind, and soul away from our relationship with God. People, money, and things can sometimes call for our attention and allure us away from what matters most.

Protect your soul. Guard your heart. Pay attention to where, who, and what you have made priorities in your life. Why not pause today, ask, and allow God to examine your heart. Is there anything or anyone that is blurring your allegiance? Nothing or no one in this world is worth losing your soul over. Pledge and profess your love for Christ today.

PRAYER

Dear Jesus, I realize that my soul was worth your death on the cross. Please help me to value my soul over the things of this world. Amen.

Follow the Light

Jesus spoke to the people once more and said, "I am the light of the world. If you follow me, you won't have to walk in darkness, because you will have the light that leads to life." John 8:12 NLT

We are now in the Advent season and it is a good time to review our lives and loves. Advent is a time of looking forward with anticipation and hope. We hope for the second return or advent of Jesus Christ. That hope is based on our relationship with him.

It is true that God promises many things in his Word. Nothing is clearer in Scripture than the fact that obedience matters to God. Yes, we are saved by grace; but from Genesis to Revelation he calls us to follow him and obey him. It's simple really. Read his Word, follow his commands and principles, and put him first. Always put him first.

Jesus spoke words of hope when he said: "I am the light of the world." Everybody loves light. Most of us prefer light to darkness. Light provides a lot of things including security, guidance, sight, and freedom from darkness. Most of us have heard this statement of Jesus quoted before or we have read it, but there is a condition to the promise for light.

You can have the light, but Jesus says: "IF you follow me ... you won't have to walk in darkness." The implication is that if you choose to not follow him you will eventually wind up in darkness. But why wouldn't we follow him? What choices face us that trump a genuine relationship with the Savior of the world?

Jesus also says if we follow him we will have "the light that leads to life." There is hope and it is always and only found in Christ. In this month of reflection and anticipation, make sure that nothing is, or comes, between your soul and the Savior.

PRAYER

Dear Jesus, so often this world and the culture around me are distracting and discouraging. I will follow you, and I will walk in your light. Give me courage and self-awareness today in my relationship with you. Amen.

The Morning Light

John the Baptist's father proclaimed these words:

"And you, my little son, will be called the prophet of the Most High, because you will prepare the way for the Lord. You will tell his people how to find salvation through forgiveness of their sins. Because of God's tender mercy, the morning light from heaven is about to break upon us, to give light to those who sit in darkness and in the shadow of death, and to guide us to the path of peace" (Luke 1:76-79 NLT).

What an incredible moment in history! The one who would prepare the way for Jesus' earthly ministry was born. John the Baptist, like Jesus, would give his life for this message of salvation through the forgiveness of sins.

All of the good things that come to us come because of God's tender mercy. Sometimes we may not think of the tender side of God, but his love and mercy exceed any you can find on earth. For Zechariah, the Light was about to dawn. This Light of the world would bring light to the dark places and those walking in the shadow of death. This Light would also be available to guide us to a pathway of peace.

These are some reasons to celebrate the advent of our Lord. He brought salvation and forgiveness of sins. He brings light, comfort, and peace. He is for you today and knows what is happening in your life. He wants to be your Lord today. Reach out to him. Call on him. Trust him.

PRAYER

Dear Jesus, thank you for bringing light to this dark world and for sharing that light with me. Your light is the light I want to follow always. I am thankful for your light today! Amen.

Believing Brings Blessings!

You are blessed because you believed that the Lord would do what he said. Luke 1:45 NLT

Elizabeth, the mother of John the Baptist, spoke these words to Mary, the soon-to-be-mother of Jesus. They are words of blessing, faith, and encouragement. They are words that speak to the heart of our faith in Jesus Christ.

It is not uncommon for us to face situations in life that test and try us. Sometimes these circumstances may seem insurmountable and leave us struggling to see a way out. What are our options when life has turned upside down and we absolutely don't have answers? As authentic followers of Jesus Christ we have one option.

We are to believe. Believe always.

The Bible is full of promises, stories, and guidance. We can read about others who struggled in their lives. Sometimes there was a miraculous delivery and sometimes not. Sometimes lives were spared and sometimes they were not. What we learn when we read these stories is that God is God no matter what. We learn to trust him, lean on him, and love him regardless of what is happening around us.

This blind faith is what the mother of Jesus possessed. Her life was turned upside down for sure. There was no logical explanation for her pregnancy. Who would believe her that the Holy Spirit had planted this child inside of her and that he would be the Son of God? And yet she believed.

This belief and unwavering faith brought her the blessing she could have never achieved on her own. We know that her life was filled with sorrow at the foot of the cross, but she never quit believing.

Blessed are you among women, Mary; and blessed are you and I if we can only believe.

PRAYER

Dear Jesus, give me the courage of Mary to believe quickly when you speak. Help my unbelief, and please let my faith be strong. Amen.

Fear Not!

And, lo, the angel of the Lord came upon them, and the glory of the Lord shone round about them: and they were sore afraid. And the angel said unto them, Fear not: for, behold, I bring you good tidings of great joy, which shall be to all people. For unto you is born this day in the city of David a Savior, which is Christ the Lord. Luke 2:9-11 KJV

These verses are some of the most familiar Christmas related verses that are read and known worldwide. Maybe we remember them so well because they were given to regular guys and most of us are "regular" people. Like these shepherds, some of us may even work third shift. Like them, we don't feel wealthy even if our needs are met every day.

We may also remember these verses because all of us have dealt with fear in our lives; and one thing is sure, these shepherds were very shocked and afraid. There is a message here that goes way beyond a few sleepy shepherds watching over their sheep. There is a message of hope and salvation, and it is for everyone. The gospel is not exclusive. It absolutely is for everyone on this earth.

Maybe this outline will be helpful to process this event that happened so long ago.

"Unto you" makes it personal.

"This day" makes it present.

"A Savior" makes it precious.

Christmas is about Christ. That is all. Everything else we do has been added over the last 2,000 plus years. Because it is about Christ we all must deal with that message. We deal with it personally and we decide to accept this great gift of salvation or reject it. The shepherds could have ignored it like many do today and stayed out in the dark and cold, but they believed it and acted on what they believed.

It's a relevant message for today. It has never changed no matter how much the world changes around us. Even as you read this, God is offering you the best gift ever known to men and women the world over. Your sins can be forgiven. You can have joy and peace in your soul.

What makes this gift and message precious is that all of us need a Savior. When this world wraps up and our time on earth is over, eternity looms for everyone. How glad you will be that you accepted the gift of Jesus. How precious he will be to you on that day. The apostle Paul wrote about the "precious truth that has been entrusted to you."

Today make sure you are following the Christ of Christmas. Let his light shine in and through you. Let go of things that are worrying you or causing anxiety. "Fear not." It is a day of good news! It is a day for great joy, and that trumps anything happening around you.

PRAYER

Dear Jesus, fear often tries to invade my life. Anxiety can be very real and distracting, but I am asking you to help me overcome unhealthy fear. Because of you, I will not be afraid. Amen.

The Great Exchange

You know the generous grace of our Lord Jesus Christ. Though he was rich, yet for your sakes he became poor, so that by his poverty he could make you rich. 2 Corinthians 8:9 NLT

You may not feel rich today, but if you have received the grace of Christ in your life, you are wealthy beyond measure. Jesus came to earth as a baby and gave up heaven so that we might have eternal life through him. He gave his life for our salvation. Don't miss the best exchange gift ever.

The riches promised by Jesus far exceed cars, houses, and money. His generous grace sustains us in this journey called life. When we accept him as our Savior and allow him to forgive our sins, we are accepting the gift of salvation. Along with the gift of salvation come the gifts of the Spirit and the gift of the Holy Spirit who will guide us into truth and empower us for holy living.

Whatever you do, make sure that you have received this precious gift offered by Jesus. He came to give life everlasting to whoever would believe. He loves all humans that much.

PRAYER

Dear Jesus, I accept the gift of salvation that You offered by Your death and resurrection. You forgive my sins and I want to follow you all the days of my life. Amen

With God!

For with God nothing will be impossible. Luke 1:37 NKJV

These words were spoken to Mary by the angel telling her she was going to be the mother of Jesus. No matter what is going on in your life today, remember these words. Nothing is impossible for God.

When Mary was told she would become pregnant but not in the usual way, one could understand if she struggled to believe what was being said. There is no evidence that she struggled at all to believe or accept what was being touted as God's will for her life.

It was complicated. There would be shame, scorn, and people that would not believe the story she would tell. There would be the challenge of making her husband understand that she was pregnant from the Holy Spirit and not from cheating in their relationship.

It is good to remember that with God all things are indeed possible. You may not be in the same spot as Mary or dealing with anything close to what she was facing, but we have the same God. This message of hope for her is good for us as well. So today, remind yourself often: "For with God nothing will be impossible."

PRAYER

Dear Jesus, there are times I forget this or maybe doubt it. I know that it is true, and today I will remind myself of this and deepen my confidence in you! Amen.

Anna

Anna, a prophet, was also there in the Temple. She was the daugh-
ter of Phanuel from the tribe of Asher, and she was very old. Her
husband died when they had been married only seven years. Then
she lived as a widow to the age of eighty-four. She never left the
Temple but stayed there day and night, worshiping God with fast-
ing and prayer. 38 She came along just as Simeon was talking with
Mary and Joseph, and she began praising God. She talked about
the child to everyone who had been waiting expectantly for God to
rescue Jerusalem. Luke 2:36-38 NLT

She was a very old lady who had been through a lot in her life. She was
in the temple at the same time as Simeon, Joseph, Mary, and the in-
fant Jesus. She overheard the news that this little baby was the promised
Messiah. What can we learn from her story? We don't have much. Her
mention in the Scriptures is all contained in the above paragraph. Here
are some takeaways from her life:

She survived a personal tragic event: It made her better, not bitter
"Her husband died when they had been married only seven years.
Then she lived as a widow to the age of eighty-four."

What a tragic thing to endure, and yet we find her decades later serving God and waiting hopefully for the coming Messiah. She persevered
and stayed faithful even when her life fell apart. God honored her for it.

**She stayed in the temple every day and night: It made her a wor-
shiper, not a worrier**
"She never left the Temple but stayed there day and night, worshiping God with fasting and prayer."

Over the years she learned to draw close to God. She literally stayed
in his presence in the temple; and while most of us can't do that, we have
a friend in Jesus Christ that will never leave us or forsake us. Stay close
to God. Don't drift away because of negative circumstances or people.

She shared the good news with everyone: It made her passionate, not passive

"She talked about the child to everyone who had been waiting expectantly for God to rescue Jerusalem."

At her age, Anna could have legitimately not been active. She could have passively spent her remaining years disengaged from God's work, but she wasn't about to quit. She was passionate about the message of the Messiah. Who knows how much longer she lived, but I am sure she never quit sharing the message of hope and good news.

I guess there is lot to learn from Anna's paragraph after all. She loved her God and she was full of hope and praise for his great mercy. She served him with fasting and prayer, and she waited to see the salvation of the Lord.

PRAYER

Dear Jesus, may I be filled with Anna's kind of passion. May the circumstances of my life push me closer to you and make me a better person. May I discover the power of worship this Advent season as I wait expectantly for your return. Amen.

Elizabeth

When Zechariah's week of service in the Temple was over, he returned home. Soon afterward his wife, Elizabeth, became pregnant and went into seclusion for five months. "How kind the Lord is!" she exclaimed. "He has taken away my disgrace of having no children." Luke 1:23-25 NLT

Elizabeth was past the child-bearing stage of life, so this pregnancy was a miracle of God and a gift to her at the same time. She believed. She accepted God at his word. She had a baby boy and they named him John. Prior to this birth, Mary, the soon-to-be-mother of Jesus, came to visit Elizabeth her cousin. This happened when she greeted her:

"She entered the house and greeted Elizabeth. At the sound of Mary's greeting, Elizabeth's child leaped within her, and Elizabeth was filled with the Holy Spirit" (Luke 1:40-42 NLT).

What happened when Elizabeth was filled with God's Spirit? She uttered affirming and confirming words to the much younger virgin Mary. She proclaimed these historic words of blessing:

"Elizabeth gave a glad cry and exclaimed to Mary, 'God has blessed you above all women, and your child is blessed. Why am I so honored, that the mother of my Lord should visit me? When I heard your greeting, the baby in my womb jumped for joy. You are blessed because you believed that the Lord would do what he said'" (Luke 1:42-34 NLT).

When Zechariah's and Elizabeth's baby was born we read:

"Awe fell upon the whole neighborhood, and the news of what had happened spread throughout the Judean hills. Everyone who heard about it reflected on these events and asked, 'What will this child turn out to be?' For the hand of the Lord was surely upon him in a special way" (Luke 1:65-66 NLT).

What can we learn from Elizabeth? What can we take away and apply to our own journey?
- God uses common people to do great things!
- God uses obedient people to answer His call!
- God uses willing people.
- God uses people like us to bless others and affect our communities!

Purpose to follow hard after God. Pursue and love Him with all of your heart, mind, soul and strength. Love your neighbors as much as you love yourself. Stand back and watch God work through you as you surrender to Him daily. Elizabeth helped prepare the way for the salvation that came to us through Jesus Christ our Lord. You never know what God wants to do through you!

PRAYER

Dear Jesus, help me to be willing to let you work in my life regardless of notoriety, applause or affirmation. Just help me to always be willing to do Your will. Amen.

Zechariah

Zechariah and Elizabeth were righteous in God's eyes, careful to obey all of the Lord's commandments and regulations. They had no children because Elizabeth was unable to conceive, and they were both very old. Luke 1:6-7 NLT

While Zechariah was in the sanctuary, an angel of the Lord appeared to him, standing to the right of the incense altar. Zechariah was shaken and overwhelmed with fear when he saw him. But the angel said, "Don't be afraid, Zechariah! God has heard your prayer. Your wife, Elizabeth, will give you a son, and you are to name him John. You will have great joy and gladness, and many will rejoice at his birth, for he will be great in the eyes of the Lord." Luke 1:11-14 NLT

Zechariah said to the angel, "How can I be sure this will happen? I'm an old man now, and my wife is also well along in years." Then the angel said, "I am Gabriel! I stand in the very presence of God. It was he who sent me to bring you this good news! But now, since you didn't believe what I said, you will be silent and unable to speak until the child is born. For my words will certainly be fulfilled at the proper time." Luke 1:18-20 NLT

This is a very fascinating story for several reasons. To bring focus on Zechariah it is important to see the dynamics of this encounter. He was a faithful man. He and his wife were careful to obey all the commands of God. When faced with the prospect of childbirth at an older age he wondered out loud how this could happen.

He got in trouble for questioning the angel, but it didn't keep God from using him and his wife. His silence in the long run was probably a gift. He was a worshiping man. He worked hard at serving God in the temple, which meant he was "in the ministry."

I wonder what lessons God spoke to his heart and mind in those days of silence? Do you ever practice silence? Often we turn on electronics to fill in the quiet around us. We are accustomed to noise, and we sometimes use it to keep us from engaging our thoughts. God wants to speak to us. He wants us at times to remain quiet before him and listen deep in our hearts for his nudging and nurturing. Find some time this season of the year to turn things off and be silent. Embrace the quiet and let the Holy Spirit of God have access to your mind, heart, and soul.

When the baby was born, Zechariah was allowed to speak: "Instantly Zechariah could speak again, and he began praising God. Awe fell upon the whole neighborhood, and the news of what had happened spread throughout the Judean hills. Everyone who heard about it reflected on these events and asked, 'What will this child turn out to be?' For the hand of the Lord was surely upon him in a special way" (Luke 1:64-66 NLT).

The first words out of his mouth were praise for God! Later in this chapter he breaks out into song. I wonder what God could fill up our hearts with this Christmas if we listened to him in the quiet times of our lives.

PRAYER

Dear Jesus, let my first words always be praise for you and your works in my life. Thanks for the testimony of your hand being on and in our lives. Amen.

Herod

Not all the characters in the Christmas story are positive. King Herod, or Herod the Great as he was also known, was apparently a very insecure man and didn't mind murdering the innocent that he thought might pose a threat.

In an effort to kill this fabled Messiah, he ordered what is known as the Massacre of the Innocents. Joseph was warned about it in a dream and moved with his family to Egypt. Matthew writes about it:

Herod was furious when he realized that the wise men had outwitted him. He sent soldiers to kill all the boys in and around Bethlehem who were two years old and under, based on the wise men's report of the star's first appearance. Herod's brutal action fulfilled what God had spoken through the prophet Jeremiah: "A cry was heard in Ramah—weeping and great mourning. Rachel weeps for her children, refusing to be comforted, for they are dead." Matthew 2:16-18 NLT

Nobody reading this is in a position to take the lives of others at the stroke of a pen, but I wonder sometimes how often our insecurities get us in trouble. It is easy to become obsessed about our titles, positions, status, and whether or not people like us. Sometimes it may be within our families and relationships. There are times when we find ourselves so far from what we know is right and we wonder if it is possible to return.

What many people don't know is that Herod the Great was a Jew. He was the client king of Judea working for the Roman Empire. He should have been looking for the Messiah and anticipating his coming.

This wasn't about killing the Messiah as much as it was protecting his own interests. He was aware of the prophecies of a coming Messiah but obviously wasn't living in a way that engaged his faith. He was about self-preservation. He was on the throne of his own heart.

We will always get in trouble when we take God off the throne of our hearts. Too often we replace God with someone else. It could be our parents, our children, someone we are in relationship with, or even a hobby or business. It could be a thousand different things; but when we do this, we are taking the wrong path. It is a path for sure destruction.

What does it mean to have God on the throne of our heart?

It means that we will live our lives to please God above and before anyone else. When I first heard this expressed I was taken back. The speaker said in essence that if I was living my life based on what someone else wanted instead of God that I had taken God off of the throne of my heart. He then went on to express in very clear terms that this was idolatry and needed to be repented of. It can be a real struggle at times. We want to keep him there, but there are things that happen that cause us to choose other paths.

Do your best to surrender yourself, your desires, your wants to God. If you find yourself with anything or anyone other than God in charge of your heart, do whatever you have to do to make him first. What a great time of the year to once again bow at the sacred manger and bask in the shadow of the cross.

PRAYER

Dear Jesus, even in this story of King Herod, I find myself wanting to make sure that you and you alone are on the throne of my heart. I want your ways not my ways. Amen.

DECEMBER 14

Bethlehem

And you, O Bethlehem in the land of Judah, are not least among the ruling cities of Judah, for a ruler will come from you who will be the shepherd for my people Israel. Matthew 2:6 NLT

Phillips Brooks was burned out. He was known as the most dynamic and inspirational preacher of his time, but he had lost his fervor and could not seem to recover. In his mid-twenties he had become pastor of the Holy Trinity Church in Philadelphia. He recruited a super sales-man named Lewis Redner to be his Sunday school superintendent and organist. The church exploded in growth. They began with 30 children and within a year there were 1,000. The next two years the numbers increased, partly because of Brooks' dynamic preaching, partly because of Redner's music.

But then the Civil War came and the mood in the church became somber. The national spirit was dying, women were wearing black due to a husband or son killed in battle, and darkness fell over every facet of the worship services. Brooks tried to be inspirational and encourage his church, but it was draining him. When the war ended he thought the vitality and joy would return immediately, but it did not.

Abraham Lincoln was assassinated and the pain intensified. Phillips Brooks was not the president's pastor, but because he was such a great orator, he was asked to preach the president's funeral. He reached down deep and found the appropriate words to say for the moment, but later he was so burned out that he could not rekindle his own spiritual flame. So he asked the church for time off and took a trip to the Holy Land.

On Christmas Eve in Jerusalem, he mounted a horse and went off riding. At dusk, when the first stars were out, he rode into the tiny village of Bethlehem. The town had changed little since the birth of Christ. It lifted Brooks' spirits to be within a few feet of the very spot where Jesus was born. There was singing in the Church of the Nativity, and he felt surrounded by the Spirit of God.

Brooks wrote about his horseback journey from Jerusalem to Bethlehem, where he assisted with the midnight service on Christmas Eve, 1865: "I remember standing in the old church in Bethlehem, close to the

499

spot where Jesus was born, when the whole church was ringing hour after hour with splendid hymns of praise to God, how again and again it seemed as if I could hear voices I knew well, telling each other of the wonderful night of the Savior's birth."

When he returned he wanted some way to express the stirring in his soul, and he decided it would be best communicated in the form of a poem. He sat and penned the words to the song, *O, Little Town of Bethlehem*. The final verse of this song is spoken or sung directly to Jesus. Jesus is still the answer for our lives, our nation, and our world. He knows you. He knows all about you. He knows your successes and your failures in this past year. He knows the challenges, burdens, and blessing that are coming in the New Year. Jesus is still the only answer.

PRAYER

O holy Child of Bethlehem,
Descend to us, we pray
Cast out our sin and enter in,
Be born to us today
We hear the Christmas angels,
The great glad tidings tell
O come to us, abide with us,
Our Lord Emmanuel. Amen.

Joseph

Joseph is the father of Jesus. . . sort of. It certainly wasn't a perfect situation that is for sure. This is his story as recorded by Matthew's gospel:

This is how Jesus the Messiah was born. His mother, Mary, was engaged to be married to Joseph. But before the marriage took place, while she was still a virgin, she became pregnant through the power of the Holy Spirit. Joseph, to whom she was engaged, was a righteous man and did not want to disgrace her publicly, so he decided to break the engagement quietly. Matthew 1:18-19 NLT

"When Joseph woke up, he did as the angel of the Lord commanded and took Mary as his wife. But he did not have sexual relations with her until her son was born. And Joseph named him Jesus" (Matthew 24-25 NLT).

He was faithful. He was faithful to God and faithful to Mary. Ultimately he was faithful to Jesus. He took Jesus on as his own son even though he really had no earthly blood relation to him. He was a man that could have easily run in the face of such adversity. God offers us adoption into his family through his Son, Jesus Christ; but in Joseph's case, he adopted Jesus as his own.

Sometimes circumstances in our lives change and we find ourselves in situations that we wouldn't pick to be in or walk through. The struggle is real. By the power and grace of God, we are enabled to endure much. We find strength we didn't know we possessed. I am sure Joseph was overwhelmed with his role at first. What we know about him is that he remained faithful.

That's it. He was Joe faithful. He didn't run away. He didn't come up with excuses. He stayed and took on the task of being a father. He worked his trade. He helped raise a son. He exits pretty quietly from the biblical narrative. Most of the light is shed on Mary, but I love Joseph's example.

As I look at the figure of Joseph in my nativity I have a deep appreciation for his role and for the legacy he leaves for us to follow. He did what he was called to do. May God grant us the strength and fortitude to do what we know we ought to do always.

Dear Jesus, I am moved by Joseph's willingness to play this role in your earthly birth and life. In some ways he adopted you as his own. He was willing to fill a role as your earthly father. May I always be willing to do things that aren't conventional as I follow you. Amen.

Mary

"Handpicked by God to be the mother of Jesus" is a pretty good resume addition. In reality she was just like all of us. She was just a normal woman who answered the call of God and allowed herself to be used by him for his purposes.

Several months before delivering her baby and while visiting her cousin Elizabeth, the soon-to-be-mother of John the Baptist, Mary broke out into a spontaneous time of worship. We are going to focus our attention on what she was celebrating, and maybe we can find reason to share in her great joy.

Mary Celebrated Personal Grace: She had been redeemed, regarded, and rewarded.

And Mary said: "My soul glorifies the Lord, and my spirit rejoices in God my Savior, for he has been mindful of the humble state of his servant. From now on all generations will call me blessed, for the Mighty One has done great things for me—holy is his name." Luke 1: 46-49 NLT

Personal grace is accepting the fact that Jesus Christ was born over 2,000 years ago to bring you salvation. He wants to redeem you from all the sins and mistakes you have made. Mary was redeemed: Salvation had come to her life.

Mary was regarded: She was singing about the fact that she was a nobody but God had looked favorably on her. Mary was rewarded: She was feeling rewarded because she realized that God was using her to bless others.

Mary Celebrated Perpetual Grace: She sings of permanence, performance, and promise.

"His mercy extends to those who fear him, from generation to generation. He has performed mighty deeds with his arm; he has scattered those who are proud in their inmost thoughts. He has brought down rulers from their thrones but has lifted up the humble. He has filled the hungry with good things but has sent the rich away empty" (Luke 1:50-53 NLT).

Mary celebrated the permanence of this coming grace. It is still available today for all who turn to Jesus as their Savior.

Mary celebrated the performance of a Savior that came not to impress the proud and mighty but to bring salvation to those that would humble themselves and follow Jesus.

Mary celebrated the promise of good things to come.

Mary Celebrated Performing Grace: She remembers his passion for his people.

"He has helped his servant Israel, remembering to be merciful to Abraham and his descendants forever, even as he said to our fathers" (Luke 1:54-55 NLT).

Jesus never fails, and the performance of his grace in our lives is beyond what we can imagine or ever earn.

A young boy went to the local store with his mother. The shop owner, a kindly man, passed him a large jar of suckers and invited him to help himself to a handful. Uncharacteristically, the boy held back. So the shop owner pulled out a handful for him. When outside, the boy's mother asked why he had suddenly been so shy and wouldn't take a handful of suckers when offered.

The boy replied, "Because his hand is much bigger than mine!"

Sometimes I think we spend a whole lot of wasted time trying to work everything out on our own when all we need to do is trust this God of grace with our lives. His hands are bigger than our hands. His power is more powerful than our power. His grace is sufficient.

Mary saw it coming and it filled her heart with a song!

PRAYER

Dear Jesus, I thank you for picking Mary to be your mother. Her role in your life must have been amazing as she did her best to raise you, the Son of God. I am humbled by her faithfulness and thank you for her story and testimony. Amen.

The Donkey and the Ox

I was on a search for a nativity scene for my office. This soon turned into a bit of a passionate pursuit. I quickly dismissed all of the scenes with the wise men in them because I do not believe they were anywhere near the manger. The longer I searched the more upset I became with the portrayal of the wise men being there, and usually it was three to one (wise men versus shepherds) in every set. I write this with some humor, realizing I am being a bit picky about the whole thing.

Much to my delight I found an unusual nativity at the local Catholic Bookstore in Canton, Ohio. It was simply the baby Jesus in a manger and an ox and a donkey. I knew it was different but had no idea why. Later I began to think about it and realized there had to be a reason someone made this simplistic nativity scene. Here is what I found out, and I offer it to you as a devotional thought.

Apparently the earliest example of a nativity is found on a fourth century tomb and contains only the child in the manger, the ox at his head, and the donkey at his feet.

What is then this relationship that is worthy of our devotional thoughts today? Traditionally the ox is viewed as Israel and the donkey represents the Gentiles. This comes from the distinction that is made between the two animals. The ox is a "clean" animal and the donkey is considered to be an "unclean" animal according to the dietary laws of the Old Testament.

The mixing of these two animals is symbolic of the message of Jesus Christ. It is not a message just for Jews. It is a message to the whole world! It includes you and me! The Ephesian writer wrote about this very separation that was in existence prior to the coming of Jesus Christ:

For Christ himself has brought peace to us. He united Jews and Gentiles into one people when, in his own body on the cross, he broke down the wall of hostility that separated us. He did this by ending the system of law with its commandments and regulations. He made peace between Jews and Gentiles by creating in himself one new people from the two groups. Together as one body, Christ reconciled both groups to God by means of his death on the cross, and our hostility toward each other was put to death. He brought this Good News of peace to you Gentiles who were far away from him, and peace to the Jews who were near. Now all of us can come to the Father through the same Holy Spirit because of what Christ has done for us. Ephesians 2:14-18 NLT

During this sacred season, pause and thank God for the ox and the donkey and the door of salvation that opened for all the world on this glorious evening. What a Savior! He came to take on the sins of the whole world. The Ephesian writer leaves us with this benediction of grace and truth:

"So now you Gentiles are no longer strangers and foreigners. You are citizens along with all of God's holy people. You are members of God's family. Together, we are his house, built on the foundation of the apostles and the prophets. And the cornerstone is Christ Jesus himself" (Ephesians 2:19-20 NLT).

What child is this, who, laid to rest,
On Mary's lap is sleeping?
Whom angels greet with anthems sweet,
While shepherds watch are keeping?
This, this is Christ the King....
Why lies he in such mean estate
Where ox and ass are feeding?
Good Christian, fear: for sinners here
The silent Word is pleading

PRAYER

Dear Jesus, thank you for breaking down any barriers that would keep us from coming to you for our salvation. I am unworthy, but through your work in this world I am able to come before you just as these two animals that no doubt shared your stable. Amen.

Simeon

He was in the temple a few days after Jesus was born. His faith was a rarity after 400 years of silence from God in a nation that was used to hearing from God. He was devout enough that he was still hoping for a Messiah to come. Here is his story from the Bible:

"At that time there was a man in Jerusalem named Simeon. He was righteous and devout and was eagerly waiting for the Messiah to come and rescue Israel. The Holy Spirit was upon him and had revealed to him that he would not die until he had seen the Lord's Messiah. That day the Spirit led him to the Temple. So when Mary and Joseph came to present the baby Jesus to the Lord as the law required, Simeon was there. He took the child in his arms and praised God, saying, 'Sovereign Lord, now let your servant die in peace, as you have promised. I have seen your salvation, which you have prepared for all people. He is a light to reveal God to the nations, and he is the glory of your people Israel!'

Jesus' parents were amazed at what was being said about him. Then Simeon blessed them, and he said to Mary, the baby's mother, "This child is destined to cause many in Israel to fall, and many others to rise. He has been sent as a sign from God, but many will oppose him. As a result, the deepest thoughts of many hearts will be revealed. And a sword will pierce your very soul." Luke 2:25-35 NLT

What an amazing moment it must have been for Mary and Joseph as this devoted elderly man gave a clear word of proclamation from God about their Son. His words contained both blessing and burden for them.

Our lives, much like Simeon prophesied, have in them the same kinds of extreme experiences that Mary and Joseph would go on to live out. Some of you this Christmas season are not filled with joy. There are things that you are walking through that don't seem to have an answer. You are carrying a burden, and perhaps the happiness of Christmases past are but a dim memory. Some of you feel alone and are trying to navigate the loss of people that have moved out of your reach either by death or location.

Simeon was a not a prophet. He was just a man that followed God in the darkness with great devotion. He had remained faithful when all around there seemed to be little or no faith left in Judaism. There was no light, and then Jesus came. When Jesus came and he saw him for the first time, he cried out: "He is a light to reveal God to the nations."

Jesus' light has never gone out. No matter how much the darkness of our circumstances threaten to engulf us, his light is brighter and will light our way. He is the light of the world, but he is also our personal source of light. In the book of John, we read these words:

"Jesus spoke to the people once more and said, 'I am the light of the world. If you follow me, you won't have to walk in darkness, because you will have the light that leads to life'" (John 8:12 NLT).

PRAYER

Dear Jesus, I am thankful to have seen your light and for the fact that it shines in my life. Let your light shine through me to others. Amen.

Jesus is the Rose

The wilderness and the wasteland shall be glad for them, and the desert shall rejoice and blossom as the rose; it shall blossom abundantly and rejoice, even with joy and singing. Isaiah 35:1-2 NKJV

A few years ago, I experienced the shame of moral failure. I am not proud of it in any way, but I am still amazed at the love of Jesus that pursued me. Of course, I resigned from my position as lead pastor of an amazing church. I left so much of what had been normal for me my whole life. Even attending church was not an option because I had no idea where to attend. People don't take kindly to pastors that fail.

I went to see a retired pastor known for his ability to counsel and help people in my condition. I will never forget the December day when he told me I had entered a desert place. Jesus would be with me, but everything would be different. There would be no rules. Time wouldn't be important. He encouraged me to let Jesus find me and bring me back to himself. He suggested that I learn as much as I could about the Lord and not be in a hurry to rush out of this desert place.

That Sunday I made my way to a more formal or liturgical worship service than I am used to attending. The first song we sang was an ancient hymn not sung in most churches.

Lo, How a Rose E'er Blooming is a familiar and beloved Advent hymn. The hymn's origins may be traced back to the late 16th century in a manuscript found in St. Alban's Carthusian monastery in Trier in the original German, *Es ist ein Ros entsprungen*.

I was reduced to tears as I sang the words. Jesus is the rose blooming in the desert. Once again he found me in my desert and showed his grace to me in these historic words. Make them part of your prayerful thoughts today.

PRAYER

Lo, how a Rose e'er blooming
From tender stem hath sprung!
Of Jesse's lineage coming,
As those of old have sung.
It came, a flower bright,
Amid the cold of winter,
When half spent was the night.

Isaiah 'twas foretold it,
This Rose I have in mind,
With Mary we behold it,
The Virgin Mother kind.
To show God's love aright,
She bore to us a Savior,
When half spent was the night.

O Flow'r, whose fragrance tender
With sweetness fills the air,
Dispel in glorious splendor
The darkness ev'rywhere;
True man, yet very God,
From sin and death now save us,
And share our ev'ry load.

Rejoice! This Rose has bloomed even in the deserts of life.

And Streams in the Desert

Then the eyes of the blind shall be opened, and the ears of the deaf shall be unstopped. Then the lame shall leap like a deer, And the tongue of the dumb sing. For waters shall burst forth in the wilderness, And streams in the desert. Isaiah 35:5-6 NKJV

These wonderful words of promise are a continuation of yesterday's devotion. This Old Testament prophecy declared that when Jesus came to earth the desert would bloom and flourish, but Isaiah also wrote the above promises.

Blinded eyes would be opened.

Deaf ears would hear.

Lame folks would leap.

The dumb would speak.

This living water would burst forth in the wilderness, and streams would run in the desert! When Jesus came, all of this happened. It is still happening! We share the gospel because we believe that Jesus and this message of hope truly changes lives.

Whatever is going on in your life today, I pray that your eyes will be open to see the Savior and your ears would hear of the goodness of the Lord. I pray that you will be delivered from any lameness caused by sin or discouragement. Lift up your head and look around. Open up your mouth and praise the God who came to earth and who makes the desert come alive.

PRAYER

Dear Jesus, I do go through deserts in my life at times. I am comforted by the promise of your presence. Give me eyes to see what you are doing even when I am discouraged. Help me to always sing your praise. Amen.

Small Things Matter

But you, O Bethlehem Ephrata, are only a small village among all the people of Judah. Yet a ruler of Israel, whose origins are in the distant past, will come from you on my behalf. Micah 5:2 NLT

The Old Testament is filled with references to the coming of the Messiah. Many of them have to do directly with Jesus or the main characters in this wonderful story of redemption, peace and hope.

The prophet Micah reminds us that God uses small things. In this verse, Micah feels the need to remark about the size of the village of Bethlehem. Out of this small, obscure village will come the Savior of the world. From the time of Christ's birth until now, Bethlehem is a place of pilgrimage and worship.

I wonder what you are being asked to do that you think might be too small to matter. I am made to wonder what things in my life I have written off as of little consequence because they weren't grand in their scope or size. Let this tiny village be a reminder to you that God uses people and places that this world may never deem worthy. It's just the way God does things. He does what he does in a way that brings the glory to him and not us, and that's okay because he is worthy to be praised.

Being in God's story may take you places you can't imagine, but if you are in his story it's the best place to be. Reminds me of a verse and chorus from an old gospel song.

> *Does the place you're called to labor*
> *Seem so small and little known?*
> *It is great if God is in it,*
> *And he'll not forget his own.*
> *Little is much when God is in it!*
> *Labor not for wealth or fame;*
> *There's a crown, and you can win it,*
> *If you go in Jesus' name.*

Stables, mangers, shepherds, Bethlehem... Nothing impressive to see here until you put the Savior of the world in the middle of it. Let him be in the center of your life and nothing you do will be in vain. He knows where you are at all times, and he will work in and through you if you let him.

PRAYER

Lord Jesus, I know that you are in the little things of my life. I believe that you know the tiniest details about me and that you will use little things to bring honor to your name. Please help me never forget. Amen.

And Now For Some Good News!

All right then, the Lord himself will give you the sign. Look! The virgin will conceive a child! She will give birth to a son and will call him Immanuel (which means "God is with us"). Isaiah 7:14 NLT

Seven hundred years before Christ was born, the prophet Isaiah uttered these words speaking of a coming Messiah, a miraculous birth and the fact that "God would be with us." They were words of promise and hope for the Jewish people. It took a long time for them to be fulfilled.

The most important takeaway from this prophecy is the name Immanuel. The incarnation of Christ to this earth means that he came in the flesh and lived among us. He came and brought redemption to this earth.

He came to be with us and in us. The invitation is extended to whoever will respond and open themselves up to a relationship with Jesus Christ. Here are some things to think about when "God is with you." When God is with us:

We won't need to be afraid: "Suddenly, an angel of the Lord appeared among them, and the radiance of the Lord's glory surrounded them. They were terrified, but the angel reassured them. 'Don't be afraid!' he said" (Luke 2:9-10 NLT).

The presence of Jesus in our lives should help us when we are afraid. He came and was one of us and faced the things that make us afraid. He is praying for us daily at the right hand of the Father.

We will have an abundance of joy: "I bring you good news that will bring great joy to all people" (Luke 2:10b NLT).

The joy of the Lord is our strength! His joy is everlasting and should be the constant underlying emotion of our hearts. Even when everything looks and feels sad, the knowledge of our salvation and the relationship we experience with Christ should always give us joy to fall back on.

We will have atonement for our sins: "The Savior—yes, the Messiah, the Lord—has been born today in Bethlehem, the city of David!" (Luke 2:11 NLT).

Isaiah wrote his words as a prophecy of hope. We have been given a sign, and that sign was fulfilled in the coming of the Christ child. He is coming again, and our thoughts are directed to the hope of this second Advent.

PRAYER

Dear Jesus, thanks for coming to this world and for bringing good news. You take away our fears. You give us joy, and you forgive our sins. I rejoice in this today. I praise you today. Amen.

God with Us!

Therefore the Lord Himself will give you a sign: Behold, the virgin shall conceive and bear a Son, and shall call His name Immanuel.
Isaiah 7:14 NKJV

The word Immanuel only appears three times in the Bible. The word means, "God with us." This season of the year we celebrate the coming of Jesus to earth to live among us. The significance of this advent is the fact that God came to be with us.

He came and lived among the human race. He experienced the ups and downs that we experience. He must have felt the ebb and flow of the human experience. He was tempted in all ways just like we are. (He did not sin.) I like to imagine the things he might have gone through in adolescence and even young adulthood.

His coming to live among us is what gives us the courage to approach him as a Savior. He knows what we are going through. He knows the highs and the lows. He felt the sting of losing a friend to death. He felt hunger, abuse, and even the cruelty of a torturous death.

Today, pause and let the fact that God dwelt among us in the form of Jesus really sink in. Yes, he went back to heaven; but we are told that he is sitting at the right hand of the Father interceding for those that follow him. He is praying for you today! God is still with us in the form of the Holy Spirit sent to comfort, guide, and lead us into truth.

PRAYER

Dear Jesus, thank you for being willing to come to live among us. Thank you for giving us your Spirit to be in us and around us. Amen.

The Shepherds' Words

All who heard the shepherds' story were astonished, but Mary kept all these things in her heart and thought about them often. Luke 2:19 NLT

This verse may not be the most memorized from the Christmas story. Little children are not given this verse to recite at Christmas programs unless it is part of a larger group of verses. It was a part of the shepherds' narrative.

As they are worshiping the Christ child, they are rehearsing for Mary and Joseph everything that happened to them and what they heard the angels say. It was a fantastic story and almost too much to take in on this sacred and special night.

Mary must have been overwhelmed. The miraculous conception, overcoming the shame, the trip to Bethlehem in the late stages of pregnancy, and no place to stay except a stable must have given her pause. And then the baby is born, and there must have been joy even in the stench and dirt of a stable.

When the shepherds show up, their story is almost unbelievable. Angels, the glory of the Lord shining on them, the words about a baby being born, and the confirmation that he was the Messiah (even though at this point he was still just her baby), the good news of joy for all people. It was almost unbelievable.

She kept it all in her heart and thought about them often. Wouldn't you like to know what she really thought as she raised this little boy? I wonder how often she came back to the memory of this blessed night and the words of these shepherds. I am sure she remembered them in his adolescence and young adult life. I am sure she thought about them during his popularity and ministry years, and I have no doubt she rehearsed the story in her mind as he was crucified and dying right in front of her.

Never forget what God has done for you and even the ways he has spoken to you through the years. The sermons and songs, the quiet whispers while reading his Word, and even the words spoken by someone else that moved and touched your soul.

God loves you and wants nothing more than to be in a daily relationship with you. He wants to be the air you breathe and the first thought every morning and the last moment of worship at night. Fill your heart with God things. Fill your mind with his words and think about them often. Ponder today the goodness of God and his grace to you. Grace that sent his only Son to be born in a stable in the shadow of a cross. You are loved today!

PRAYER

Dear Jesus, help me to always remember this story and what you have done in my life. Let me meditate on your goodness and mercy all the days of my life. Amen.

Always Keep a Room

And while they were there, the time came for her baby to be born. She gave birth to her firstborn son. She wrapped him snugly in strips of cloth and laid him in a manger, because there was no lodging available for them. Luke 2:6-7 NLT

Much has been written and surmised about Mary's reaction when she found out there was no room available. I can only imagine what a pregnant mother would feel in those moments. Was she upset? Did she cry out to God and ask what he was thinking? There is no indication of any such reaction. She went to a stable and laid him in a manger. For the King of Glory, the Son of God, the Fairest of Ten Thousand, it was okay because it was a place. There was no lodging, but there was a place.

You and I have the opportunity to open our hearts as a place for God to dwell. As a children we sang, "Into my heart, into my heart, come into my heart Lord Jesus. Come in today, come in to stay, come into my heart Lord Jesus."

Make sure you have an open door policy for the Lord. Always give him the freedom to come and go. Always keep a room available. Open your heart and let him in daily.

PRAYER

Dear Jesus, I will always make room in my heart for you. Even on this day we celebrate your birth, help me to not let the business of this day crowd out my time with you and for you. Amen.

The Shepherds

They were minding their own business, which meant they were protecting their sheep throughout the night. The Bible records it this way:

Suddenly, an angel of the Lord appeared among them, and the radiance of the Lord's glory surrounded them. They were terrified, but the angel reassured them. "Don't be afraid!" he said. "I bring you good news that will bring great joy to all people. The Savior—yes, the Messiah, the Lord—has been born today in Bethlehem, the city of David! And you will recognize him by this sign: You will find a baby wrapped snugly in strips of cloth, lying in a manger." Suddenly, the angel was joined by a vast host of others— the armies of heaven—praising God and saying, "Glory to God in highest heaven, and peace on earth to those with whom God is pleased."

When the angels had returned to heaven, the shepherds said to each other, "Let's go to Bethlehem! Let's see this thing that has happened, which the Lord has told us about."

They hurried to the village and found Mary and Joseph. And there was the baby, lying in the manger. After seeing him, the shepherds told everyone what had happened and what the angel had said to them about this child. All who heard the shepherds' story were astonished, but Mary kept all these things in her heart and thought about them often. The shepherds went back to their flocks, glorifying and praising God for all they had heard and seen. It was just as the angel had told them. Luke 2:9-20 NLT

Not the people you might think would receive the announcement that the Messiah had come to earth, but that's who God chose to announce it to. That's the people he thought should be the first to see and then go and tell the story.

Communication has always been a part of God's story. The call and challenge has always been to offer the hope of the gospel of Jesus. And on this night it was no different. Think for a moment with me about what happened on this night and the message that was given.

The shepherds were fearful: Message of security and hope

The Bible says they were terrified but were told to not be afraid. Fear is a major part of the human condition. Around the world people fight this emotion every day.

The shepherds were most likely faithless: Message of salvation and healing

They heard for the first time: "I bring you good news that will bring great joy to all people."

There is a really good chance that these hard-working shepherds were not part of the religious elite. The message was for them and to ALL people.

The shepherds were faithful: Message that was simple and holy

They made the trip by faith to see what had happened.

The shepherds were filled: Message worth sharing and hearing

"After seeing him, the shepherds told everyone what had happened and what the angel had said to them about this child."

PRAYER

Dear Jesus, I am thankful that the shepherds are included in your story. As you moved in their lives may you move in mine. Help me to always grow closer to you and respond quickly Your plan for my life. Amen.

Put on and Put Off . . .

If indeed you have heard Him and have been taught by Him, as the truth is in Jesus: that you put off, concerning your former conduct, the old man which grows corrupt according to the deceitful lusts, and be renewed in the spirit of your mind, and that you put on the new man which was created according to God, in true righteousness and holiness. Ephesians 4:21-24 NKJV

If there is one reoccurring theme throughout the Bible it is God's desire and intention for us to turn from sin and to walk in righteousness and holiness. This is not a shadow or suggestion. He has always meant it when he calls us to let go of this world and its filth.

The apostle Paul clearly calls for believers to put off our former conduct which only leads to corruption and to put on the new man of righteousness and holiness. This may be disconcerting for some who have been taught that we all must remain poor miserable sinners until we get to heaven. Why would God call us to something unattainable? Why would he say it over and over and not expect us to do it?

Whatever you do in the coming year, hunger and thirst for righteousness. Let God fill you with so much of his Spirit that choosing sin would become nauseating to you. Just like men and women who are faithful to their spouse, you can also be faithful to God.

Be renewed in the spirit of your mind! Put on the new man created according to God!

PRAYER

Dear Jesus, I know there are many people who believe serving you faithfully is impossible. More than anything, I want to love you with all of my heart, soul, mind and strength. Let me love you so much that sinning against You and others would become less and less of an option. Amen.

Jesus Wept

John 11:35 NKJV

Yes, the come-down-to-earth Jesus cried. I love this. I am thankful that he experienced human emotion. I understand that there are no tears in heaven, but there are plenty on earth to go around. This Jesus, who shed tears while he was here on earth more than once, is sitting today at the right hand of the Father and praying for you and me.

I am encouraged that tears are part of an emotion given to us to allow us to feel sorrow and joy. They are expressions of something stirring deep within us. Somehow, they are cathartic and eventually bring us to a place of peace.

Tears are a part of many stories throughout the Bible. The psalmist wrote, "You number my wanderings; Put my tears into Your bottle; Are they not in Your book?" If God is collecting our tears, it affirms the fact that he knows exactly what is going on with us day to day. He knows the last time you cried. Whatever may be happening today or tomorrow, don't hold back. Even Jesus cried. What a Savior we come to with our tears. He knows, he remembers what sorrow and disappointment feels like.

PRAYER

Dear Jesus, I realize that you must remember what it felt like to have tears run down your face. I know that your Word says that one day you will wipe all the tears from our lives. Thank you, Jesus, for being a friend that sticks closer than a brother. Amen.

Making the Most of Every Opportunity

So watch your step. Use your head. Make the most of every chance you get. These are desperate times! Don't live carelessly, unthinkingly. Make sure you understand what the Master wants. Ephesians 5:15-17 MSG

This is the week when we all start thinking about a new year. Some people will make resolutions and some will just have a silent resolve to try to do some things differently in the coming year. It is a transition to a fresh start. The holidays are over and we trek toward the unknown of the days ahead. There may be laughter. There may be tears. There may be joy. There may be sorrow. There may be new babies, and there may be a death. There will be some ups and there will be some downs.

What will you do this year regarding your relationship with God? What changes will you make to insure that you are living a life pleasing to him and helpful to those around you? Let me suggest an outline to help you process the above verses.

Watch your step: Examine your life: "So watch your step. Use your head." All of us should examine the steps we take. Make sure you are taking steps that lead to good things and God things.

Weigh your opportunities: Exercise good judgment: "Make the most of every chance you get. Don't live carelessly, unthinkingly." We are all faced with the same amount of time in a day. In the last year, Americans have averaged six hours and forty two minutes a day on the Internet and most of that on their phones. Make sure you are using the time you have wisely.

Want what God wants: Embrace what God is doing: God moves every day to reach people with his love. You and I are to be in the middle of that. Why not ask God to allow you to be in his story instead of trying to get him into your story. Want what he wants in your life and in your world.

PRAYER

Lord please help us to understand what You want us to do with our time, talent and treasure on a daily basis. Help us Lord to make good choices and live close to Your word and in Your presence daily.

Dwelling in His House

And I will dwell in the house of the LORD forever. Psalm 23:6 NKJV

There is something very encouraging about this last verse of the very familiar Psalm 23. There is hope in these words. There is assurance in these words. There is determination, confidence, and resolve in these words.

To purpose to dwell in the house of the Lord forever speaks of two worlds. It means you will dwell in his house both now and in eternity. Why not? Where else would you possibly want to dwell? In his house there is safety, peace, relationship, community, purpose, and direction.

Determine today that you will always live in his house forever. Stay connected. Embrace his will and Word every day. Explore the house of the Lord. Learn everything you can about what it means to dwell in his house. Like Joshua, determine that as for you and your household, you will serve the Lord.

Prayer

Dear Lord, more than anything else I can think of, I want to dwell in your house forever. I want you to be with me now, and I want to be with you forever in eternity. Thank you for pursuing me, leading me, protecting me, and being the Shepherd of my soul. Amen.

Soldiers of Christ

They all hold swords. Being expert in war. Every man has his sword on his thigh because of fear in the night. Song of Solomon 3:8 NKJV

Good soldiers will always be aware of the dangers around them. In this book full of allegory and metaphors, one must dig a little to understand the language. For those of the Jewish faith, they believe this book illustrates the relationship between God and Israel. Christians traditionally believe it is also an illustration of God and his bride, the church.

With that in mind, we come to understand that the people of faith will always be alert to protect the bride. It is not inconceivable that there are people seeking to destroy the effectiveness and reputation of the church. They cast doubts and point out the faults of the church.

Real followers of Christ are like the soldiers mentioned here. They will defend the church and the Lord's good name. They will not allow the church to be taken over by people with misguided intent. Satan's goal is to destroy the church on this earth. Those of us traveling through the wilderness of this world are called upon to be vigilant and active in the spiritual warfare that is all around us.

The apostle Paul wrote, "Put on the whole armor of God, that you may be able to stand against the wiles of the devil. For we do not wrestle against flesh and blood, but against principalities, against powers, against the rulers of the darkness of this age, against spiritual hosts of wickedness in the heavenly places. Therefore take up the whole armor of God, that you may be able to withstand in the evil day, and having done all, to stand" (Ephesians 6:11-13 NKJV).

As you face the coming year, be aware and stand up for Jesus even if it costs you everything.

PRAYER

Dear God, your church is not perfect, but I pray that we will come to know you better, that we all will stand for what you stand for, and that we will always do what's best for the church. Amen.

Old Testament

New Testament

535